Plumbing

DISCARD

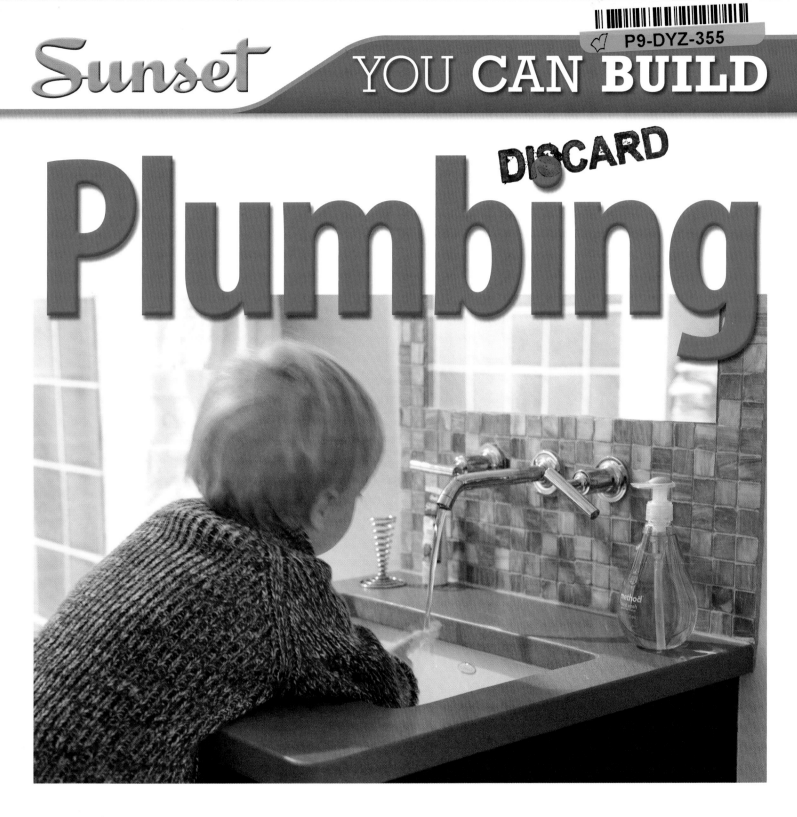

by Esther Ferington
and the Editors of
Sunset Books

ISBN-13: 978-0-376-01468-9
ISBN-10: 0-376-01468-7
Library of Congress Control Number: 2008932411

10 9 8 7 6 5 4 3 2 1
First Printing January 2010
Printed in the United States of America

Oxmoor House, Inc.
VP, Publishing Director: Jim Childs
Editorial Director: Susan Payne Dobbs
Brand Manager: Fonda Hitchcock
Managing Editor: L. Amanda Owens
Project Editors: Emily Chappell, Vanessa Lynn Rusch

You Can Build: Plumbing
Contributors
Author: Esther Ferington
Managing Editor: Bob Doyle
Editor: Ben Marks
Design & Production: Hespenheide Design—
    Gary Hespenheide, Randy Miyake
Prepress Coordinator: Eligio Hernández
Copy Editor: John Edmonds
Proofreader: Linda Bouchard
Interns: Natalie Heard, Allison Sperando,
    Christine Taylor
Indexer: Marjorie Joy
Series Designer: Vasken Guiragossian
Front cover photography by Mark Rutherford,
    styling by JoAnn Masaoka Van Atta

To order additional publications, call 1-800-765-6400
For more books to enrich your life,
    visit **oxmoorhouse.com**
Visit Sunset online at **sunset.com**
For the most comprehensive selection of Sunset books,
    visit **sunsetbooks.com**
For more exciting home and garden ideas, visit
    myhomeideas.com

Note to readers: Almost any do-it-yourself project involves risk of some sort. Your tools, materials, and skills will vary, as will conditions at your project site. Sunset Publishing Corporation and the editors of this book have made every effort to be complete and accurate in the instructions. We will, however, assume no responsibility or liability for injuries, damages, or losses incurred in the course of your home improvement or repair projects. Always follow the manufacturer's operating instructions in the use of tools, check and follow your local building codes, and observe all standard safety precautions.

How to Use This Book

You Can Build: Plumbing is organized by chapters, of course, but we have also created a number of repeating features designed to help you successfully and safely complete your masonry project.

Safety Notices

Found only on certain pages, this is usually to remind you to turn off the power before proceeding with a project. Sometimes, though, the warning is particular to a specific project on a specific page, so please read all boxes carefully and follow their instructions.

Skill Level Required

Many plumbing projects are Easy, but some are Moderate and a few are downright Challenging. The actual Degree of Difficulty will depend on your experience and skills.

Shopping Guides

In some cases, you can use the information in these boxes as the basis for your shopping list before you head off to the home improvement center. In other cases we offer tips and advice to help you shop smart.

What It Will Take

As with the Degree of Difficulty, the time it takes to complete a plumbing project will vary with your skill level and experience, but this should help you prepare for a quick plumbing project that can be completed in under an hour or a weekend-long one.

Preparation Help

Having the tools you need on hand before you begin a project saves multiple trips to the home improvement center, so give this box a quick glance before you begin your project.

For More Info

To save you a trip to the Index, we've placed Related Topics boxes on many pages in *You Can Build: Plumbing*. You may want to consult these pages before you begin a project, just in case your plumbing job is a bit of a hybrid.

Contents

1 Plumbing in Your House

2 Tools & Materials

3 Upgrading Bathroom Fixtures

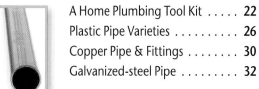

4 Fresh Options for Your Kitchen

5 Other Plumbing Projects

Pipefitting

New Plumbing Lines

Outdoor Projects

Help Section

1 Plumbing in Your House

In this chapter, you'll learn how water gets into your home, how plumbing systems distribute it throughout your house and garden, and how wastewater is removed. You'll also find out how to conserve water—and save money—by purchasing fixtures and faucets that do much of the job for you. Finally, we'll show you how to assess your home's water, from its pressure to its quality.

Chapter Contents

Home Plumbing Systems

If your plumbing experience has been limited to turning a faucet on and off, you may be pleasantly surprised to learn that the systems behind that faucet are just as simple. It all comes down to how water enters your house, gets to where you need it, and flows away after use.

Inside Connections

Inside your house, the plumbing is made up of three systems: supply, drain-waste, and vent. The drain-waste and vent systems are interconnected and are often referred to as the DWV system. Each system is described in greater detail on the following pages, but here is how they all fit together.

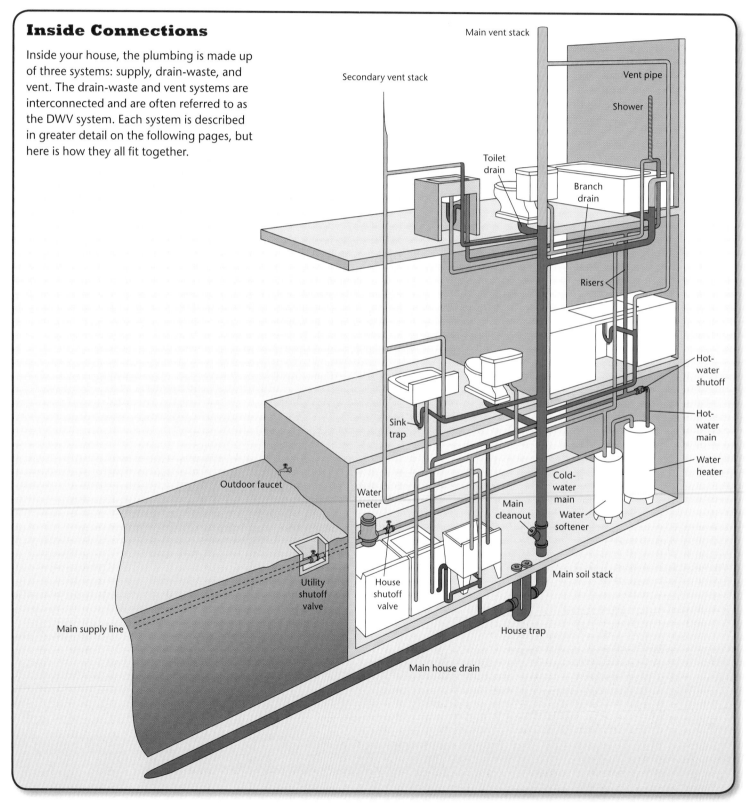

Outside Connections

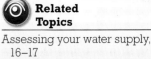
Related Topics

Assessing your water supply, 16–17
Emergency plumbing, 190–191
The DWV system, 12–13
The supply system, 10–11
Tools & materials, 20–37

Your plumbing connects to the outside world in two ways: taking in fresh water through a main supply line and releasing wastewater through the main house drain.

The water supply for a house begins as rainfall or melted snow, which collect in lakes, reservoirs, and the underground water table. Unless you're on a private or community well, the water then travels through a treatment plant. Water towers and/or pumping stations maintain the pressure that drives the treated water through a water main and meter to your house. Homes with a private well connect directly to the water table instead.

Wastewater from the house flows from the main drain to a main sewer, which in turn leads to a sewage treatment plant. After it's treated, the water evaporates, completing the water cycle as it returns to the sky. Houses with no sewer connection use underground septic systems or holding tanks.

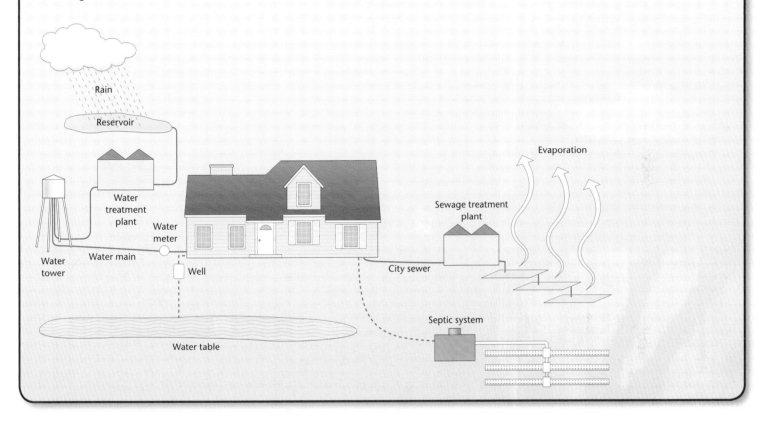

Three Plumbing Systems

Your home has three separate but interdependent pipe systems:

WATER SUPPLY

Water from the main supply line to the house travels to a meter, while water from a private well is typically pumped into a pressure tank. The house shutoff valve, which can stop water from flowing anywhere in the house, is usually near the meter or pressure tank. Cold water may pass through a water softener or filter. The water branches into separate lines for hot and cold water. These lines provide water to plumbing fixtures and appliances throughout the house, often with hot and cold lines running beside each other.

DRAIN & WASTE

The drain-waste system relies on gravity to carry water and waste out of the house, which means each fixture's drainpipe is installed at a precise slope. At the center of the drain-waste system is the main soil stack, a vertical section of 3- or 4-inch-diameter pipe that carries waste away from toilets and other fixtures and connects with the main house drain.

VENT

The vent system gets rid of dangerous sewer gases. It also maintains atmospheric pressure inside the drain-waste system to help waste flow downhill. This works on the same principle as the second hole on a gas can.

When a drainpipe is empty, sewer gases rise through the vent stack and go out through the roof. Below each drain, a P- or S-shaped trap remains filled with just enough water to keep the gases from getting into the house instead.

The Supply System

The supply lines in your house depend on water pressure. Because of this constant pressure, opening a faucet or valve immediately produces a supply of water—as will a leaky pipe or worn-out fixture.

Your Home's Supply System

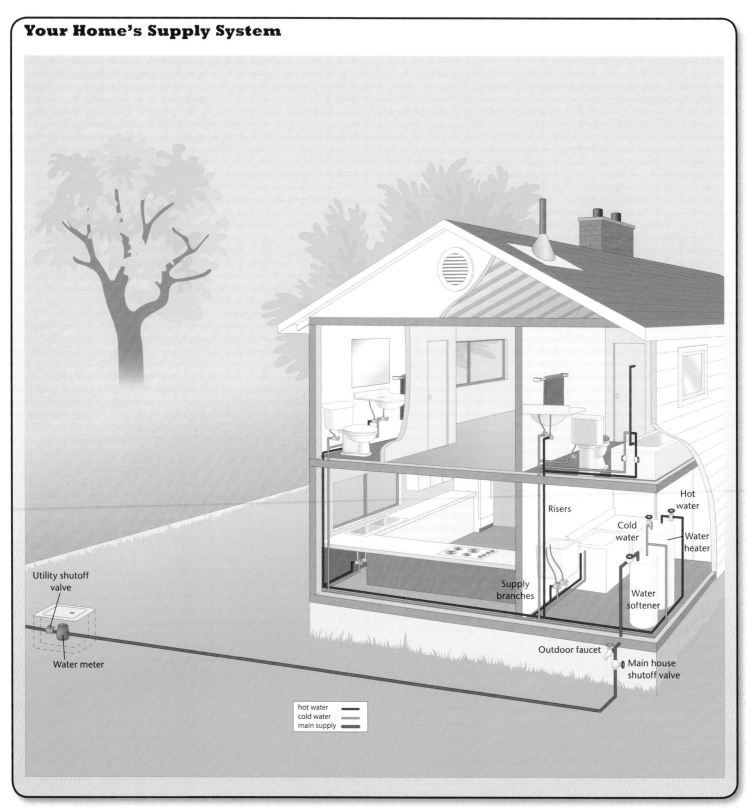

Utility shutoff valve

Water meter

Risers

Cold water

Hot water

Water heater

Supply branches

Water softener

Outdoor faucet

Main house shutoff valve

hot water
cold water
main supply

How Water Works

If you get your water from a utility, it's probably delivered by an underground water main regulated by a utility shutoff valve and measured by a water meter. In cold climates, look for the valve and meter just inside the house, basement, or crawl space. If your water is provided by a utility but is not metered, the utility's shutoff valve is likely to be at your property line.

If your water is metered, look for the main shutoff valve—your on/off switch for water flow to the home—on the house side of the meter, either inside or outside the house. For water from a private well, look for a shutoff valve just before the pressure tank or at the wellhead. You may have a valve in both places. Be sure to turn off the well pump before you shut off the water. Wherever it's located, the main shutoff valve should be a full-flow type—ideally a ball valve—so it won't restrict water flow into the house.

RUNNING HOT & COLD

Once inside the house, the main supply line divides into two. One pipe leads to the water heater, which supplies the hot-water lines in the house, and the other pipe supplies the house's cold-water lines. If you have a water softener, it may be on the main supply line before it divides, or on the leg supplying the water heater.

For most of their distance, hot- and cold-supply branches run parallel and horizontally, fastened to floor joists or buried under a concrete slab. Many supply pipes are installed with a slight pitch in their runs so that all pipes can be drained through a valve or hose bibb at the lowest point. Vertical branches called risers connect the supply lines to groups of fixtures and appliances.

PIPES & FIXTURES

Hot- and cold-water branches are typically ¾ inch in diameter. Risers that feed fixtures are generally ½-inch galvanized iron, copper, or plastic pipe. Local codes and the age of your house will determine the kinds of pipe and fittings you'll find. Many fixtures and water-using appliances have their own shutoff valves, enabling you to work in one place without cutting off water to the entire house.

When everything is working properly, the supply system is the only branch of a home's overall plumbing system with which most of us will come into contact.

The DWV System

Unlike the supply system, which brings water in under pressure, the drain-waste-vent system uses gravity to channel away wastewater. In any house, drains occasionally clog, making cleanouts a vital part of the system to make access easy.

Gravity & Waste

To ensure a smooth flow, drainpipes lead away from fixtures and appliances at a carefully calculated slope. If the slope is too steep, water runs off too fast, leaving solids behind. If the slope is not steep enough, the drain empties too slowly and water backs up into the fixtures. The normal pitch is $1/4$ inch for every horizontal foot of pipe.

DRAINPIPES & FITTINGS

The central element in the drain-waste-vent system is the main soil stack, a vertical section of 3- or 4-inch-diameter pipe that carries away wastewater from toilets, other fixtures, appliances, and branch drains, and then connects with the main house drain.

Many older main soil stacks are made of cast iron with branch drains of galvanized steel. Newer drainpipes are typically plastic. Unlike supply and vent fittings, drain fittings have smoother, more curved angles that don't restrict the flow of water and waste.

CLEANOUTS

Cleanouts are placed in drainpipes to provide access for removing clogs. Ideally, there should be one cleanout in each horizontal section of drainpipe, plus a U-shaped house trap (sometimes located outdoors) for the main house drain. A cleanout is usually a 45-degree Y-fitting or a 90-degree T-fitting with a removable cap on one end.

P-Trap

Cleanout (90° T-Fitting)

S-Trap (older homes only)

In a kitchen, the drain-waste-vent system begins at the bottom of sinks and in drainpipes connected to appliances such as dishwashers.

Venting the System

To keep out dangerous sewer gases, each fixture must have a trap and must be vented. A trap is essentially a bend of pipe that's always filled with water. The water blocks gases from coming up through the drain so they instead escape into the vent and are released above the house.

P-traps, which have a horizontal tailpiece leading to the wall, are most common. In an older home, you may find S-traps, which exit through the floor. S-traps are no longer allowed by code, but stores still carry replacement parts. Toilets have built-in traps.

The upper part of your home's main soil stack is the main vent stack, which runs out through the roof. Additional 1½- to 2-inch-diameter vent pipes connect to it. In many houses, widely separated fixtures make a single main vent stack impractical, so some fixtures or fixture groups have secondary vent stacks, which exit through the roof as well.

Like drainpipes, vent pipes in older homes may be made of cast iron or, for vent sizes up to 2 inches, galvanized steel. Newer vents are typically made of plastic.

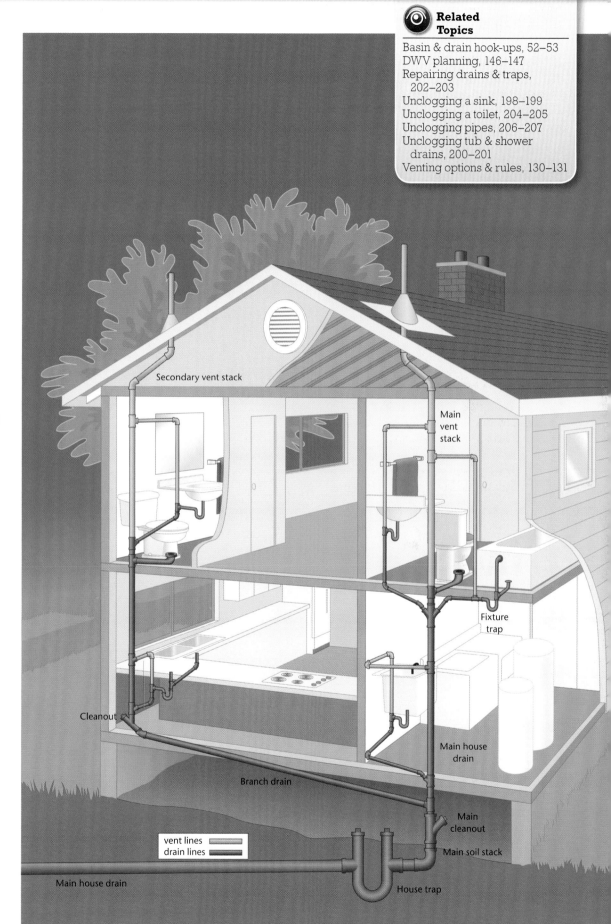

Secondary vent stack

Main vent stack

Fixture trap

Cleanout

Main house drain

Branch drain

Main cleanout

Main soil stack

vent lines
drain lines

Main house drain

House trap

Conserving Water

Saving water saves you money, and it helps the environment, too. Water isn't just a scarce resource; treatment and pumping also consume power, producing carbon emissions. Your first step? Put a stop to leaks or drips—a tactic that also avoids future headaches.

Why Save Water?

In some parts of the United States, rainfall is frequent and drinking water is plentiful. But whether or not you live in the land of aquatic plenty, it's smart to conserve water. For one thing, water isn't free. Even well water takes power to pump and chemicals to treat, not to mention maintenance and repair on the well system.

Keeping track of water use is also a good way to discover a hidden leak inside the walls or floors, allowing you to fix it before more damage occurs.

Equally important, water use is becoming a key environmental concern, not just because of water scarcity but also because of the energy and carbon effects of water use. Extracting, treating, and pumping the water you use (and treating the wastewater that results) all consume electricity.

FIXING DRIPS & LEAKS

The first step in saving water is simple: repair leaks and drips. A leaking toilet can consume up to 200 gallons a day, and a dripping faucet might waste 2,000 gallons a year. Fixing these problems will reduce your water bill and improve your daily life. Nobody likes the drip-drip sound of a leaking faucet or the hiss of a toilet that refills in the middle of the night.

CHANGING HABITS

By paying attention to how you use water, you may spot some changes that will be easy to make. In the bathroom, for example, avoid overfilling the tub or letting the water run while you brush your teeth. You could even switch from baths to showers, as a bath requires 70 gallons of water while a typical shower takes only 10 to 25 gallons. It's also a good idea to shorten long showers and avoid running the water as you shampoo or condition your hair. In the kitchen, wait to run the dishwasher until it's fully loaded, and don't let the faucet run as you wash dishes by hand. Similarly, don't run a clothes washer until you have a full load.

OUTDOOR WATER USE

By government estimates, a typical suburban American home uses 30 percent of its water outdoors. In dry climates, that figure can reach 70 percent. Here, too, repairs are the first order of business. A bad hose connection wastes water just like a dripping faucet indoors, and it may go unnoticed longer. A leaking swimming pool can cause even greater water loss.

Next, consider other changes. Clean off sidewalks with a broom, not a hose. Put in new plants in spring or fall, when less watering is needed. Add mulch around

There are good drips and bad drips. Running a drip-irrigation system through a vegetable garden (above left) conserves water, while letting a faucet leak day and night (above right) is a costly and wasteful oversight.

existing plants to conserve water, and let grass grow taller to make it more drought-resistant. If your garden requires watering, consider drip irrigation or explore alternative water sources (see opposite page). Keep a cover on your swimming pool to cut evaporation by 90 percent.

Related Topics

Fixing a running toilet, 220–221
Fixing faucets, 208–217
Leaking or cracked pipes,
   192–193
Sprinklers & drip systems,
   162–163

Making Smart Upgrades

Plumbing manufacturers offer a growing list of water-saving faucets, showerheads, toilets, and other fixtures and appliances. Usually, the switch to a water-efficient product has no noticeable effect other than a smaller water bill.

To find out whether the appliance or fixture you are considering is water-efficient, look for the WaterSense logo, which is placed on products as part of an Environmental Protection Agency partnership program. The WaterSense logo identifies products that work as well as or better than others in the same category but reduce water use by 20 percent.

The Eco-Flow by Waterpik uses 40 percent less water then standard showerheads.

Alternative Water Sources

For some uses, you may be able to save on city water by substituting water from another source, such as rain or lightly used waste-water. Garden irrigation is a good application for these alternatives.

One classic choice is a rain barrel to collect and store runoff from the roof. Modern barrels have a closed or fine-mesh screen top, a spigot to which you can attach a hose, and an overflow that releases excess water to a remote area. Rain barrels rely on gravity to dispense water, so install the barrel above ground level on two or three rows of cinder blocks, bricks, or railroad ties to make the water flow well at the spigot. You can install a barrel for every downspout, but add only as many as you can regularly use. A full rain barrel serves no purpose when it rains, and water left to sit will develop algae.

Some state and local codes are increasingly open to gray-water recycling, especially in drier regions. Be sure to check your local codes. Gray water is non-sewage wastewater, like the water from a clothes washer. The idea is to drain the water through pipes that lead to a filtering system and, in some cases, a holding tank, then disperse the water into the garden soil, often through underground pipes. The design of such a system depends on many factors, including the climate, the terrain and plantings in your garden, your fixtures and appliances, and local codes. Research the best systems for your area and consider hiring a specialist to create and install yours. Gray-water systems may be much cheaper in new construction or additions, as they often require a parallel drainpipe system.

Assessing Your Water Supply

You can learn a lot about your home's water supply just by reading the water meter, checking the pressure, and testing the water. Check your meter regularly, and assess the water pressure from time to time. Test water quality often if you have a well.

Reading the Meter

By reading your water meter, you can keep track of water use in your home and detect any leaks in the system. To track down a possible leak, turn off all the water outlets in the house and note the position of the 1-cubic-foot dial on the meter. After 30 minutes, check the dial. If the needle has moved, you have a leak. In the same way, you can monitor the water an appliance uses by making sure it's the only part of the plumbing system in operation, then subtracting the "before" reading from the "after" reading.

SIX-DIAL METER

Your home's water consumption is probably measured by one of three meter types. A six-dial meter is the most common. Five dials divided into tenths are labeled 10; 100; 1,000; 10,000; and 100,000 for the cubic feet of water per revolution. The needles of the 10,000 and 100 meters move clockwise, while the other three move counterclockwise. The sixth dial, usually undivided, measures 1 cubic foot per revolution.

To read the meter, begin with the 100,000 dial, noting the smaller of the two numbers nearest the needle. Then read the dial labeled 10,000 and so on.

This meter reads 628,260 cubic feet.

FIVE-DIAL METER

A five-dial meter is read in exactly the same way as a six-dial meter, except that single cubic feet are measured by a large needle that sweeps over the entire face of the meter. The meter in this example reads 458,540 cubic feet.

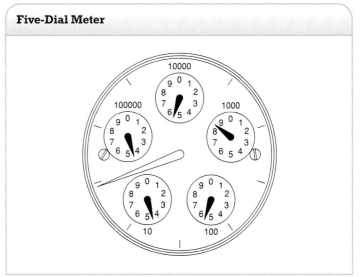

Five-Dial Meter

DIGITAL-READOUT METER

The digital-readout meter looks like an automobile odometer. This type of meter may also have a small dial that measures a single cubic foot per revolution.

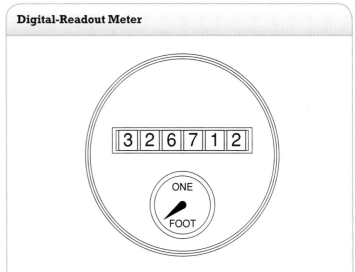

Digital-Readout Meter

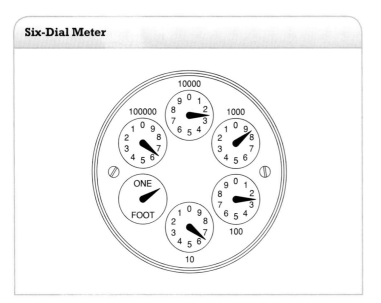

Six-Dial Meter

Related Topics

Conserving water, 14–15
Leaking or cracked pipes,
  192–193
Money-saving upgrades,
  196–197
Whole-house water treatments,
  100–101

Measuring Water Pressure

Water is delivered to homes at widely varying pressures, from as high as 150 pounds per square inch (psi) to as low as 10 psi, depending on the location and time of day. But most appliances, valves, and fixtures are engineered to operate at 50 to 60 psi. Outdoor drip and sprinkler systems can also be sensitive to pressure levels.

If you're having trouble with your current fixtures and appliances, or if you plan to add a new one, you'll need to find out whether your water pressure is adequate or perhaps too high. You can check by attaching a water-pressure gauge to an outside hose bibb or to one for a laundry hookup.

Water-Pressure Gauge

Testing Water Quality

If you suspect that your drinking water is unhealthful, contact your local water department to have it tested.

Hard water, which contains lots of minerals, has not been shown to have health implications, but can be a nuisance. It leaves deposits that can clog aerators and showerheads, and it does not produce as much soap lather, making it difficult to wash clothes and dishes or take a satisfying bath or shower. You can check for water hardness with a test kit. A whole-house water softener, installed on the main supply line, is often the best solution.

Water that simply tastes bad can be made more palatable with an easy-to-install water filter. Consult a plumber or your local water supplier for the best type of filter for your water. You may prefer to add one at the kitchen sink or, more ambitiously, to install a whole-house filter.

A small, inexpensive carbon filter added to the sink will remove chlorine taste and reduce sulfur, which causes water to smell like rotten eggs. A bulkier and more expensive reverse-osmosis filter will eliminate nearly all bacteria as well as any harmful chemicals.

Testing kits identify harmful levels of common water contaminants, including bacteria, chlorine, and lead.

Working Safely & Hiring a Pro

Most plumbing projects are fairly straightforward, but hiring a professional may be the best choice for large, complicated projects, and is sometimes required by law. For any project, be sure you know your local codes—and keep safety concerns in mind.

Checking the Codes

Faulty plumbing can pose serious health and safety hazards. Before you begin any work, be sure your plumbing plans conform to local codes and ordinances. Almost any improvement that adds pipe to the system will require approval from local building department officials before you start, plus inspection of the work before you close up the walls and floor.

Although there are model national codes, regulations regarding methods, materials, and design differ from one state, county, or municipality to the next. Local codes supersede national codes.

Doing It Yourself

If you plan to tackle a plumbing project yourself, at a minimum you should understand the basic principles of plumbing and your own home's pipe systems, and learn how and where to turn off the water supply, which is required for many plumbing jobs. If you need advice, a good inspector or plumbing-supply retailer can walk you through a wealth of local knowledge in a short time. They've both been there before.

Commonsense Safety

As with any home repair or improvement project, it's important to play it safe at all times. Wear appropriate safety gear, shut off the water before beginning any plumbing job, and always consult your local plumbing code. Be sure you can distinguish gas and heating lines from the supply and DWV pipes in the house plumbing system. (This book does not include projects or techniques for dealing with gas or heating lines.) Allow plenty of time for the job so you won't feel rushed.

WHAT TO WEAR

Wear safety goggles whenever you cut or hang pipe or tubing, drive nails, or work with power tools. Also use goggles when you do sweat soldering or when you use drain cleaners. Leather work gloves will protect your hands from abrasions while you are cutting or threading pipe. Wear rubber gloves to clean out drain clogs or when using drain cleaners, and be careful not to rub your eyes as you work. Disposable latex gloves are great for working with adhesives and soldering compounds.

USEFUL ADDITIONS

A pair of cushy knee pads can keep you comfortable and prevent possible infection from abrasions in dusty or waste-soaked surroundings. A small headlamp instead of a flashlight will allow you to work with both hands in a dark crawl space or attic.

VENTILATION & FIRE SAFETY

The work area should be well ventilated, especially when you're working with solvents and adhesives. For soldering copper pipe in close quarters, you'll need a metal or fiber flame protector to shield surrounding wood framing. Keep a fire extinguisher nearby. If you remove a toilet or a trap, plug the drainpipe with a rag so you won't let sewer gases into the house (but make sure the rag is too big to go down the drain).

HANDLING POWER TOOLS

Exercise common sense when using any hand or power tools. If you don't know how to use them, find out first. Choose double-insulated power tools and plug them into a GFCI-protected receptacle or extension cord. Better yet, use cordless power tools, which offer extra protection against electrical shock.

When to Hire a Pro

There is a downside to working on your plumbing: It's messy, dirty, and needs to be done right. There's nothing inherently tricky about the basics, with the possible exception of soldering, which takes a little practice to master. Still, it can take a lot of sweat and stamina to pull off a major job, especially if you're extending existing pipes below floors and through walls. Even simple repairs under a sink may require lots of patience and physical flexibility if you don't have easy access.

Some codes stipulate that a licensed plumber must perform certain types of work. You should also consider hiring help if you are at all unsure of your abilities on a given project.

Tools & Materials

In this chapter, we'll show you the tools you really need for a well equipped home plumbing kit. You'll learn the differences between various types of plastic pipe, from PVC to ABS, as well as the situations when copper and galvanized-steel pipe and fittings should be used. We'll also help you choose the right transition fittings and valves, including shutoff valves.

Chapter Contents

A Home Plumbing Tool Kit

Most plumbing projects require only a handful of tools, from general items like adjustable wrenches to specialized devices like basin wrenches and plungers. Your choice of tools also depends on whether your pipes are plastic, copper, steel, or iron.

Adjustable Wrenches

- Smooth jaws fit small nuts, bolts, and square and hexagonal fittings
- Good for a range of nut sizes, depending on how far the jaw opens
- Sizes range from 6 to 12 inches long; buy a single 10-inch or a set of 8- and 12-inch wrenches

Pipe Wrenches

- Adjustable, toothed jaws grip pipes and fittings
- For some jobs, you'll need two pipe wrenches
- Sizes vary from 10 to 24 inches; a 14-inch pipe wrench is a good all-around choice
- Aluminum reduces weight and fatigue in longer versions
- Can turn a stubborn nut if necessary but is likely to damage it

Slip-Joint Pliers

- Adjustable; open wide enough to remove drain traps
- Use curved-jaw versions for pipes, straight versions for nuts and fittings
- Not intended for heavy turning power (torque); for strong turning, try a pipe wrench or an adjustable wrench

Basin Wrench

- Pivoting jaws and an extension handle provide access to nuts in hard-to-reach places, such as under a basin
- Shaft at the base of the handle adds turning leverage

Spud Wrench

- Wide and toothless jaws adjust to fit large nuts on toilets and sinks
- Large slip-joint pliers may also work

Long-Nose Pliers

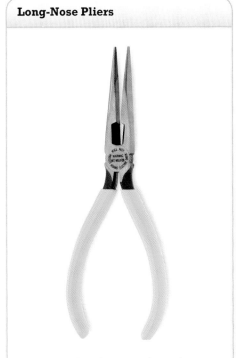

- Can reach tight spots that other gripping tools can't
- Useful for delicate work, such as removing seals and springs during faucet repairs

Valve-Seat Wrench

- Used to remove worn or damaged valve seats from faucets
- One end is square and the other hexagonal, so it fits valve seats of either shape

Valve-Seat Dresser

- This specialty tool grinds and smoothes faulty non-replaceable valve seats in old faucets
- Look for one with variously sized cutters

How the Pros Do It

"For a cartridge faucet, it's a good idea to invest in a special-purpose cartridge puller. It's tempting to reach in and pull out the cartridge with pliers, but if only the center part of the cartridge comes out, the other part can get stuck inside. A cartridge puller is designed to remove the whole cartridge."

Tim Miller, J. Kittelberger & Sons

Faucet-Handle Puller

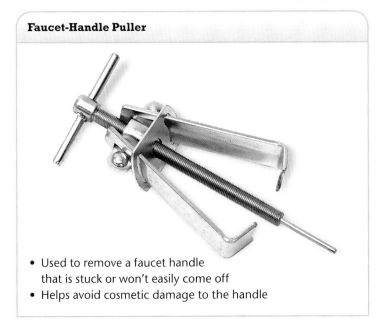

- Used to remove a faucet handle that is stuck or won't easily come off
- Helps avoid cosmetic damage to the handle

Shower Socket

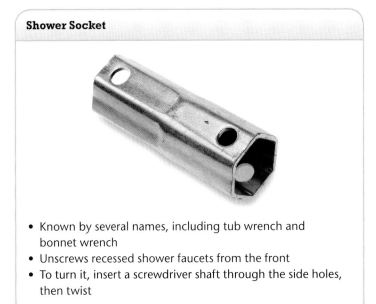

- Known by several names, including tub wrench and bonnet wrench
- Unscrews recessed shower faucets from the front
- To turn it, insert a screwdriver shaft through the side holes, then twist

PVC Scissors

- For cutting plastic pipes and tubing up to an inch or so in diameter
- Ratcheted jaws clamp down on the pipe as you squeeze
- For larger pipes, use a PVC saw

Tubing Cutters

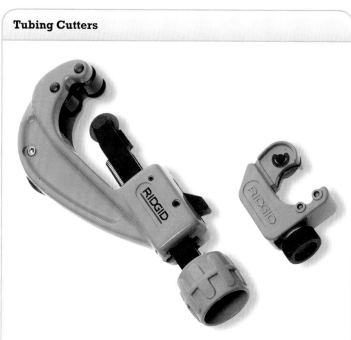

- Designed to cut copper tubing cleanly and accurately
- Use the large ratcheted cutter for pipes up to 1 inch in diameter
- Use the smaller version for tighter spots
- For galvanized steel pipe, rent a larger tubing cutter

Plungers

- Dislodge clogs with alternating pressure and suction
- Also called plumber's helpers
- A sink plunger has a flat face for strainers and drain openings
- A toilet plunger has a funnel-cup tip to fit the toilet bowl; some fold flat to work on sinks as well
- Replace every few years, as cups can become rigid and fragile over time

Drain & Trap Auger

- Extends 10 to 25 feet to remove drain blockages deep inside the plumbing system; also called a snake
- Snakes can be of poor quality; use a high-quality snake with a housing and crank

PVC Saw

- Cuts rigid plastic pipes (PVC and ABS) that are too big for PVC scissors
- For straight cuts, guide the saw with a miter box
- A power miter saw will also cut plastic

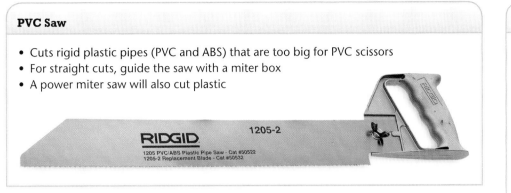

Tubing Bender

- Needed only for rare projects involving flexible copper tubing
- Shapes the tubing without crimping it
- Slide it over the pipe and bend
- Different sizes are made for different pipe diameters

Soil Pipe (Snap) Cutter

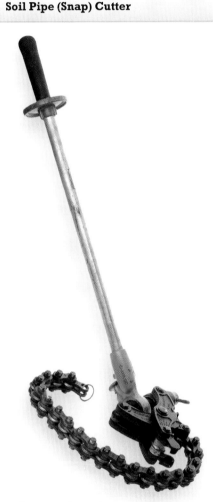

- Cuts cast-iron pipes
- Clamp the chain with cutting wheels around the pipe, then work the ratcheted handle until the pipe snaps
- Usually a rental item, not a purchase; rent the right one for the size of your pipes

Soldering Torch & Accessories

- Used to solder copper pipes and fittings
- Portable torches, not tank-and-hose setups, are best for home users
- Use a propane canister, not MAPP gas; propane costs less and doesn't burn as hot
- A striker tool (flint) lights the torch; torches with push-button ignition won't need one
- A fiber or metal flame guard helps shield wood framing around pipe that's in place

Toilet (Closet) Auger

- Works like a drain-and-trap auger (snake) but is designed for toilets; 3 to 6 feet long with a bent housing to reach into the toilet's trap
- Look for a housing with rubber or plastic padding to avoid scratching the toilet bowl

Plastic Pipe Varieties

Most homeowners who have worked with different types of pipe prefer plastic. That's because plastic pipe is lightweight, inexpensive, and easy to cut and fit. Make sure which varieties are permitted by your local code, and for what uses.

Pros & Cons

Besides being light, cheap, and simple to work with, plastic pipe is resistant to damage from chemicals and won't be corroded by acidic water. Plastic's smooth interior surface provides less flow resistance and avoids building up flow-restricting deposits from hard water. All major plumbing codes accept at least some types of plastic pipe, although your local codes may not.

Unlike metal pipe, plastic pipe cannot be used to ground electrical systems. Rigid plastic is also less sturdy, so a hard hit is more likely to crack plastic than steel or copper. In addition, CPVC projects take longer to finish, as the solvent cement may require a few hours (check the label for specifics) before you can restore water pressure to the line.

Plastic Pipe Varieties

Plastic pipe can be rigid or flexible. Rigid plastic pipe has been used for both supply and drain lines in the United States for decades. Flexible PEX (cross-linked polyethylene, pronounced "pex") is still relatively new in the United States, but it has been used for decades overseas. PE (polyethylene) pipe is also flexible but is used only for cold water.

For the best quality, look for a designation from the American Society for Testing and Materials. If the pipe is to carry potable water, it also should have the National Sanitation Foundation's certification seal.

Plastic pipe is stamped with pressure ratings known as schedules. Use the schedule number prescribed by your building department. The pressure ratings for plastic are lower than those for metal, so it is also important to install water-hammer arresters at fixtures and appliances (except toilets).

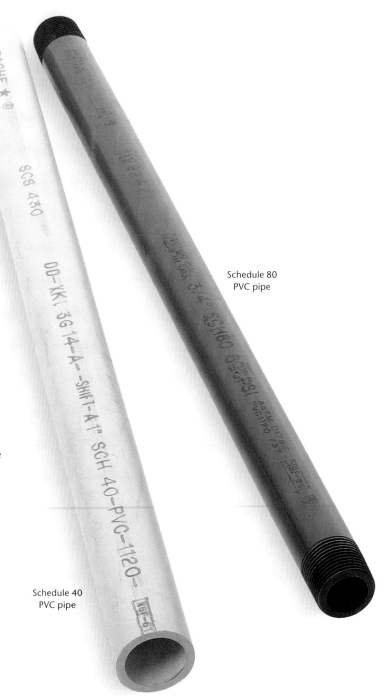

Schedule 80 PVC pipe

Schedule 40 PVC pipe

CPVC or PVC primer

PVC cement

Storage Tip

Take care not to store plastic pipe in direct sunlight for longer than a week or so. The accumulation of ultraviolet rays can make it brittle.

Rigid Supply Pipe

Two types of rigid plastic supply pipe are used indoors: polyvinyl chloride (PVC) for cold-water supply only and chlorinated polyvinyl chloride (CPVC) for both hot- and cold-water systems. Never use PVC for hot-water supply lines. CPVC was developed for safe use with hot and cold water, and it is rated for that range of temperatures.

PVC and CPVC pipes are commonly available in 10- and 20-foot lengths, although some home stores carry precut 2-foot pieces. Common sizes include 1/2-, 3/4-, and 1-inch nominal diameters. (Nominal diameters are the sizes used for matching fittings; actual diameters may be different.)

PVC and CPVC fittings slip over the ends of the pipes and are fixed in place with a permanent solvent cement. Supply fittings are smaller than drain-waste-vent fittings. They are designed to work under pressurized conditions, unlike DWV fittings, which work with the flow of gravity.

CPVC Fittings

Related Topics

Adding a sprinkler system, 168–169
Leaking or cracked pipes, 192–193
Making the connections, 118–121
Tying old to new, 122–123
Valves & transitions, 34–35
Working with plastic pipe, 104–107

PVC Fittings

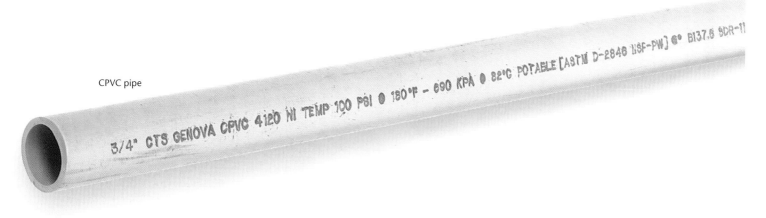

CPVC pipe

3/4" CTS GENOVA CPVC 4120 HI TEMP 100 PSI @ 180°F - 690 KPA @ 82°C POTABLE [ASTM D-2846 NSF-PW] @° B137.6 SDR-11

Drain-Waste-Vent Pipe

Two types of plastic pipe are used to repair or extend drain-waste-vent systems: acrylonitrile-butadiene-styrene (ABS) and polyvinyl chloride (PVC). You can tell the difference by the color. ABS is black, and PVC is typically off-white. Basin traps and other short connectors to DWV lines are often fabricated from a third plastic, known as polypropylene (PP), which is identifiable by its stark-white color.

Both ABS and PVC are less expensive, lighter in weight, and easier to connect and hang than cast-iron pipe. For this reason, plastic pipe is a common choice for new work, for extending a cast-iron system, and for replacing a leaking section of cast-iron drainpipe.

As always, check your local code. While both plastics are widely accepted, some codes may allow only ABS or PVC rather than both. Each of the two materials is also found more or less frequently in stores in different parts of the United States. Both ABS and PVC drainpipe are sold in lengths of 10 and 20 feet. Drainpipe for tubs, sinks, and lavatories normally has a 1½- or 2-inch nominal diameter. Toilets require 3- or 4-inch-diameter drains. Vent pipe can range from 1¼ to 4 inches in nominal diameter.

Plastic DWV Fittings

DWV fittings differ from supply fittings in that they have no interior shoulders, which would catch waste. There are many change-of-direction and reducer fittings. Always direct the flow from the smaller pipe diameter to the larger.

Fittings for PVC and ABS are not readily interchangeable. Use PVC fittings for PVC, and use ABS fittings for ABS. Connect most PVC or ABS fittings to drainpipes with solvent cement. Some ABS and PVC fittings are threaded, especially those intended to be disassembled for maintenance, like cleanout plugs. Other types of fittings or pipe can be connected to plastic pipe with no-hub couplings and special compression fittings.

ABS PIPE

ABS FITTINGS

Flexible Supply Pipe

Flexible plastic pipe can follow a winding course without requiring a lot of fittings, and it is easier to fit into cramped spaces. For that reason, it may be used in new construction.

Cross-threaded polyethylene (PEX) is a versatile flexible pipe. Used for many years in Europe, it has come to the United States more recently. PEX is suitable for both hot- and cold-water supply lines. (Another kind of PEX, which is not rated for drinking water, is used in radiant floors.) PEX is well-suited to new construction, in which separate lines are run to each individual fixture from cold- and hot-water manifolds. Attaching PEX lines and fittings, however, requires special tools, making it an impractical choice for homeowner projects.

Polyethylene (PE) pipe is used for cold-water lines only. It is a common choice for well systems, in which acidic groundwater can corrode copper pipe. PE is also handy for outdoor projects, such as running lines for sprinkler systems. Join lengths of PE pipe with barbed insert fittings. Insert fittings have hollow, corrugated nipples held in place by stainless-steel clamps. Transition fittings have a socket on one end for joining to rigid plastic pipe.

FLEXIBLE PE PIPE

STAINLESS-STEEL CLAMPS

BARBED INSERT FITTINGS

Copper Pipe & Fittings

Copper replaced galvanized-steel pipe decades ago and remains a popular choice for supply lines today. Compared with steel, copper is lightweight, easier to work with, and less prone to corrosion or mineral buildup.

Types of Copper Pipe

Most copper supply lines use hard-temper copper; soft-temper copper lines are used for limited plumbing purposes. Larger-diameter copper pipe can also be used with drain-waste-vent systems, although the price of copper makes that a very costly option today.

Copper supply lines are often compared with the CPVC plastic alternative. Compared with plastic, copper is stronger but more expensive. It's also ready to use (and test) as soon as you complete the job, whereas rigid CPVC lines require a wait of several hours for the solvent cement to set.

HARD-TEMPER COPPER

Hard-temper copper is sold in straight lengths of 20 feet or less. Because it cannot be bent without crimping, it must be cut and joined with fittings wherever a length is extended or a section changes direction. The pipe comes in three thicknesses: K (thick wall), L (medium wall), and M (thin wall). M is usually adequate for home plumbing, while L is typically used underground outdoors.

Nominal diameters range from ¼ to 1½ inches and larger. The actual diameters are greater.

SOFT-TEMPER COPPER

Soft-temper copper, sold in coils, may also be used (depending on local codes) for many non-plumbing purposes, including fire-protection systems, air conditioning, fuel oil, diesel oil, compressed air, and so on. Although it can be used for plumbing, it is more expensive than hard-temper copper, and in practice it is limited to a few applications, such as running a long, seamless underground supply line to a house. Soft-temper copper comes in K and L thicknesses. Nominal diameters range from ¼ to 1 inch. Actual diameters are slightly greater.

Soft-temper copper tubing

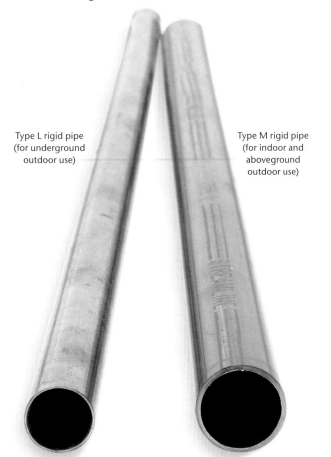

Type L rigid pipe (for underground outdoor use)

Type M rigid pipe (for indoor and aboveground outdoor use)

COPPER DWV PIPE

Copper drainpipe is so costly compared with plastic that it is rarely used in new work. You'll sometimes see copper drainpipes in kitchen areas because their smooth interiors minimize grease buildup and corrosion. Copper drain or vent pipe is usually sold in nominal diameters of 1½, 2, and 3 inches. Copper DWV pipe with a nominal diameter larger than 2 inches is very expensive and is not readily available. Because DWV pipe is not under pressure, copper DWV has thinner walls than supply tubing.

COPPER FITTINGS

As with other pipe varieties, fittings designed specifically for copper are available and should be used. Rigid, hard-temper copper fittings are soldered in place, except where there may be a need for disassembly. In that case, fittings may be soldered on one side and threaded on the other.

Brass compression and flare fittings are used for joining soft-temper copper flexible tubing. Flare fittings are required for some valves and fixtures. Compression fittings are more commonly employed because they are easier and faster to use.

Use transition fittings to connect copper pipe to other kinds of pipes, such as steel and plastic.

FLEXIBLE COPPER PIPE FITTINGS

RIGID COPPER PIPE FITTINGS

T-fitting

90° elbow

45° elbow

Coupling

Reducer

Compression fittings

Flare fittings

Union

Threaded-to-slip couplings

Galvanized-steel Pipe

Once the norm for water supply lines, galvanized-steel pipe is no longer used in new plumbing. (Inside the house, uncoated black steel pipes carry natural gas.) There are occasions, however, when you may wish to use galvanized pipe for a repair.

A Pipe from the Past

Galvanized-steel pipe was long ago replaced in new work by copper and, in recent years, plastic pipe. It corrodes faster than copper, and its rough interior surface collects mineral deposits over time, reducing water flow.

Still, you may prefer to replace a leaking length of galvanized-steel pipe with the same material. This often requires less equipment and expense than using copper or plastic for such a small section.

When you are extending a supply system of galvanized pipe, however, use copper or plastic. Special-purpose transition fittings can make the connection.

Buying Steel Pipe

Galvanized-steel pipe and fittings are coated with zinc to guard against corrosion. (The steel pipe used in indoor gas lines, by contrast, is uncoated, while outdoor gas lines are coated in green). Fittings are connected to the pipe by tapered pipe threads, and galvanized-steel pipe is sold threaded on both ends.

As a result, if you need to replace a bad section of steel pipe, you will have to cut through it (after draining the line), unscrew both of the resulting pieces from the nearest fittings, and replace them with two threaded lengths of new pipe joined with a union. The union allows you to tighten both new lengths.

Galvanized-steel pipe is available in nominal diameters of $1/4$ to $2\frac{1}{2}$ inches and can be custom-cut to length. Threading the cut ends is not particularly difficult, but it requires special tools. Some stores will thread the pipe for you, though they will need precise measurements. If you can, have the store do the job when you buy the pipe, as it's usually simpler and less costly than renting pipe-threading tools yourself. Short threaded pieces called nipples are also available in lengths from $1/2$ to 12 inches.

When you buy the pipe, also pick up some thread tape or joint compound. Wrap the tape around male pipe threads to ensure a proper connection. (A different type of pipe-thread tape is used for gas connections.) Alternatively, you can use pipe-joint compound on the male threads.

Black steel pipe, used for indoor gas lines

Green (coated) steel pipe, used for buried outdoor gas lines

Zinc-coated galvanized-steel pipe, used for plumbing supply lines

Related Topics

Making the connections, 118–121
Tying old to new, 122–123
Valves & transitions, 34–35
Working with steel pipe, 114–115

Cross

T-fitting

45° elbow

45° elbow

Plug

Union

Coupling

RECTORSEAL
Pipe Thread Sealant

Pipe-joint compound

TEFLON※THREAD SEAL TAPE
MIL-SPEC. T-27730A

Pipe-thread tape

Cap

Male-to-female elbow

Valves & Transitions

Supply valves control the flow of water through pipes at several stages in the system. In many plumbing projects, you're also likely to need transition fittings to connect one pipe material to another.

All About Valves

There are different types of valves for different uses. Some valves restrict the flow of water even when fully open, while others allow unrestricted flow when open. The three most commonly used types are ball, gate, and globe valves. Fixture shutoff valves control the flow at each fixture or appliance.

Valves are available in a variety of materials. Those used in home plumbing are most commonly made of cast bronze, while plastic valves are sold for use with plastic pipe. Valves are sized to match all common supply-pipe sizes.

BALL VALVES

Ball valves are the cream of the crop. A straight handle twirls an interior sphere, which has a channel through it. When aligned with the pipe, the channel lets water flow smoothly. To shut off the water, simply turn the handle 90 degrees to rotate the sphere, ensuring that the flow stops promptly without time-consuming, multiple turns. Although a ball valve is the most expensive option, it's the best choice for a main-supply shutoff.

GATE VALVES

Gate valves have a wedge at the end of a stem that moves across the water flow like a gate opening and closing. While gate valves are often used as main-supply shutoffs, a gate valve is better suited to shut down branch supply lines.

Because it takes half a dozen or more turns to fully open a gate valve, many people unknowingly open the valve only partially. Slightly opening a gate valve permits partial flow, but the pressure of the water moving across the wedge wears down its surface, resulting in an imperfect seal and a leaking valve. Because of this reason, water should never be allowed to flow through a gate valve that is only partially open.

GLOBE VALVES

Globe valves, by design, reduce water pressure. When the valve is open, water is forced to flow around two partitions, which slow the water down. By turning the handle of a globe valve, you enlarge or diminish the opening for the water to pass through. Branch supply lines are sometimes equipped with globe valves, but the valves tend to break down from the constant pressure. It's a good idea to replace them with ball or gate valves.

Gate valve

FIXTURE SHUTOFF VALVES

Throughout the house, fixture shutoff valves allow you to turn off the water flow to a fixture for repairs or in an emergency. Select a shutoff valve that is compatible with the supply-pipe material. Copper tubing takes brass valves, plastic pipe uses plastic valves, and so on. You'll probably want a chrome- or brass-finished valve if it will be visible.

Ball valve

Fixture shutoff valve

Related Topics

Adding shutoff valves, 36–37
Copper pipe & fittings, 30–31
Galvanized-steel pipe, 32–33
Plastic pipe varieties, 26–29
The supply system, 10–11

Transition Fittings

Depending on your project, you may find yourself connecting different pipe materials together—an old galvanized-steel supply pipe to a copper line, say, or a cast-iron drain to a plastic section. Transition fittings are available at many home centers, but for an even wider selection, visit your local plumbing supplier. Be sure to double-check local codes for approved fittings.

To switch from copper to plastic or from galvanized to plastic, look for threaded adapters. They're available in both female and male versions, though some inspectors allow only male plastic threads to meet female metal threads.

It's essential to use a dielectric (nonconductive) union to connect copper supply lines to galvanized steel. Copper and steel in direct contact are a sure recipe for corrosion due to a reaction called electrolysis. A dielectric union, which contains steel and copper portions, keeps the two metals apart with an insulating washer and an insulating sleeve.

To switch from cast-iron to plastic DWV pipe, use a no-hub coupling that's labeled for plastic. (This type of fitting is different from ones designed for cast-iron connections only.) No-hub couplings are also available as reducer fittings, allowing you to change pipe size when you change pipe type.

No-hub coupling

Dielectric union

Female adapter

Male adapter

Adding Shutoff Valves

Shutoff valves at your home's fixtures and appliances allow you to turn off the water only where you need to for repairs or in an emergency. With a valve closed, you can work on a project or a repair while the rest of the house has full access to water.

Checking for Fixture Shutoffs

If you have a fixture shutoff in good repair, turn the valve handle clockwise until it's fully closed. Then open the faucet or faucets to drain the pipes (or, in the case of a toilet, empty the tank) and start working. A local shutoff also saves time, allowing you to turn off water instantly if a fixture leaks or overflows.

Take a few minutes to conduct a shutoff-valve survey in your house to make sure there's a shutoff everywhere you need one. Every sink, tub, shower, and washing machine should have shutoffs for both hot- and cold-water pipes. Toilets require only one shutoff valve because they use only cold water, and dishwashers need only one shutoff because they use only hot water. The shutoff valve for a dishwasher is usually in the base cabinet below an adjacent sink. Other shutoffs are right at the fixtures or appliances. Outdoor faucets should also have shutoff valves inside the house so you can drain the faucets before winter.

What to Buy

When you shop for a shutoff valve, you'll need to choose either an angled valve or a straight one. Angled valves are used when the stubout (the end of the supply pipe from the plumbing system) comes out from the wall. Straight valves are used for pipes that come up from the floor. The kind of stubout dictates the type of valve and adapter fittings you'll need. A threaded pipe or fitting, for example, requires a threaded valve, while an unthreaded copper stubout takes a compression valve. Plastic pipe requires yet another variety.

Lengths of flexible supply tubing run from the shutoff valve to the fixture. They come in a variety of materials, including woven stainless steel; woven vinyl; plain copper; and corrugated,

Leaving the shiny shutoff valves exposed under a bathroom sink goes well with a rustic decor.

Fixture shutoff valve with supply tube

chrome-plated copper. Most homeowners find that woven stainless steel is easiest to work with because it is easier to flex. All are available in a variety of lengths and with preinstalled fittings on each end. Err on the long side, as a supply tube that's too long can always be curved, or even looped, between shutoff and fixture.

Be sure the fittings at the ends of the supply tube match your shutoff valve and your fixture inlet shank. Fittings supplied on supply tubes are either threaded or compression and are commonly available in $3/8$-, $7/16$-, and $1/2$-inch diameters.

 **Stuff to Buy**	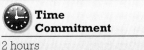 **Time Commitment**	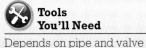 **Tools You'll Need**	**Related Topics**
SHUTOFF VALVE Either angled or straight, depending on pipe, and suited to pipe material **SUPPLY TUBE** Braided metal tubes work well; always replace an old tube **BASIC SUPPLIES** Pipe-thread tape	2 hours	Depends on pipe and valve	Emergency plumbing, 190–191 Hooking up a washer, 92–93 Valves & transitions, 34–35

1 Prepare the stubout

- Turn off the house water supply and open faucets on the lowest level to drain the lines
- If you're replacing an old valve, remove it
- If you're installing a valve for the first time, you may have to add a threaded nipple or supply adapter to the stubout
- Slip an escutcheon (trim plate) over the stubout

2 Add the valve

- Secure the shutoff valve to the stubout
- Depending on the pipe material, you may need a threaded connector, a compression ring and nut, or CPVC solvent cement

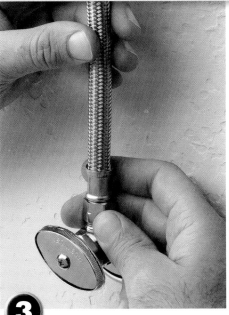

3 Attach the supply tube

- Run a supply tube from the shutoff to the matching inlet on the fixture or appliance (hot to hot, cold to cold) and tighten each coupling
- If you used CPVC solvent cement, wait the recommended time before proceeding
- Restore the water supply, remembering to close all the faucets that drained the lines
- Open the new shutoff valve

FLEXIBLE SUPPLY TUBES

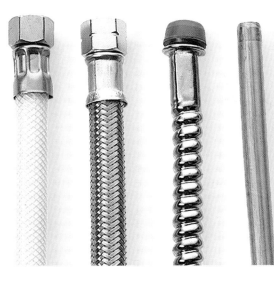

SHUTOFF VALVES

Angled shutoff valve

Straight shutoff valve

Upgrading Bathroom Fixtures

I n this chapter, you'll learn about different traditional and contemporary styles of bathroom sinks, showers, bathtubs, and toilets. We show you how to install a variety of sink types (countertop, above-counter, pedestal, wall-mounted), hook up a basin drain, and install a drain pop-up. Finally, we help you choose tubs, toilets, and showers, with particular attention paid to the water use of each fixture.

Chapter Contents

Sink & Vanity Options

Faucets, sinks, and vanities help set the style and provide interesting visual details in bathrooms. They also offer the practical features that keep your house operating smoothly, efficiently, and reliably.

New & Classic Styles

Bathroom sink materials include enameled cast iron or vitreous china for traditional bathrooms, and metal, glass, crystal, stone, or solid-surface resins for contemporary styles. Save the most delicate sinks for little-used bathrooms, such as powder rooms and guest baths, where you might want to make a design statement. Use the most durable sinks for the kids' bathroom.

Not all sinks are combined with vanities, but those that are provide a wealth of options for setting the tone and style of your bathroom. A common variation is a console (essentially a vanity with feet) or a more open frame that exposes some of the plumbing lines. When you choose plumbing materials, keep in mind whether the drains and supply lines will be visible.

A simple basin and counter is a clean contrast to patterned backsplash tile.

These sinks appear to float above the cabinets below.

The built-in stepstool in this kids' bathroom rolls out from the cabinet on spring-mounted casters. When a child steps on the box, the casters retract and the box drops to the floor. Once the child is done washing up, the caster springs back so that the stepstool can be returned to its hiding place.

This sculptural, one-piece counter features a built-in sink.

The floor drain below this shower taps into the branch drain for the tub to the right.

If you want to install a sink that does not sit in a counter, position it close to shelving.

This ceramic sink sits below the counter, making the top surface easy to clean.

Fresh Sink & Vanity Options **41**

Installing Bathroom Faucets

A new faucet can be just the thing to spruce up an existing bathroom. There's sure to be a style to express your taste. Most faucets mount to the sink, so buy a faucet that fits the hole spacing. A well-known brand will have repair kits and parts available for future use.

Faucet Control Options

Bathroom sink faucets are available with single, center-set, or spread-fit controls. A single-control fitting has a combined faucet and lever or knob controlling water flow and temperature. A center-set control (opposite page) has separate hot- and cold-water controls and a faucet, all mounted on a shared base. A spread-fit control has separate hot- and cold-water controls and an independently mounted faucet.

Preparing for the Job

Clean the surface where the new faucet will sit. Most faucets have a rubber gasket on the bottom. If yours doesn't, apply plumber's putty (Step 1) before you set the faucet in position. If your faucet comes with integral supply tubes, carefully straighten the tubes before you mount the faucet, and then feed the tubes through the appropriate hole or holes.

SINGLE-CONTROL FAUCET

Washer

Nut

Integral supply tubes

SPREAD-FIT FAUCET

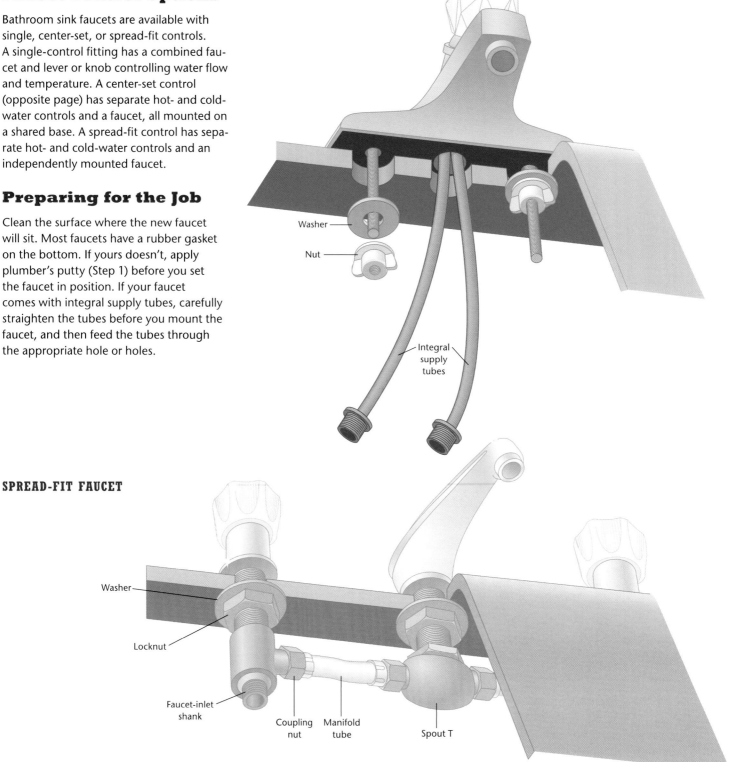

Washer

Locknut

Faucet-inlet shank

Coupling nut

Manifold tube

Spout T

Stuff to Buy

FAUCET Most come with hardware and instructions
SUPPLY TUBES It's best to replace supply tubes when you change faucets
BASIC SUPPLIES Plumber's putty, if there's no gasket

Time Commitment

1 to 2 hours

Tools You'll Need

Basin wrench or adjustable wrench

Related Topics

Fixing faucets, 208-217
Installing bathroom sinks, 46–51
Sink & vanity options, 40–41

Installing the Faucet

1 Apply plumber's putty

- For faucets with no rubber gasket, use plumber's putty
- Roll putty between your hands into a long, thin string
- Apply the string to the outside of the faucet body where it will make contact

2 Mount the faucet

- Slip the faucet into the mounting holes
- Align the faucet front to back and side to side
- Press it down on the mounting surface

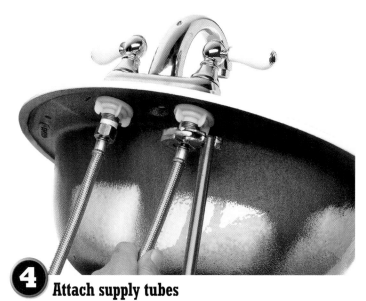

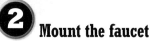

3 Secure the locknuts

- Working from below, thread the locknuts onto the sink's inlet shanks or mounting bolts
- Tighten plastic wing nuts by hand
- Use a wrench for metal nuts

4 Attach supply tubes

- Run supply tubes from the shutoffs to the faucet's inlet shanks or integral supply tubes
- Tighten the coupling nuts with a basin wrench
- Turn the water on at the shutoffs and check for leaks

Basin Choices

As the number and type of bathrooms in the average home have expanded, so has the selection of bathroom sinks. Designers have created a diverse range of high-style bathroom lavatories that turn what were once mundane fixtures into works of art.

Bathroom Sink Basics

A bathroom sink, called a lavatory or lav, usually has a pop-up stopper and an overflow hole that prevents water from spilling over the sides. Bathroom sinks, faucets, and traps also tend to be smaller than their kitchen counterparts. Most bathroom sinks are available with holes for 4-, 6-, or 8-inch faucet assemblies.

The biggest practical difference between bathroom sinks is the way they are mounted. There is no one standard or best way to mount a bathroom sink; the available options create different looks and have different uses. For example, a vanity with a countertop sink may offer welcome storage and counter space in a family bathroom, while a pedestal sink may make a powder room feel less crowded.

COUNTERTOP SINKS

Countertop or deck-mounted sinks fit into a specially cut hole in a vanity top. If you're replacing an existing sink, measure the hole in the countertop and take the measurements with you when you go shopping.

The methods of attaching sinks to countertops varies. Traditional countertop sinks may have a rim that sits on or is clamped to the countertop, or is recessed below it.

SELF-RIMMED SINK

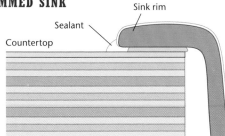

RECESSED SINK

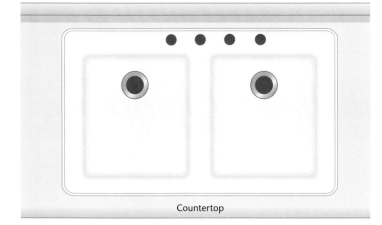

Countertop

ABOVE-COUNTER SINKS

Above-counter sinks, often called vessel sinks, are also mounted to a countertop, but part or all of the sink sits above the counter. (Since this increases the overall height, you may wish to lower your vanity or console a bit to compensate.) Vessel sinks require a very accurate cutout. Mounting systems differ, so follow the manufacturer's instructions.

This style of sink may be more suited to a lightly used space, such as a powder room or entertainment area, than a family bathroom. Often, the faucet is mounted behind the sink instead of on it. Choose a tall, special-purpose faucet to fit the sink height.

Above-Counter Sink

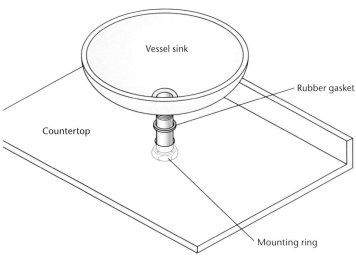

PARTIALLY RECESSED SINK

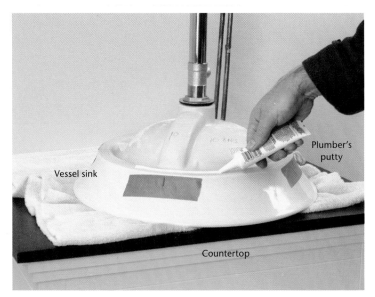

Related Topics

Installing bathroom faucets, 42-43
Installing bathroom sinks, 46–51
Sink & vanity options, 40–41

MOLDED SINKS

For small bathrooms or simpler installations, you can buy a vanity countertop with a sink molded in. The seamless, one-piece assembly is installed all at once, with no worries about a possible gap or leaks around the sink as in a two-piece arrangement. The downsides are less surface area around the sink and fewer design options.

Integral Sink

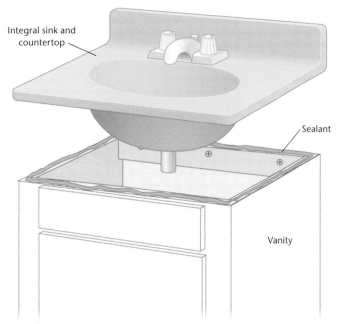

Integral sink and countertop

Sealant

Vanity

PEDESTAL SINKS

These often elegant towers, typically of vitreous china, can make great design accents. If a pedestal sink's trap, supply tubes, and shutoff valves will be visible, you may wish to buy decorative versions of these components to complement other bathroom accents. Pedestal sinks require support framing inside the adjacent wall, much like wall-mounted sinks. Making the plumbing connections within the available space and access area can take time and care.

Pedestal Sink

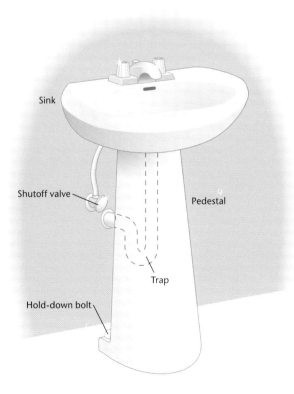

Sink

Shutoff valve

Pedestal

Trap

Hold-down bolt

WALL-MOUNTED SINKS

Wall-mounted sinks, also called wall-hung sinks, are no longer a common sight, but new versions are available and others are still found in many traditional designs. For a first-time installation, you will need to mount a backing board, which requires opening and then refinishing a part of the wall.

Wall-Mounted Sink

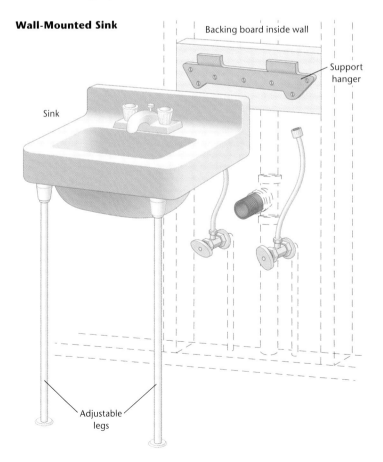

Backing board inside wall

Support hanger

Sink

Adjustable legs

Installing Bathroom Sinks

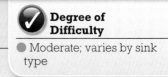
Bathroom sinks, or lavatories, can be categorized by the method used to mount them: countertop, wall-mounted, pedestal, above-counter (also called vessel), and recessed (also called under-mounted). Each is installed in a different way.

Installing a Countertop Sink

Countertop sinks are a common choice for vanities, and a classic element of many American family bathrooms. Vanities remain popular because they provide counter space on top and storage below, while concealing the plumbing connections from view. If you're buying a new vanity to go with your new sink, you may want to consider a back-saver version. Slightly higher than the traditional variety, a back-saving sink can relieve taller family members from bending over to use the sink and mirror and, as the name suggests, spare everyone's back in the bargain.

The steps shown here are for putting in a self-rimming, drop-in bowl, which is the easiest type to install. The rim of the sink hides slight irregularities, making installation forgiving. If you are installing a self-rimming sink in a new countertop, start by making a cutout for the bowl. Hire a professional to do this if the countertop is of a material that is difficult to cut.

Most sinks are sold with a template for marking this hole. Position the cutout according to the manufacturer's directions. A sink is typically centered from front to back.

When installing a heavy sink, such as a cast-iron unit, you can simply use a bead of plumber's putty rather than adhesive to seal the edges. The sink's weight will hold it in place. If you are installing a frame-mounted sink, attach the sink with the mounting clips or metal strip included with the unit.

❶ Mark for the cutout

- Use the manufacturer's template to draw the cutout line on the countertop
- If there's no template, set the bowl upside down on the countertop and trace it, then draw the cut line about ¾ inch inside the traced outline

❷ Cut out the opening

- For a countertop like this one, carefully drill a ⅜-inch starter hole inside the cut line
- Using a saber saw, begin cutting along the line
- Before finishing the cut, screw a scrap board wider than the cutout to the center of the cutout to prevent it from falling
- Lift out the support and cutout when you finish cutting

Stuff to Buy

SINK Countertop, recessed, or above-counter for a vanity; wall-mounted or pedestal are stand-alone
FAUCET & DRAIN ASSEMBLY Buy new ones for a new sink
BASIC SUPPLIES Plumber's putty, silicone adhesive; for some sinks, mounting clips or wall and floor fasteners

Time Commitment

Varies by sink type

Tools You'll Need

Saber saw
Socket wrenches
Combination wrenches
Basin wrench
Drill with masonry bit

Related Topics

Basin choices, 44–45
Basin & drain hookups, 52–53
Basin & tub pop-ups, 54–55
Installing bathroom faucets, 42–43
Sink & vanity options, 40–41

3 Attach the drain & tailpiece

- Place a bead of plumber's putty around the drain hole of the sink
- Press the housing into the drain hole
- Slip on the gasket, washer, and locknut below
- Tighten the locknut; keep the housing from turning as you go, using the handles of pliers to hold the screwdriver in the housing
- Remove any excess plumber's putty
- Attach the tailpiece to the housing

4 Pivot-rod option

- If you don't have a lot of room below your sink, consider installing the pivot rod for the sink's pop-up stopper now
- For more instructions on installing a pop-up stopper and pivot rod, please see page 53

5 Prepare the sink

- Turn the sink upside down
- Run a bead of silicone adhesive under the molded lip; adhesive is included with some sinks

6 Seat the sink

- Turn the sink and carefully align it with the countertop's front edge
- Press firmly around the lip to form a tight seal
- After the adhesive sets, apply a bead of latex caulk around the edge
- Smooth it with a wet finger

Installing a Wall-mounted Sink

Wall-mounted sinks are either hung on a metal bracket attached to the wall's framing or bolted directly to the framing. These sinks come with manufacturer's installation instructions, which you should follow exactly.

Unless you are replacing an existing sink that already has appropriate framing inside the bathroom wall, you will probably need to remove a small section of drywall so you can attach blocking between wall studs. Repairing and refinishing the wall section can make this a significant undertaking. For a new bathroom, the blocking can be installed ahead of time while the wall is open.

To add the blocking, determine where support will be needed, based on the instructions, the sink's measurements, and the mounting height (typically 30 inches above the floor). Remove drywall in that area and install 2 × 6 or 2 × 8 blocking between the studs. Then repair the drywall.

❶ Prepare the wall

- Add blocking inside the wall, as described above
- Position the mounting plate or sink and mark the wall through the holes
- Drill pilot holes for lag screws or for fasteners supplied with the sink; for a tile wall, use a masonry bit

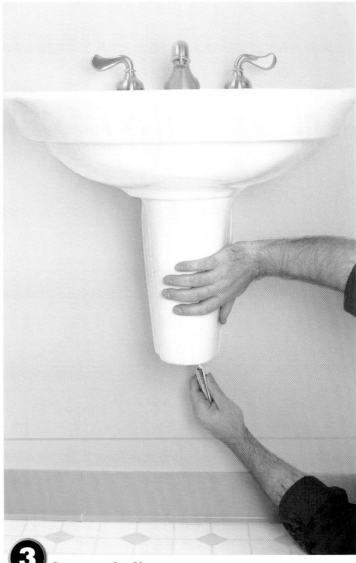

❷ Mount the sink

- Before hanging the sink, install the faucet, drain, and pop-up assemblies
- Secure the sink or mounting plate with lag screws or manufacturer-recommended fasteners
- After driving the first fastener, check that the sink or plate is level
- Drive in the other fasteners

❸ Connect the lines

- Connect the P-trap and drain arm to the drain stubout
- Connect the supply tubes to the shutoff valves
- Some sinks have a trim piece like this one to hide the plumbing lines; attach it as directed, typically with lag screws

Installing a Pedestal Sink

Pedestal sinks are made up of two parts: the sink and the pedestal, or base. Most pedestal sinks are, in effect, a variation on a wall-mounted sink, with much of the support for the sink provided by the wall framing, though the pedestal may bear some of the weight. Just as with a wall-mounted sink, you need blocking inside the wall.

Pedestal sinks come with manufacturer's installation instructions, which should be followed exactly. They also commonly come with the materials necessary for making water-supply and drain connections. As with most sinks, the faucet is purchased separately.

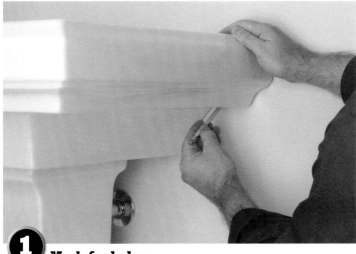

1 Mark for holes

- As needed, add blocking inside the wall and then refinish the wall
- Put the sink and pedestal in place temporarily
- Level and square the assembly
- Mark for mounting holes on the wall and floor

2 Prepare the wall and sink

- Drill pilot holes for fasteners in the wall and floor, using a masonry bit for a tile wall
- If you are drilling tile, put tape on the area to be drilled to keep the bit centered
- Install the drain assembly and faucet on the sink

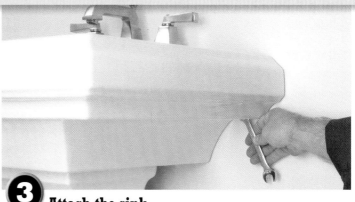

3 Attach the sink

- In most cases, secure the sink with lag screws or manufacturer-supplied fasteners
- Connect the drain, the trap, and the supply tubes
- For some pedestal sinks, you must connect the plumbing before attaching the sink, temporarily resting it on the pedestal near the wall

4 Bolt the pedestal to the floor

- Drill pilot holes in the floor for bolts that will secure the pedestal
- Insert the bolts
- To avoid porcelain and tile cracks, do not overtighten the bolts

5 Attach the sink to the pedestal

- If the sink has a nut or rod to mount it to the pedestal, secure the connection

Installing an Above-counter Sink

An above-counter bathroom sink, also called a vessel sink, is an excellent choice to make a design statement. These stylish features appear to sit on top of the counter, but the drain attaches underneath, just as with a countertop sink. Above-counter sinks install much like a countertop sink, but the hole in the countertop is smaller—in the most extreme scenario, just large enough for the drain. Most manufacturers include instructions, as well as a pattern for cutting the countertop, so be sure to follow the directions precisely. Some manufacturers of above-counter sinks provide precut countertops that make installation a snap.

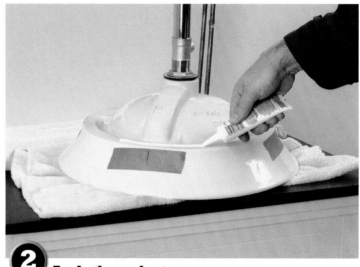

1 Dry-fit the sink

- Mark for the cutout, then make the cut, working very accurately for a good fit
- Mount the faucet and drain assembly (you can wait to install a counter-mounted faucet)
- Temporarily position the sink in the cutout to check for alignment and clearance
- Mark the countertop and sink with masking tape to guide the installation

2 Apply the sealant

- For a model like this one, turn the sink upside down on a soft surface like a towel
- Apply a bead of sealant under the counter rim, following the label directions

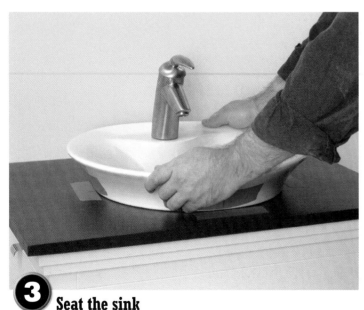

3 Seat the sink

- Position the sink in the opening
- Align the guide marks and press down

4 Apply finishing touches

- Smooth away excess sealant
- Allow the sealant to set according to label directions
- Connect the drainpipes and supply tubes

Installing a Recessed Sink

A recessed or undermount sink is another variation on the counter-top sink. Recessed sinks offer a sleek, uninterrupted look and make the counter easy to clean. They can also be installed in practically any type of counter. The method of attachment varies by manufacturer, and installation instructions are included with all models.

In addition to the sink, many manufacturers offer complementary countertops that are precut, predrilled, and pre-fitted to work with the sink. You simply apply a bead of sealant and tighten some screws.

1 Prepare the countertop and sink

- Locate and cut the opening
- Mount the drain assembly to the sink
- For a small to medium-size countertop, turn the countertop upside down (make sure you and a helper will be able to flip it over later with the sink attached)
- Position the sink and mark for the mounting clips
- Attach the clips to what will be the underside of the countertop
- Apply sealant around the sink rim

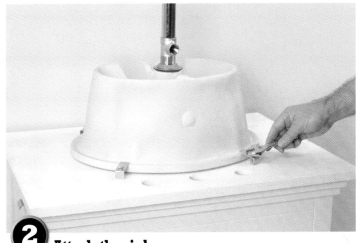

2 Attach the sink

- Turn the sink upside down, set it in place, and secure it with the clips
- Allow the sealant to set according to label directions

3 Install the faucet

- If you wish, install the faucet before seating the countertop
- You can also install the pop-up mechanism now, or do it later

4 Seat the assembly

- Prep the top edges of the vanity with adhesive
- With a helper, turn over the sink and countertop assembly and install it
- If you haven't already, install the faucet and pop-up mechanism
- Connect the drain assembly and supply tubes

Basin & Drain Hookups

For most types of bathroom sinks, the drain connections are installed in the same way. The parts include a sink flange and drain body, a tailpiece, a P-trap, a waste arm, and usually a pop-up assembly. Only the materials vary.

Drain & Pop-Up

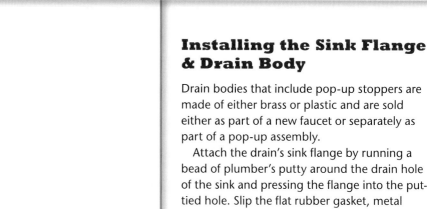

Lift-rod knob

Pop-up stopper

Sink flange

Clevis

Rubber gasket

Metal washer

Locknut

Spring clip

Drain body

Pivot rod

Tailpiece

Pivot ball

Installing the Sink Flange & Drain Body

Drain bodies that include pop-up stoppers are made of either brass or plastic and are sold either as part of a new faucet or separately as part of a pop-up assembly.

Attach the drain's sink flange by running a bead of plumber's putty around the drain hole of the sink and pressing the flange into the puttied hole. Slip the flat rubber gasket, metal washer, and locknut over the drain body (see left). Insert the threaded top of the drain body into the bottom of the sink and screw it onto the flange.

Tighten a metal locknut with slip-joint pliers or a spud wrench until it is snug, but be careful not to overtighten it. Plastic nuts should be tightened by hand and then tightened slightly more with a tool.

Adjusting the Trap & Drain Arm

Bathroom P-traps come in chromed brass, plastic ABS or PVC, and 17-gauge brass. Plastic is usually the best choice for traps that won't be seen, but check your local code.

Traps and drain arms may require some care and attention to get just right. Be patient and don't rush the job. First, connect the trap to the drain body, then add the waste arm, working the parts back and forth to get the right length and angle to align with both the drain body and the drain stubout.

Measure and cut the waste arm as required to meet the drain stubout correctly. If necessary, add a threaded trap adapter to the end of the drain stubout. Usually, the trap's slip fitting has enough play to line up with the drain body. If it doesn't, you can add a separate tailpiece to make up the difference.

The couplings on plastic traps need hand tightening only; metal couplings may need half a turn or so past hand-tight with adjustable pliers. If in doubt, err on the loose side. Hand-tighten, turn on the water, and check for leaks. If there's a leak, tighten the offending coupling slightly, then recheck.

$ Stuff to Buy	**Time Commitment**	**Tools You'll Need**	**Related Topics**
	1 to 2 hours	Slip-joint pliers or spud wrench	Basin & tub pop-ups, 54–55

DRAIN ASSEMBLY COMPONENTS Plastic parts are lighter, cheaper, and easier to work with; metal is an option for exposed drains
BASIC SUPPLIES Plumber's putty

Repairing drains and traps, 202–203
Unclogging a sink, 198–199

Installing the Pop-Up

If you're installing a new pop-up assembly, follow the manufacturer's instructions. Be sure to test the stopper when you're done. If it won't open or close properly, remove the spring clip and move the pivot rod to a higher or lower hole on the clevis.

❶ Secure the flange & drain body

- Run plumber's putty around the sink opening
- Slip the sink flange through the opening, pressing against the putty
- Working from below, secure the drain body with a rubber gasket, metal washer, and locknut
- Tighten a metal locknut with slip-joint pliers
- Tighten a plastic one by hand, then tighten slightly more with pliers

❷ Connect the trap

- Position slip nuts or couplings on the drain arm and the tailpiece as needed
- Slip the drain arm into the drain stubout
- Slip one end of a P-trap onto the tailpiece
- Join the free end of the trap to the drain arm
- Adjust heights and angles until the assembly fits snugly
- Tighten down all couplings

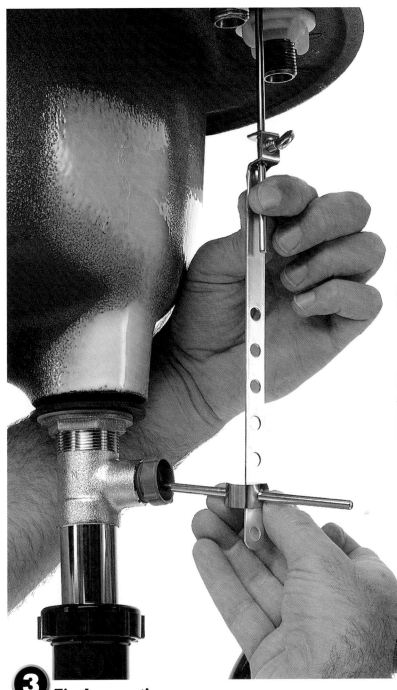

❸ Final connections

- Slip the pop-up stopper through the sink flange from above
- Insert the pivot rod through the side of the drain body
- Run the pivot rod through a hole in the clevis and secure it with a spring clip
- Secure the clevis to the faucet's lift rod

Basin & Tub Pop-ups

Pop-up mechanisms are signature elements of bathroom plumbing, found primarily in bathroom sinks and tubs. As the pop-up's name implies, it pops up or down to open or close the drain. It's easy to make small adjustments for a better fit.

Bathroom Sink Pop-Ups

A sink pop-up opens or closes the drain depending on the position of the lift rod, which is raised or lowered at the faucet. The lift rod and clevis can be adjusted to fix a pop-up that doesn't close properly or open fully. The spring clip that holds the pivot ball may also need adjustment to prevent leaks. Clogs can be addressed with disassembly and cleaning.

SINK POP-UP

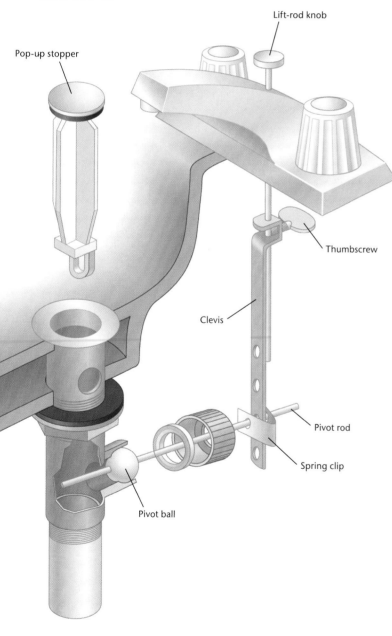

Pop-up stopper

Lift-rod knob

Thumbscrew

Clevis

Pivot rod

Spring clip

Pivot ball

TROUBLESHOOTING SINK POP-UPS

If the pop-up stopper in a sink doesn't open far enough for proper drainage, loosen the thumbscrew and retighten it lower on the lift rod. If there's not enough room left on the rod, move the spring clip and pivot rod to a lower hole.

If the pop-up stopper isn't seating snugly, pull it out. An unattached type is simply pulled out, while the slotted type must be twisted and then pulled. For the attached type, you'll need to undo the spring clip and pull out the pivot rod before you can take out the stopper. Once the stopper has been freed, clean off any hair or debris. Also check the rubber seal. If it's damaged, pry off the seal and slip on a new one.

If the pop-up still doesn't seat correctly, loosen the thumbscrew, push the stopper down, and retighten the screw higher on the lift rod. When the drain is closed, the pivot rod should slope downhill from the clevis to the drain body.

If the pop-up seems to be seated well but water is still draining from the basin, try tightening the retaining nut that holds the ball in place. Still draining? Replace the washer behind the ball, then adjust the pivot rod.

Unattached

Slotted

Attached

RELEASING AN ATTACHED POP-UP

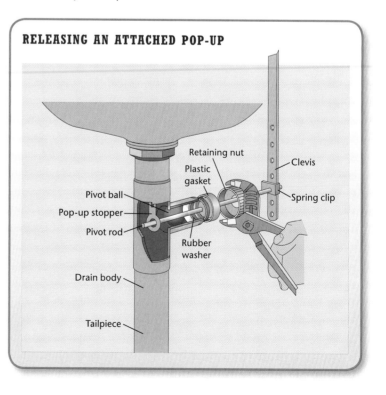

Retaining nut

Plastic gasket

Clevis

Spring clip

Pivot ball

Pop-up stopper

Pivot rod

Rubber washer

Drain body

Tailpiece

Bathtub Pop-ups

In a bathtub, the pop-up stopper is part of the waste-and-overflow fitting, which includes the all-important overflow plate that helps prevent bathroom floods.

The two systems shown here are common. A lift-lever unit is analogous to the pop-up in a sink but with a different mechanism. You operate the pop-up from a distance by flipping the lever up and down. The toe-tap is a stand-alone add-on, a modern alternative to an old-fashioned drain plug.

LIFT-LEVER UNIT

Overflow plate
Lift lever
Striker rod
Adjusting nut
Middle link
Striker spring
Pop-up stopper
Rocker arm

TOE-TAP FITTING

Overflow plate
Toe-tap fitting

SERVICING A TUB POP-UP

If the stopper of a lift-lever unit doesn't seat properly, or if water drains slowly, remove the pop-up stopper and rocker arm by pulling the stopper straight up. Then unscrew and remove the tub's overflow plate and pull the entire assembly out through the overflow. For a stopper that isn't seating well, loosen the adjusting nuts and slide the middle link up to shorten the striker rod. The striker spring rests unattached on top of the rocker arm. For a sluggish drain, lower the middle link to lengthen the assembly. Before reassembling it, clean the pop-up stopper.

Instead of a pop-up assembly or a toe-tap, some tubs have a plunger assembly consisting of a strainer at the drain opening and an internal plunger that blocks the back of the drain to stop the flow of water. The lift mechanism and plunger can be removed through the overflow in the same way.

Overflow plate

Toe-tap stopper

Related Topics

Basin & drain hookups, 52–53
Installing bathroom sinks, 46–51
Planning for a new shower, 62–63
Planning a new tub, 58–59
Repairing drains & traps, 202-203
Unclogging a sink, 198–199
Unclogged tub & shower drains, 200-201

How the Pros Do It

"A toe-tap depends on a spring, and the spring can wear out, usually with the stopper in the closed position. If there isn't a pop-up mechanism, I like a lift-and-turn plug because it doesn't use a spring."

Tim Miller, J. Kittelberger & Sons

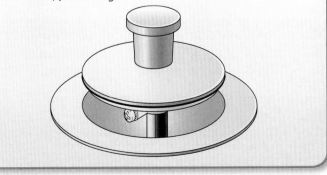

Showerheads

Showerheads offer a great opportunity for quick, simple upgrades that can make your daily routine more pleasant. Take some care as you work, however, as a broken pipe behind the wall can turn a simple upgrade into a major project.

Removing an Old Showerhead

In principle, you can detach any showerhead, old or new, by unscrewing the collar that attaches it to the shower arm, a threaded section outside the finished wall of the shower. When changing a showerhead, make sure the shower arm doesn't start to turn or move. Turning the arm could damage the plumbing inside the wall, creating an immediate mess followed by a serious repair job.

If you're removing a collar that has been in place for years or decades, it may require more force to turn than a newer one, making it especially important to steady the arm.

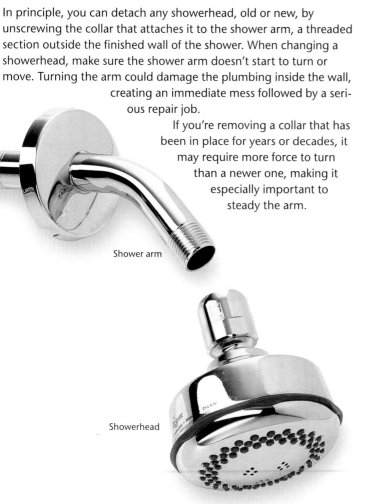

Shower arm

Showerhead

How the Pros Do It

"Let's say you have to hold the shower arm in place but you don't want to scar the chrome. The jaws on an adjustable wrench will munch right into the finish. I use a strap wrench for a good grip without scarring the arm."

Tim Miller, J. Kittelberger & Sons

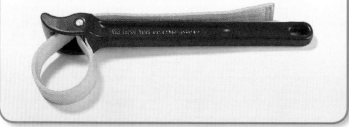

Installing a Fixed Showerhead

1 **Prepare the shower arm**

- Once the old showerhead is off, clean the pipe threads
- Wrap the threads with pipe-thread tape about three times
- Alternatively, apply pipe-joint compound to the threads

2 **Add the showerhead**

- Wrap the jaws of an adjustable wrench with tape to avoid scratches
- Steadying the showerhead, tighten the collar, but avoid overtightening it

 **Time Commitment**
1 hour

 **Tools You'll Need**
Adjustable wrench

Related Topics
Minor clogs & leaks, 218-219
New shower possibilities, 60–61
Planning for a new shower, 62–63

Showerhead Options

Many modern showerheads offer a group of selectable spray options, from soothing to invigorating, to suit different family members and times of day. Adjustable-height showerheads can be raised or lowered, much like a desk lamp, to accommodate the person taking a shower. Other showerheads have much wider heads, creating a rain-shower effect instead of a directed spray.

If your house has low water pressure, your shower time doesn't have to suffer for it. Look for a special-purpose showerhead designed for low-pressure conditions.

Showerhead flow rates are limited by law to no more than 2.5 gallons a minute at a standard water pressure, but low-flow or water-efficient showerheads will save even more money. Another way to save water is to buy a showerhead with a shampoo switch right beside the head. You flip the switch to turn the water off until you need to rinse.

Low-flow showerheads with "shampoo" switches

HANDHELD SHOWERHEADS

A handheld showerhead lets you direct the water more freely than the fixed variety. One type attaches directly to the shower arm. Another is an integral part of a tub spout, which allows you to add a shower outlet to a tub that doesn't have shower pipes behind the wall. Handhelds can usually be clipped into place on the wall, offering the advantages of a fixed showerhead as well. They are convenient for anyone taking a shower, and they are especially useful if you're helping an older person or a child to shower.

To install one at the shower arm, replace the existing showerhead with a diverter valve, then fasten the handheld shower's hose to the outlet on the diverter. For a handheld that hooks up to a tub spout, you'll need to replace the spout with one that has a diverter-valve knob and a built-in hose outlet.

Most handheld showerhead kits come with a wall bracket for hanging the unit. Position the bracket at a convenient height. Mark and drill screw holes into the wall, using a masonry bit for tile. If there's no wall stud to accept screws, fasten the bracket with toggle bolts.

To prevent water from siphoning back through a handheld showerhead into the water supply, local codes may require the installation of a vacuum-breaker assembly. Manufacturers typically include instructions for installation of this device.

Planning a New Tub

Tub installations range from one-for-one replacements to the freer choices of a full remodel. Combine a tub and a shower to maximize your choices.

Practical Considerations

A bathtub filled with water is extremely heavy. Check local building codes for floor framing requirements and consider getting professional help for framing and support or for the entire installation. Even a one-for-one bathtub replacement is a challenging project to undertake because of the awkward size and weight of tubs. If you're remodeling, you may have to remove doors and even some trim to get a tub in or out.

A cast-iron tub is bulky and very heavy. If you're removing one, it can be broken into pieces with a sledgehammer, lifted out in sections, and then recycled.

Planning a New Tub

Bathtubs come in four basic styles—recessed, corner, drop-in, and freestanding—which reflect their installation methods. Tubs are available in right- and left-handed versions, depending on which end contains the drain hole.

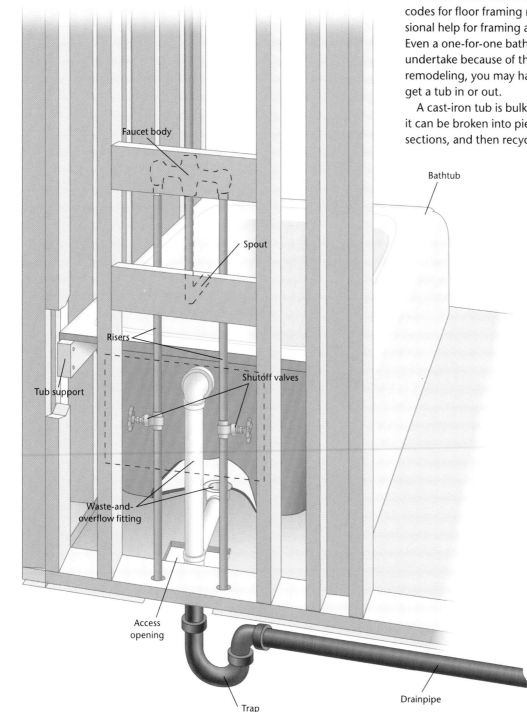

Faucet body

Spout

Risers

Tub support

Shutoff valves

Waste-and-overflow fitting

Bathtub

Access opening

Trap

Drainpipe

Whirlpool Tubs

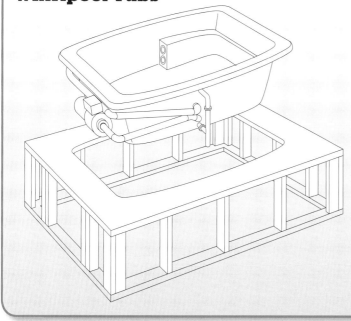

Whirlpool tubs offer motorized circulation jets that provide a soothing hydromassage. Such tubs are available in recessed, corner, drop-in, and freestanding styles, but most are built for platform installation. The pump can be located separately for noise control and ease of service with some models. Whirlpool tubs may require special framing, an additional water heater, or a dedicated electrical circuit.

Some types of whirlpools have variable-speed pumps with electronic controls that adjust the power of the massage. Those controls also set temperatures and cycle times. Jets vary in size, number, and power. Air jets are smaller and less powerful than water jets, which mix water with air. They provide a lighter massage but keep mildew and other substances from accumulating.

RECESSED TUBS

Also called a three-wall-alcove tub, the recessed style is the most popular because of its space efficiency, affordability, and availability. Only the front has a decorative finish, because alcove walls conceal the other sides. The standard length is 60 inches and the standard depth is 14 inches, but 72-inch-long models and 16-inch-deep tubs are also available. Recessed tubs are typically made of enameled steel, which is relatively lightweight and inexpensive but is also noisy and prone to chipping. A better choice is expensive enameled cast iron, but the bathroom floor may need reinforcement to support the tub's heavy weight.

DROP-IN TUBS

Drop-in tubs are usually mounted on a platform, but they can be sunk below floor level. Some overlap the deck, while others are undermounted, with only the inside of the tub finished. Drop-in tubs are made of lightweight acrylic or fiberglass-reinforced plastic, both of which are susceptible to scratching and dulling, or of enameled cast iron, which may require structural reinforcement of the bathroom floor.

CORNER TUBS

While the term "corner tub" applies specifically to a triangular tub with a finished front and two unfinished sides, it more generally refers to any shape of tub installed in a corner with at least two sides against a wall and one decorative side visible.

FREESTANDING TUBS

Most freestanding tubs are built with four legs (though some are designed to fit into a frame), with completely finished exteriors. Reproductions of antique claw-foot tubs in lightweight materials are easy to find, as are reconditioned antiques. A true antique will be made of cast iron, so floor buttressing may be required.

New Shower Possibilities

Showers are often the showpieces of large bathrooms, offering a wealth of features and design choices. Many showers are more practical than tubs, which typically use more water and can't be adapted to the available space.

A World of Shower Options

Showers, which must be at least 36 inches square, range from pre-fabricated stalls to custom-built shower spas with steam-shower functions, programmable shower panels, seats, and other features. A typical stall can be built from scratch or assembled from manu-factured components. More elaborate installations are likely to be specially designed and custom-framed.

If you are concerned about saving water, a classic shower setup with one showerhead uses far less water than a bath. Shower walls or ceilings with multiple sprays (opposite page) may use more water than a bath.

PREFABRICATED VERSUS CUSTOM

One-piece showers are common in new construction but are usu-ally too large for a remodel unless some walls are knocked down. For remodels, manufactured shower-wall panels are preferred. The panels lap over a molded shower base and are attached to a water-proof wall.

A custom shower can be built from the ground up or with a pre-fabricated shower base, which saves time and money. The shower's adjoining walls must be waterproof. For a custom shower, walls typically include a layer of water-resistant drywall covered with waterproof cement board and finished with ceramic tile, slate, granite, marble, or solid surface.

Sometimes all it takes to install a new shower is to make the most of the plumbing you already have. In these cases, all it took was a sus-pended shower curtain and some simple hardware.

Left: A wall separates this shower and toilet, but the shower door itself is glass, which makes this small bathroom feel a bit more spacious.

Related Topics

Planning a new tub, 58–59
Planning for a new shower, 62–63
Showerheads, 56–57

Surrounded by Spray

More elaborate showers offer multiple spray heads in the walls, and sometimes the ceiling, which can be custom-programmed as you take your shower. (Digital panels may also let you select light levels, audio, and steam settings.) Behind the scenes, these installations typically use pipes that run from a manifold to the separate sprayers. The controller operates each line to create the total effect.

Planning for a New Shower

Unlike a bathtub, a new shower can be designed for the size and shape of your bathroom, as long as it's at least 36 inches square. The plumbing is straightforward but must be tucked behind a wall. Make sure to include an access panel in your plan.

SHOWER BASES

With the exception of one-piece models, all showers begin with a base, sometimes called a receptor or a pan, which can be purchased ready-made or built by hand. Most bases are made of plastic, terrazzo, cast polymer, or solid-surface acrylic and come in standard square, rectangular, or corner configurations with a hole for the drain. Some include the drain flange. Of course, you could also have a tile professional float a traditional mortar base and line it with the tile of your choice.

A pan needs to be waterproofed and sloped precisely to the drain, which must be set at the right height for perfect drainage. Be sure to select a prefabricated shower pan with a drain opening that matches the existing location of your drainpipe. Your shower will require a single, double, or triple threshold, depending on whether it is set into three walls, into two walls, or against a single wall.

SHOWER DOORS

Traditionalists may prefer a shower curtain, but a shower door keeps in warmth and moisture and may better fit the look you're aiming for. Shower doors may swing open, fold back, slide, or pivot. Some are hinged directly to the shower entrance, but most are framed with aluminum that comes in many finishes, including epoxy-coated colors. Doors are made from inexpensive plastic or tempered glass that can be clear, frosted, mirrored, or patterned.

For a steam shower, the door must be airtight, and the shower must also include an airtight overhead panel.

ADDING A SHOWER STALL

Whether you install the shower yourself or hire a professional, the first step is to construct a frame to contain the shower unit. Be especially careful to make all measurements accurately and the framing square and plumb. Run supply pipes and drainpipes to the desired locations and install the shower pipes and trap.

If necessary, drill holes through the surface of the stall or wall panel for the valve assembly and shower-arm stubout. Refer to the manufacturer's installation instructions for exact locations and other specifications.

INSTALLING DIFFERENT UNITS

Slide a one-piece shower stall into place. Attach the stall as you would an acrylic tub, nailing the flange to wall studs. It will probably take some maneuvering to line up the shower unit with the drain, shower-arm stubout, and faucet body. Many pros leave access behind and below the shower, then add these fittings after the shower is in place.

To install a molded shower base, it's best to first spread a layer of mortar over the area, then use the mortar to both support and help level the base. Position the base atop the drain outlet and connect them by screwing in the drain flange. Cover the opening with rags.

Once the base is secured, you're ready to cover the shower's side and back walls with tile or panels.

With the shower anchored in place, caulk around all openings. Then, attach the showerhead and faucet handles.

In a small and narrow bath, a curbless shower makes the space feel much larger. The wall-mounted sink contributes to the clean theme.

A Safe, Accessible Shower

If you've ever experienced a pressure drop or an abrupt change of water temperature when someone starts a washer or flushes a toilet, or if you worry about children or slow-moving family members being exposed to very hot water, you'll appreciate the value of a pressure-balancing valve. Also known as a temperature-limiting or anti-scald valve, it takes the place of a standard faucet body and shower control to prevent scalds via a built-in pressure-balancing diaphragm. Such valves are increasingly required by code for new construction and are a great safety feature for remodels.

Like stairs and bathtubs, a shower can be a likely spot for a fall. Try to minimize the risk when you choose the surface of the shower base and the flooring nearby. Bathroom designers also recommend properly anchored grab bars—rather than towel bars, which aren't designed to support a person—inside the shower, as well as by the tub and the toilet.

Grab bars in the shower can be especially helpful for family members who need extra support. For more accessibility, consider a zero-threshold shower, also referred to as a barrier-free or roll-in design.

PRESSURE-BALANCING VALVE

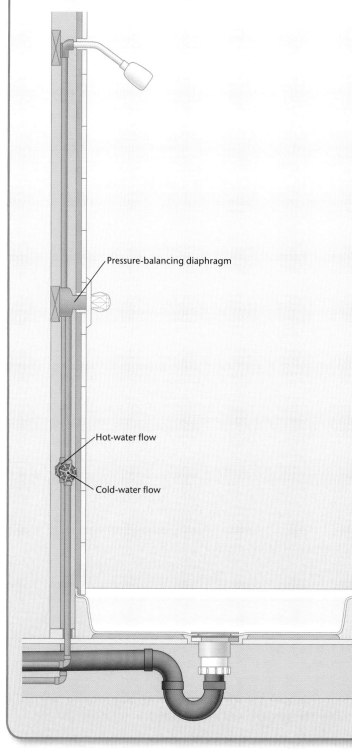

Pressure-balancing diaphragm

Hot-water flow

Cold-water flow

In this shower, a wooden stool plays the roll of a shelf for shampoos. If you like this look, choose a stool without bolts or screws to avoid rust stains.

Toilets

Toilets have changed since the advent of low-flush requirements in 1994. For the most part, today's models are far more reliable than some early low-flush designs. They also offer a host of refinements, such as warm seats, quiet lids, and new colors and designs.

New & Improved

As of January 1, 1994, new toilets in the United States are required to use no more than 1.6 gallons of water per flush, compared with older models that used 3.6 gallons or, in earlier years, 5 to 7 gallons. A number of early low-flush toilets did not have adequate flushing power, requiring frustrated users to flush twice or more and cope with more clogs. Pressure-assisted flush systems became alternative choices in some homes, as their reliable performance outweighed the louder noise and typically higher repair costs.

Today, most manufacturers have re-engineered the geometry and other design aspects of their toilets, often widening the flush valve between the tank and the bowl. Most modern toilets are dependable and effective.

Options & Alternatives

Toilets are available in many colors and designs, although white is most common and usually less expensive. Both traditional gravity toilets and pressure-assisted models are common in one- and two-piece versions. Two-piece toilets employ a separate tank and bowl. One-piece toilets, also called low-profile, merge the tank and bowl into a single unit. A two-piece model costs less, but the exterior of a one-piece toilet is easier to clean. One-piece toilets often include a seat with the unit, while most two-piece units do not.

For small baths, wall-mounted toilets are available, but they can be hard to find and expensive to buy and install. Taller toilets are available for people who need or prefer a higher seat. Heights and seat shapes vary, so make sure to pick what's comfortable.

A two-piece toilet looks at home in a traditional bathroom. Though old-fashioned in appearance, this one has a glazed trap-way that practically eliminates clogs.

A dual-flush toilet saves water by allowing you to choose between a standard 1.6-gallon flush and one that uses half that amount.

What the Experts Say

"The quiet-closing seats are great, but if you have kids, there are some pros and cons. Tell them that not all toilet seats are like that, or they'll go to a friend's house and make a big noise when they drop the seat."

Tim Miller,
J. Kittelberger & Sons

Toilet bowls are either round or elongated. The latter are 2 inches longer, with a larger water surface. Seats come in different materials —including wood, plastic, and polypropylene—and must match the bowl's shape. Some seats are cushioned, contoured, or even heated for extra comfort, and some automatically trigger the flush mechanism when the top is closed. Quiet seats close slowly and silently when you drop them, instead of slamming loudly from a height.

Before shopping for a new toilet, measure the rough-in, the distance from the wall to the center of the toilet drain. A 12-inch rough-in is standard, but some are 10 or 14 inches.

Bidets & Washing Toilets

Bidets are floor-mounted and plumbed with hot and cold water (unlike a toilet, which requires only a cold-water supply). They're best installed next to toilets. Styles and finishes are available that match new toilets, and units come with either a horizontal spray mount or a vertical spray in the center of the bowl. Some models have deck-mounted faucets, while others use wall-mounted controls.

A space-saving alternative to the classic bidet is a washing toilet or washlet, which essentially combines the function of a bidet and a toilet through a special-purpose seat. Most washlet toilets have plug-in heaters that use the toilet's cold-water supply, so no

hot-water supply line is needed. Warm water circulates inside the seat to heat it, and a timer can save energy when the house is empty. A retractable washing sprayer is tucked out of the way, then extended for use. Increasingly, some manufacturers use the term "bidet" for these seats as well.

Fresh Options for Your Kitchen

I n this chapter, you'll learn everything about the kitchen sink, from types to installation techniques; how to choose and install a new faucet, with or without a sprayer; and your options when it comes to water filters. We also show you how to hook up your kitchen sink's drain, replace or add a garbage disposer and hot-water dispenser, and make the connections for a dishwasher.

Chapter Contents

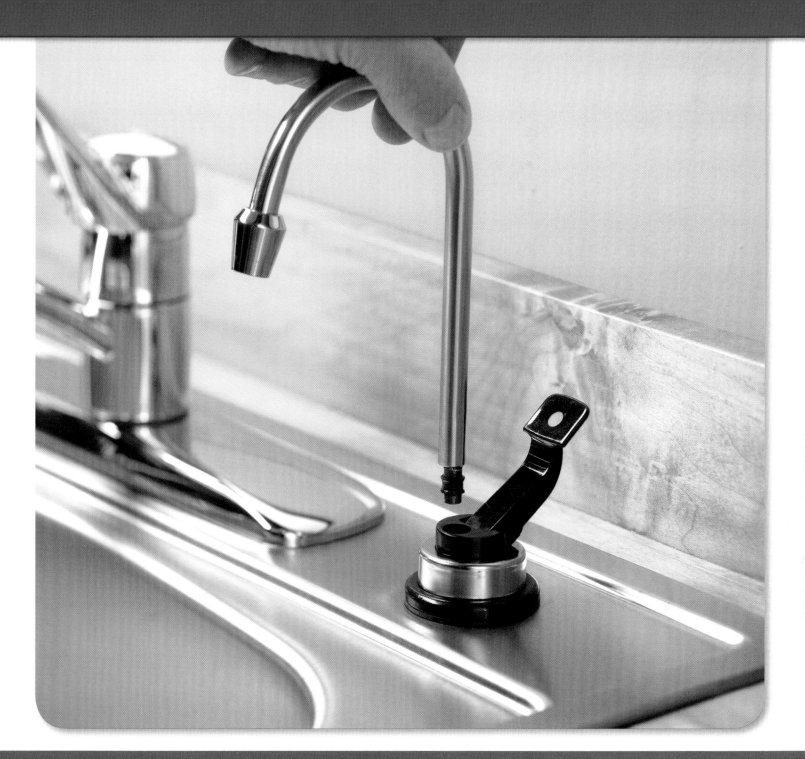

Installing a Dishwasher
page 82

Hot-water Dispensers
page 84

Adding an Ice Maker
page 86

page 74

New Looks for Kitchen Sinks

One of the hardest-working fixtures in your home is the kitchen sink. In most homes, it's used up to an hour a day, and that can include some rugged tasks. Look for kitchen sinks that are durable and easy to clean, then choose one that suits your style.

A popular choice for spray units is a separate faucet that features a gooseneck and a restaurant-style sprayer and is high enough to fill large pots.

Sizes & Combinations

The standard kitchen sink is 22 × 30 inches, with two equally sized bowls that are 8 inches deep. But specialty sinks can cater to your preferences. There are sinks with 9- or 10-inch-deep bowls if you frequently use large pots, high-set shallow bowls that go between two basins for peeling and washing vegetables, large single basins, unequally sized basins, and basins that fit into tight corners.

Pot fillers, which began as a necessity in commercial kitchens, have since been embraced by home chefs who want to give their kitchens a professional look.

This stainless-steel sink set in a granite countertop has a soap dispenser, a hot-water dispenser, and a spray head that detaches from the faucet so you can bring the water to whatever needs rinsing.

A Choice of Materials

Materials include stainless steel (the heavier the gauge, the better); easy-clean enameled cast iron, which provides the greatest number of color choices and an elegant, hard finish; integral solid surface, which forms part of a solid-surface countertop; composite ("quartz" composite is the most durable of the choices); old-fashioned soapstone; and new-style concrete. For a kitchen sink, it's best to avoid delicate and decorative materials, such as vitreous china, brass, and copper.

Self-rimming sinks, which sit on the countertop, are the easiest to install but can collect dirt at the seams. Recessed sinks, which attach to the underside of the counter, stay cleaner but are more difficult to seat. Kitchen sinks generally come with four holes for mounting faucets, sprayers, and dispensers for hot water, liquid soap, or purified water.

Sinks need not be merely functional. This old-school, porcelain-covered cast-iron sink is the centerpiece of a colorful kitchen. Pipes have been left exposed for a farmhouse look.

The self-rimming sink above was installed to function as the countertop, so seating it was not an issue. The one at upper right is set within a countertop and features a smaller basin on the left that drains through a garbage disposer.

In this custom kitchen, a colored-concrete countertop and backsplash blend seamlessly with a concrete sink of the same hue. Vintage faucets give this contemporary kitchen a retro feel.

Installing a Faucet

Putting a faucet on a brand-new sink is relatively simple. If you do it before the sink goes into place, access is easy. To add a new faucet to an existing sink, you'll need to work under the sink, making the task a bit more awkward.

Choosing the Faucet

Most faucets are made of brass. The better ones are cast in molds and are then finished with chrome, brass plating, nickel, porcelain, pewter, or powder-coated enamel. Brush-coated metal finishes hide water spots better than high-polish finishes.

Every faucet contains an inner valve that controls water flow. The quality of that valve determines how drip-free, reliable, and durable the faucet will be. Disc faucets, which use ceramic discs, are the best and most expensive. They are very durable and nearly maintenance-free. Compression faucets, in which a stem rises and falls to open and close the waterway, are the least expensive and least durable. Ball faucets and cartridge faucets are common alternatives.

Common Configurations

Kitchen faucets come in many configurations. One of the most practical is a single-lever faucet, which allows for easy one-handed temperature adjustment. A popular variation, shown in the steps at right, has a pullout spout-sprayer that adds cleanup flexibility. Other kitchen faucets include the two-handle center-set and the two-handle spread-fit type. Also popular are single-spout swing-arm faucets mounted at the back of the stove for filling pots easily.

Preparing for the Job

Remove the old faucet if there is one. Start by closing the shutoff valves and draining the faucet. With a basin wrench, undo the mounting nuts that attach the old faucet and base plate to the sink, then detach the old supply tubes from the faucet and the shutoffs.

Clean the surface of the sink where the new faucet will sit. Some faucets come with a rubber gasket on the bottom. If yours doesn't, apply a bead of plumber's putty to the base, as shown on page 72. Some plumbers pack the entire faucet base with putty for extra protection, even if it has a gasket.

SINGLE-LEVER FAUCET WITH SPRAYER

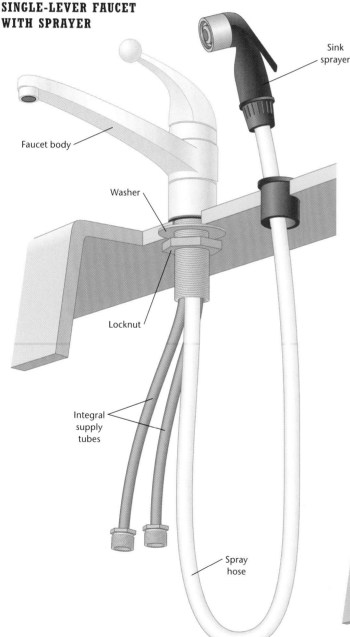

Sink sprayer

Faucet body

Washer

Locknut

Integral supply tubes

Spray hose

TWO-HANDLE CENTER-SET FAUCET

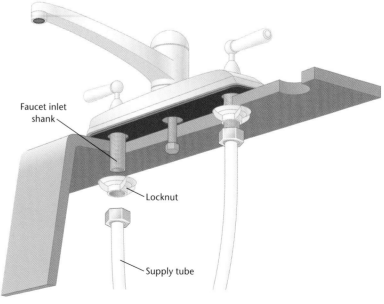

Faucet inlet shank

Locknut

Supply tube

 Stuff to Buy

BASIC SUPPLIES Plumber's putty if there's no gasket; pipe-thread tape
FAUCET Make sure your new faucet fits the holes in the sink
SUPPLY TUBES Replace old supply tubes whenever you put in a new faucet

Time Commitment

2 hours

Tools You'll Need

Adjustable wrench
Basin wrench

Related Topics

Adding a faucet & sprayer, 72–73
Filters at the sink, 74–75
Hot-water dispensers, 84–85
New looks for kitchen sinks, 68–69
Upgrading to a new sink, 76–79

How to Do It

① Prepare the faucet

- Check the instructions to see whether any assembly is required
- For pullout spout-sprayer faucets, thread the sprayer hose through the faucet body

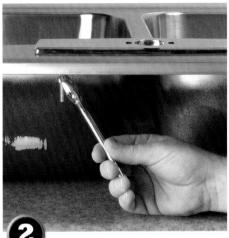

② Attach the base plate

- Insert the gasket under the base plate of the faucet and attach the base plate
- If there is no gasket, use plumber's putty as described in **Preparing for the Job** on page 70

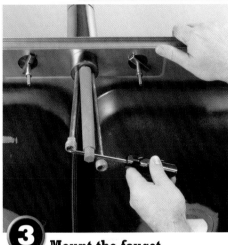

③ Mount the faucet

- Insert the faucet body, if it is separate from the base plate
- Slip the washer onto the faucet body from below, then loosely thread the lock-nut onto the body
- Center the faucet body in the hole before tightening it down
- Tighten the locknut with a long socket, if one is provided, using a screwdriver in the two holes to turn it

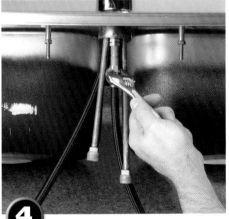

④ Attach the sprayer

- Attach the sprayer hose to the faucet body, using pipe-thread tape if it's recommended
- Tighten the hose to the faucet body with an adjustable wrench, but avoid over-tightening

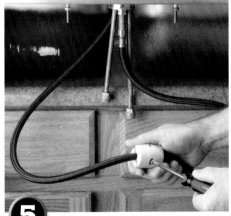

⑤ Add the counterweight

- Add a counterweight, if one is supplied, to the sprayer hose
- Follow the manufacturer's instructions on where to secure it, and avoid crimping the hose

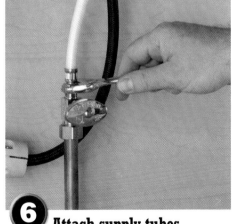

⑥ Attach supply tubes

- Connect the supply tubes to the shutoff valves, using pipe-thread tape
- Tighten snugly with an adjustable wrench, but do not overtighten
- Attach the supply tubes to the faucet's integral supply tubes; turn on the shutoff valves and check for leaks

Adding a Faucet & Sprayer

If you prefer not to install a kitchen faucet with a pullout sprayer in the spout, the usual alternative is a separate sprayer. Although the sprayer takes up another hole, this setup lets you choose among more faucets. Also, any sprayer repairs don't affect the faucet.

Replacing a Faucet

1 Apply plumber's putty

- Unless a rubber gasket is supplied, use putty
- Roll a string of plumber's putty between your hands
- Shape it around the outside of the faucet body or base plate where it will meet the sink or countertop

2 Mount the faucet

- Use the mounting nuts supplied with the faucet to secure it from below
- Hand-tighten the plastic wing nuts
- Snug up metal locknuts with a wrench, but do not overtighten

3 Connect the supply tubes

- Attach the supply tubes to the shutoff valves
- Connect each tube to the faucet's integral supply tubes
- Tighten with a basin wrench

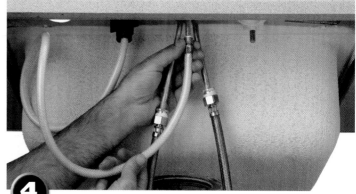

4 Attach the spray hose

- If a separate sprayer base is supplied, secure it at the hole
- Thread the end of the spray hose through the sink hole from above
- Connect the hose to the faucet body below the sink, using pipe-thread tape if it's needed
- You may need to bend integral supply tubes gently to make them reach the faucet body

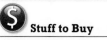 **Stuff to Buy**

BASIC SUPPLIES Plumber's putty if there's no gasket; pipe-thread tape
FAUCET Make sure it matches the holes in your sink
SPRAYER Sprayers may be supplied with the faucet

 **Time Commitment**

2 hours

 Tools You'll Need

Adjustable wrench
Basin wrench

 **Related Topics**

Replacing a Sprayer

❶ Remove the old sprayer

- Turn off water to the sink and then drain the faucet
- With a basin wrench, loosen the nut connecting the old spray hose to the faucet body
- Remove the nut and remove the old hose from the faucet body
- Drain any water from the hose, then use the existing sprayer head to pull out the old hose

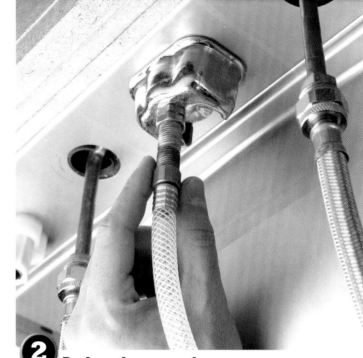

❷ Replace the sprayer base

- If you can, gently remove the old sprayer base
- Avoid scarring the sink as you work
- Mount the new sprayer base and secure it

❸ Connect the hose

- Connect the new hose to the faucet body
- Tighten the connection but avoid overtightening
- Feed the hose from below through the hole and the sprayer base

❹ Add the sprayer head

- Add the coupling to the hose end
- Attach the sprayer head to the coupling
- Turn on the water and check for leaks

Filters at the Sink

Some water conditions, such as excess sediment, may require a whole-house filter, but in many cases, water treatment at the kitchen sink is all you need. If you have questions about your water's composition, have it tested before you choose a system.

A faucet-mounted water filter is the easiest kind to install. The one above has a knob where it attaches to the faucet so water can be routed through the filter, or not. The appliance on the right also allows the user to regulate the flow. It signals the condition of the filter in the egg-shaped housing so you know when to change it.

Filter Options

A water-treatment device is a popular kitchen upgrade. Many types are available, including simple in-line filters screwed to the faucet spout. Such faucet-mounted units are quick to install, but you must remember to turn them on and off, as uses that don't require purified water will quickly exhaust the filter.

A better alternative is a water purifier that looks just like a hot-water or soap dispenser and is used only when you want filtered water (the main unit fits below the sink). Filtration systems vary widely.

Easy-to-install dual-cartridge devices like the one shown on the opposite page require no electrical power, connect directly to your cold-water line, and install in a few hours. But you must periodically change the cartridges. If you notice changes in taste, odor, or water flow, it is time to do so.

A reverse-osmosis unit is hooked up much like the dual-cartridge device, but it must also be connected to the sink's drain because it discharges wastewater. It stores the clean water in a tank beneath the sink.

Placement Options

Use an existing hole in the sink if at all possible. For example, you may be able to discard a soap dispenser, sprayer hose, or other device to free a hole.

If no hole is available, drilling a new hole is an option, but this risks serious cosmetic damage to the sink or countertop, so proceed with caution. For a stainless-steel or porcelain cast-iron sink, follow the manufacturer's instructions to drill a hole if you choose to. Never drill through a porcelain sink. You may be able to drill through the countertop instead, if the material is appropriate for drilling.

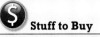

Stuff to Buy

BASIC SUPPLIES Plumber's putty if there is no gasket; pipe-thread tape

FILTRATION UNIT Choose one with a built-in indicator that shows when the filter needs to be replaced

Time Commitment

Half a day

Tools You'll Need

Screwdriver
Wrench

Related Topics

Assessing your water supply, 16–17
Whole-house water treatments, 100–101

How to Do It

① Mount the dispenser

- Center the dispenser in the hole
- Secure it with the hardware provided

④ Connect at the valve

- Cut a length of plastic tubing to go from the saddle valve to the filter system
- Make it short enough to avoid kinks but long enough for you to install a new compression fitting if needed
- Press the tubing into the compression fitting
- Thread the fitting onto the valve
- Tighten the fitting with an adjustable wrench

② Install a saddle valve

- Tap into the cold-water supply line with a saddle valve
- To install the valve, first turn off the water supply and drain the faucet
- Following the manufacturer's directions, drill a small hole in the supply line
- Turn the valve handle, exposing the lance; position the lance in the hole
- Attach the valve's back plate, tighten the nuts to lock it in place, and screw in the lance

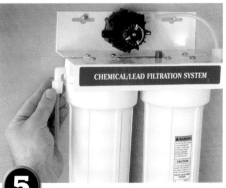

⑤ Connect at the unit

- Insert the other end of the tubing into another compression fitting
- Thread the fitting onto the inlet port of the filtration unit
- Tighten the nut by hand
- Make another turn, or turn and a half, with an adjustable wrench

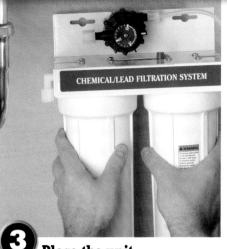

③ Place the unit

- Position the filtration unit between the cold-water line and the dispenser
- Place it so there is plenty of room underneath to remove and replace the cartridge
- Secure the device to the cabinet back or wall with the screws provided

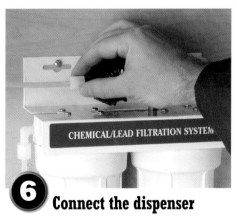

⑥ Connect the dispenser

- Cut tubing to run from the outlet port of the system to the purified-water dispenser
- Insert compression fittings on both ends and securely thread the nuts onto the dispenser and the system port
- Turn on the water, open the water dispenser, and check for leaks.
- Let the water run for about five minutes to flush carbon particles or air pockets

Upgrading to a New Sink

To many homeowners, installing a kitchen sink seems like a daunting task. But if you can trace around a template and cut out a hole, you can install a sink. Make sure you have a countertop material you can cut easily.

Planning the Job

To make sure the new sink fits your countertop and the cabinet below it, measure the width and depth (from front to back) of your lower cabinets before making a purchase. Generally, a sink up to 22 inches deep will fit in a standard 24-inch-deep cabinet if you have no back-splash. If you do have a backsplash, your countertop will take a sink only up to 20½ inches deep. Of course, your options will increase if you are also changing your cabinetry and countertop.

Mounting Methods

There are three common methods for mounting kitchen sinks. Self-rimming sinks have a molded lip that rests on the edge of the countertop cutout. Recessed, or undermount, sinks either fit flush with the countertop or attach to its underside. Frame-mounted sinks have a metal rim that hides the gap between the sink and the counter.

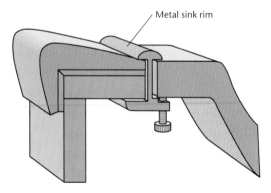

Metal sink rim

Frame-Mounted Sink

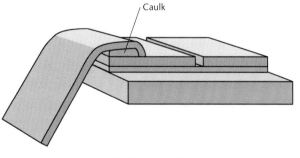

Caulk

Self-Rimming Sink

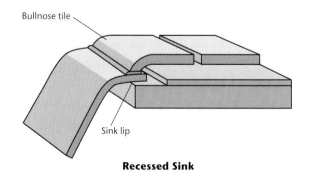

Bullnose tile

Sink lip

Recessed Sink

 **Stuff to Buy**

BASIC SUPPLIES Silicone caulk or plumber's putty; pipe-thread tape
FAUCET, DRAIN BODY Install these on the sink before putting it in
SINK Measure the sink cabinet and countertop before you buy

Time Commitment

Half a day

Tools You'll Need

Adjustable wrench
Drill and bits
Saber saw
Screwdriver
Slip-joint pliers
Spud wrench

Related Topics

Adding a faucet & sprayer, 72–73
Adding a garbage disposer, 80–81
Filters at the sink, 74–75
Hot-water dispensers, 84–85
Installing a faucet, 70–71

How to Do It

1 Trace the template

- Position the manufacturer's template so it is centered on the sink cabinet and at least 1½ inches back from the countertop's front edge
- If your countertop is deeper than 24 inches, place the sink farther back, though no more than 4 inches
- Tape the template in place
- Outline it with a marker

2 Cut the hole

- Remove the template
- Drill a ⅜-inch-diameter hole in each corner of the traced shape
- Insert a saber-saw blade into one of the holes and cut along the inside of the line
- To keep the cutout from snapping off, screw a piece of wood, a few inches wider than the opening, to the top of the cutout
- After you finish cutting, remove the cutout

3 Prepare the sink

- Turn over the sink
- Install the faucet
- Install the sink strainer and strainer body; a double-bowl sink will have two sets
- Apply a bead of silicone caulk or plumber's putty along the entire perimeter under the sink lip

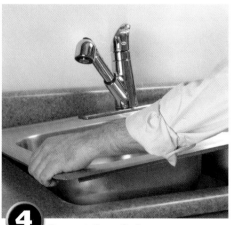

4 Insert the sink

- Carefully turn over the sink, preferably with a helper
- Insert the sink into the opening without disturbing the caulk or putty
- Consider placing a few wood scraps beside the opening to support the sink and protect you and your helper's fingers as you position it

5 Secure the mounting clips

- Frame-mounted sinks have mounting clips; space them according to the instructions and tighten them with a screwdriver or nut driver
- If caulk or putty squeezes out, remove the excess with a clean, soft rag

6 Connect the plumbing

- Connect the P-trap and attach it to the waste line
- Connect the hot- and cold-water supplies
- Remove the aerator from the faucet and run the water for a few minutes to flush the system
- Replace the aerator
- Check for leaks

DRAIN ASSEMBLY

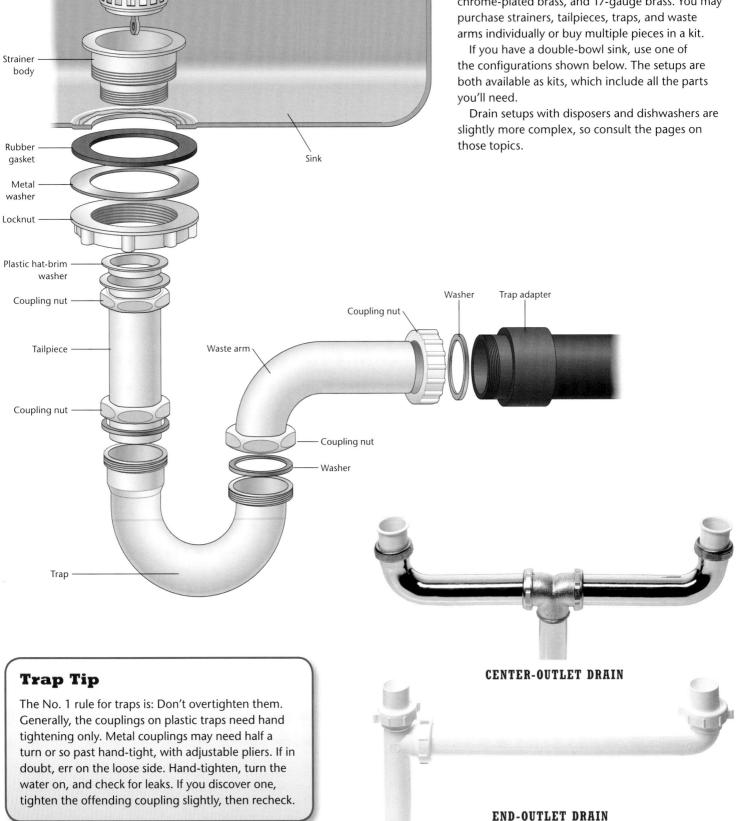

Strainer

Strainer body

Rubber gasket

Metal washer

Locknut

Plastic hat-brim washer

Coupling nut

Tailpiece

Coupling nut

Trap

Sink

Waste arm

Coupling nut

Coupling nut

Washer

Washer

Trap adapter

CENTER-OUTLET DRAIN

END-OUTLET DRAIN

Kitchen Sink Drain Hookups

Except where a garbage disposer is attached, kitchen sinks typically include a strainer in the drain assembly. Traps come in plastic (ABS or PVC), chrome-plated brass, and 17-gauge brass. You may purchase strainers, tailpieces, traps, and waste arms individually or buy multiple pieces in a kit.

If you have a double-bowl sink, use one of the configurations shown below. The setups are both available as kits, which include all the parts you'll need.

Drain setups with disposers and dishwashers are slightly more complex, so consult the pages on those topics.

Trap Tip

The No. 1 rule for traps is: Don't overtighten them. Generally, the couplings on plastic traps need hand tightening only. Metal couplings may need half a turn or so past hand-tight, with adjustable pliers. If in doubt, err on the loose side. Hand-tighten, turn the water on, and check for leaks. If you discover one, tighten the offending coupling slightly, then recheck.

How to Do It

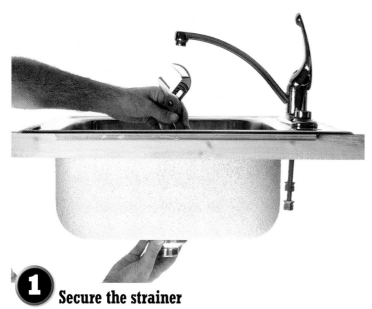

1 Secure the strainer

- Run a bead of plumber's putty around the top of the sink opening
- Press the strainer down into it
- Add the gasket, washer, and locknut from below, tightening with a spud wrench or slip-joint pliers
- If the strainer spins, wedge the handles of a pair of pliers into the strainer while you tighten

2 Add the tailpiece

- Secure the tailpiece to the strainer's threaded body with a washer and a coupling nut
- Tighten the nut with slip-joint pliers
- Tailpieces come in several lengths; they can also be cut short or lengthened with extensions

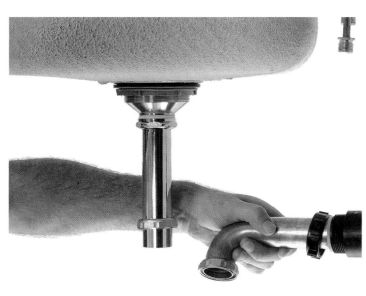
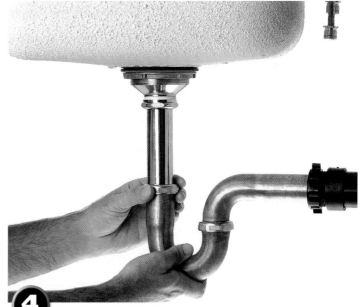

3 Place the waste arm

- If you haven't already, cement a threaded trap adapter onto the drain stubout
- Slip the trap's coupling and the trap adapter's coupling onto the waste arm
- Push the arm into the trap adapter
- As with a tailpiece, you can buy waste arms in different lengths or cut one to length

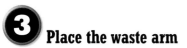

4 Add the trap

- Hold the trap in place and fit it to both the tailpiece and the waste arm
- Fine-tune by sliding the trap up onto the tailpiece, then sliding the arm in and out of the trap adapter
- Adjust the trap side to side
- Tighten the coupling nuts—first by hand, then with slip-joint pliers or an adjustable wrench

Adding a Garbage Disposer

Garbage disposers grind up and wash away kitchen refuse with the touch of a switch. Invest in a unit that delivers at least ½ horsepower, as one with less power can get stuck easily and will likely need replacing after just a few years.

STOP!
Before beginning any work, always shut off the power to the circuit that will serve the disposer. If you are replacing an old disposer, turn off the electricity to that circuit and then unplug the disposer or disconnect the wiring before removing the unit.

Disposer Basics

Garbage disposers usually fit in the standard drain outlets of kitchen sinks and mount much like a strainer. Disposers are either hardwired or plugged into a 120-volt ground-fault circuit interrupter (GFCI) receptacle. Those with plugs are easier to install. The most common disposers are switch-activated.

Local codes may determine the distance a switch must be from the sink. The farther, the safer. Disposers are never whisper-quiet, and under certain sinks, such as stainless-steel models, they can be quite noisy if they are not well-insulated. Generally, the fatter the disposer, the more quietly it will run, although you need to make sure that the model you choose fits comfortably under your sink.

A good disposer can last many years, especially if you avoid clogging it with fibrous foods like celery, potato skins, melon rinds, other fruit and vegetable peels, eggshells, and coffee grounds.

Installation Issues

Because installing a disposer requires both plumbing and electrical skills, it is a project best taken on by an experienced do-it-yourselfer. One way to simplify the task is to have a licensed electrician install a ground-fault circuit interrupter (GFCI) receptacle under the sink and a separate wall switch adjacent to the sink. The only electrical work left would be to wire a power cord to the disposer, if it doesn't come wired. If you are replacing an old disposer, the switch and receptacle may already be in place.

Space is tight under any sink. You'll get better access if you remove the cabinet doors and set them aside.

Adding a garbage disposer to a double-bowl sink requires you to re-plumb the waste line for the pair of sinks. If you are lucky, all you will need is an extension tube. Otherwise, you may need to replace the entire assembly.

GARBAGE DISPOSER WITH DISHWASHER HOOKUP

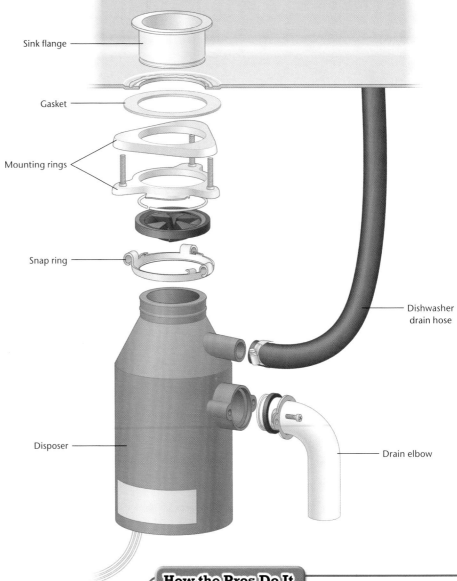

- Sink flange
- Gasket
- Mounting rings
- Snap ring
- Disposer
- Dishwasher drain hose
- Drain elbow

How the Pros Do It

"Pace yourself with a garbage disposer. Don't put in half a pot of mashed potatoes or a pot of pasta. The disposer can handle it, but if you put too much down the drain too quickly, the drain will clog up pretty fast. Also, always run the water for a while after the disposer clears, so the ground-up solids don't settle in the drain and clog it."
Tim Miller, J. Kittelberger & Sons

How to Do It

1 Install the flange

- Have towels and a bucket handy to catch water and debris
- Disconnect and remove the drain assembly from the sink flange to the trap, leaving the trap in place
- Apply a coil of plumber's putty around the sink hole
- Install the new flange and press it into place

Snap ring

2 Attach the mounting assembly

- Place a heavy object, such as a phone book, on top of the flange to hold it in place
- Remove the mounting assembly from the disposer and install it under the sink
- Follow the directions for gasket placement and slip the mounting ring over the flange
- Slide the snap ring onto the flange until it pops into the groove on the flange
- Tighten the three mounting screws until the assembly seals tightly to the sink

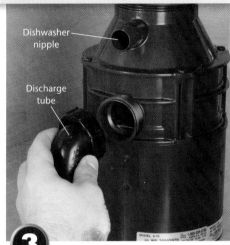

Dishwasher nipple

Discharge tube

3 Prepare the disposer

- Inspect and clean the P-trap
- Attach the discharge tube to the disposer
- If you have a dishwasher, prepare the dishwasher's drain connection
- Usually, this means knocking out a drain plug from the dishwasher nipple with a hammer and a screwdriver and later attaching the dishwasher's drain hose

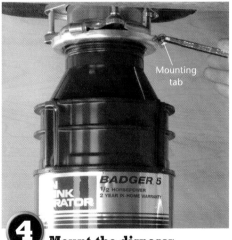

Mounting tab

4 Mount the disposer

- Position the disposer under the mounting assembly so the tabs can slide over the tracks
- Lift the disposer and insert the top into the mounting assembly
- Rotate the lower mounting ring until all three tabs lock over its ridges
- Use the wrench provided (or a screwdriver) to tighten the ring

Trap

5 Make plumbing connections

- Rotate the disposer so that the discharge tube aligns with the drain trap
- For a double-bowl sink, re-plumb the waste line as needed
- Attach the dishwasher hose securely

6 Plug in the disposer

- Plug the disposer into a nearby GFCI receptacle
- Run water and check for leaks
- With the water running, turn on the disposer with the wall switch to test the installation

Installing a Dishwasher

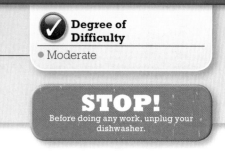

Modern dishwashers offer a variety of improvements over earlier generations, as well as the same basic benefit of saving your dishwashing labors. Look for a quiet, energy-efficient model that suits the look and scale of your kitchen.

Dishwasher Choices

The standard dishwasher is 24 inches wide, 24 inches deep, and 34 inches high. There are also 18-inch-wide versions. The better models feature stainless-steel interiors. Different dishwashers have various configurations of racks, which may include adjustable tines and trays. Exterior finishes vary. Most models offer replaceable colored panels to blend with base cabinets.

NOISE LEVEL

Improved sound insulation, sound-absorbing washtubs (particularly those made of stainless steel), vibration absorbers, and low-noise pumps make good dishwashers nearly noiseless.

ENERGY EFFICIENCY

Federal regulations require dishwashers to use half the electricity of earlier models. Stainless-steel interiors cost more but are also more efficient during the dry cycle. Air drying is always an energy-saving option.

RESIDUE ELIMINATION

Some new dishwashers include a built-in garbage disposer, also called a hard-food disposer, which grinds and flushes food residue. Just as with a sink-based disposer, don't overburden the system, as too much debris can clog the drain. Filters have also improved, but they need to be checked and cleared periodically. To prevent staining, always rinse tomato-based residue if you have a plastic tub.

CONTROLS

Electronic controls are more common than manual ones. The more expensive the machine, the more cycle choices it offers, allowing you to tailor the wash and dry cycles to the machine's contents and program a delayed start.

Installation Issues

Installing a built-in dishwasher requires only a few hand tools and a spare afternoon. Follow the manufacturer's instructions; the directions here are meant as a general guide. If you are replacing an old dishwasher, turn off the water and power and remove the machine by reversing the installation instructions.

ELECTRICAL REQUIREMENTS

A 120-volt electrical receptacle or electrical box protected by a ground-fault circuit interrupter (GFCI) must be nearby, usually at the back of the sink's base cabinet. Verify that you have a grounded 15-amp receptacle, or have an electrician install one.

PLUMBING HOOKUPS

A water supply tube connects a dishwasher to the kitchen sink's hot-water supply. A flexible hose drains wastewater to the sink trap or, if you have one, the garbage disposer.

To connect directly into the sink's trap, cut off and replace a section of the tailpiece with a dishwasher tailpiece, which has a short T-shaped nipple for the dishwasher hose.

If you have a disposer, connect the drain hose to the disposer's dishwasher inlet, as shown below. If the disposer was not previously connected to a dishwasher, unplug it or turn off its circuit, then use a hammer and screwdriver to punch out the knockout plug for the connection.

ADDING AN AIR GAP

To prevent wastewater from flowing back into the dishwasher, some codes require that the dishwasher be connected to an air gap. In some regions, codes allow you to loop the dishwasher's drain hose in a high arc under the countertop instead.

If you must install an air-gap fixture, you may be able to use an extra, unused hole in your sink. Otherwise, the task requires boring a hole in the countertop next to the sink with an electric drill and a hole saw. If your countertop is made of stone or another material that's difficult to cut, or if you are not sure about making the cut, have the sink's top drilled by a professional.

HOOKING TO A DISPOSER

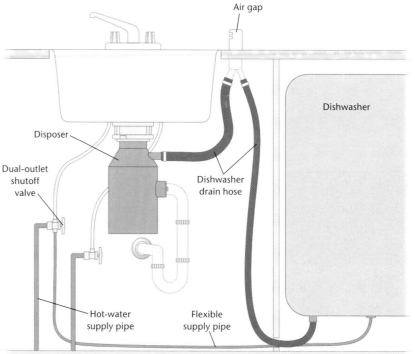

Air gap

Dishwasher

Disposer

Dual-outlet shutoff valve

Dishwasher drain hose

Hot-water supply pipe

Flexible supply pipe

$ Stuff to Buy	**⏰ Time Commitment**	**🔧 Tools You'll Need**	**◎ Related Topics**
BASIC SUPPLIES Dual-outlet shutoff valve, supply line, drain hoses, hose clamps **DISHWASHER** Look for a quiet, energy-efficient, under-counter model that fits the space	3 hours	Adjustable wrench Drill and bits Hammer Screwdriver Slip-joint pliers	Adding a garbage disposer, 80–81 Diagnosing your dishwasher, 230–231

How to Do It

① Add a dual-outlet valve

- Turn off power to the circuits near the sink
- Turn off the house water supply and, using a faucet at a lower level, drain the pipes
- To replace a shutoff valve with a dual-outlet version, disconnect the sink's water supply tube from the valve and drain it into a bucket
- Unscrew the old shutoff valve from the supply nipple with a wrench
- Wind pipe-thread tape around the nipple's threads, then screw on a dual-outlet valve
- Reconnect the sink's supply line to the dual-outlet valve

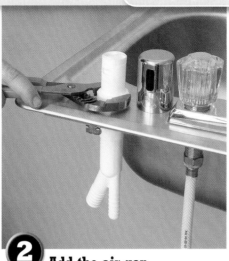

② Add the air gap

- If an air-gap fixture is required, install it through an unused hole in the sink (punch out the hole plug with a hammer)
- Insert the air gap
- Using slip-joint pliers, secure the air gap from above with a locknut and push its cover into place
- Under some local codes, a high loop in the dishwasher hose (under the countertop) can be used instead

③ Position the connectors

- Drill holes in the back corner of the sink's base cabinet for the drain hose, water supply tube, and power cord
- Position the dishwasher near the opening (use cardboard to protect the floor)
- Push the hose, supply tube, and cord through their holes
- Move the dishwasher into place without pinching or tangling these connectors

④ Attach the water supply

- Connect the dishwasher's supply line between the dual-outlet valve and the outlet on the dishwasher
- Tighten these connections with an adjustable wrench until they are snug

⑤ Add the drain hose

- For an air-gap fixture, run a drain hose from the trap to the larger outlet on the air gap, then a hose from the smaller outlet to the dishwasher's drain fitting
- Otherwise, run a single drain hose between the sink and the dishwasher, adding a high loop to create the gap
- Secure the drain hose ends with hose clamps
- Adjust the dishwasher's front feet to level it, then align the machine with the cabinets and countertop
- Anchor it with screws under the countertop
- Restore the water supply and check for leaks
- Plug in the dishwasher

Hot-water Dispensers

Consisting of only an under-counter storage tank connected to a hot-water faucet, hot-water dispensers are easy to install. The tank, which is fed by a nearby cold-water pipe, has a heating coil that keeps water at about 200 degrees Fahrenheit.

Installation Tips

Most units plug into a 120-volt grounded GFCI receptacle under the sink. The hot-water faucet commonly fits in a hole on the sink rim or mounts directly on the countertop. For countertop mounting, you'll need to drill a 1¼-inch-diameter hole near the sink. Make sure the countertop is a material you are able to cut cleanly without scarring.

For a good connection to your home's water supply, you can tap into the cold-water pipe with a standard T-fitting and a shutoff valve with an outlet that matches your dispenser's water supply tube. However, you may find it simpler to use a self-tapping saddle valve (one is often supplied with the unit), which allows you to connect to the supply line without cutting pipe or adding new fittings.

This kitchen features a hot-water dispenser next to the smaller of its two sinks so that the large sink can be free for rinsing vegetables or washing pots.

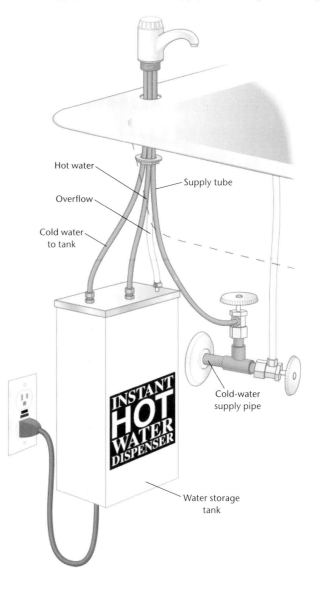

Hot water

Supply tube

Overflow

Cold water to tank

Cold-water supply pipe

INSTANT HOT WATER DISPENSER

Water storage tank

 **Stuff to Buy**

BASIC SUPPLIES Pipe-thread tape
HOT-WATER DISPENSER KIT
Make sure it includes all hardware before you start the job
SUPPLY CONNECTORS Either a saddle valve or a T-fitting with shutoff valves

 **Time Commitment**

3 to 4 hours

 Tools You'll Need

Adjustable wrench
Drill
Screwdriver

 **Related Topics**

Filters at the sink, 74–75
New looks for kitchen sinks, 68–69
Upgrading to a new sink, 78–79

How to Do It

1 Position the tank

- This type of heater hangs from its fitting at the sink
- With the handle pointing straight up, slip the heater's threaded pipe through the hole

2 Secure the tank

- With a helper keeping the faucet correctly oriented from below, slip a washer and nut over the threaded pipe
- Tighten the nut to hold the faucet in place
- In this case, the nut is covered with a decorative sleeve

3 Attach the spout

- Flip the handle back so it's out of the way of the spout
- Attach this spout by pushing it into position from above
- Make sure the spout is going in straight so it's positioned properly

4 Connect the water supply

- Tap into the cold-water supply line with a saddle valve; turn off the water and drain the faucet
- Drill a small hole in the house's cold-water supply line
- Turn the valve handle to expose the lance, then position the lance in the hole
- Attach the valve's back plate, tighten the nuts to lock it in place, and screw in the lance

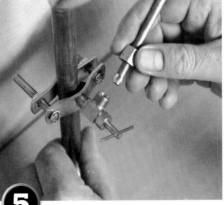

5 Connect the tubing

- Following the manufacturer's instructions, connect the cold-water line to the tank
- Connection types vary and may include snap-on fittings, barb fittings, or other systems
- Make sure each connection is tight and secure

6 Finish the job

- Turn on the water at the shutoff valve and check all connections for leaks
- With the power still off, turn on the hot-water faucet until there is a constant flow of water (which will be cold)
- Flush the system by running the faucet for a few minutes
- Plug in the tank and wait several minutes to allow it to heat fully

Adding an Ice Maker

Degree of Difficulty
● Moderate

Refrigerators often come with at least one of two terrific conveniences, an ice maker and a chilled-water dispenser. What's slightly less convenient is that you may have to do the hookup. Be sure to leave extra tubing so you can roll the refrigerator out for cleaning.

STOP!
Unplug the refrigerator before you begin the project.

Installation Basics

A refrigerator may come with an ice maker, a chilled-water dispenser, or both. If either is present, you'll need to connect the refrigerator to your home's cold-water supply. A refrigerator may be relatively far from a shutoff valve, requiring you to locate and connect to the nearest cold-water supply line. Look around to determine where that might be. In some homes, it might be a line running along a basement ceiling under the kitchen.

If the refrigerator happens to be near the sink, however, you may instead be able to connect at the valve under the sink and route the tubing to the refrigerator behind or through the base cabinets.

Whichever way you make the connection, allow at least 4 or 5 feet of extra tubing so you can easily roll the refrigerator out of place for cleaning or maintenance without disturbing the water connection.

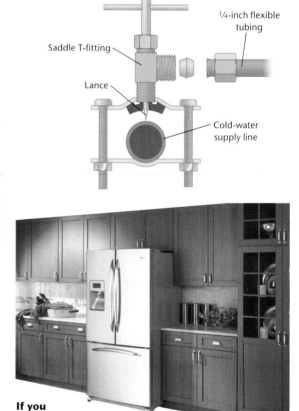

T-FITTING AT THE SHUTOFF VALVE

Cold-water shutoff

T-fitting

Ice maker shutoff

Refrigerator

Ice maker inlet valve

Saddle valve alternative

¼-inch flexible tubing

Saddle T-fitting

Lance

Cold-water supply line

Tubing & Connector

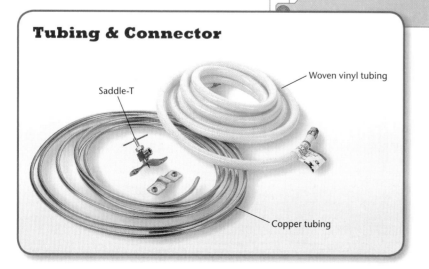

Saddle-T

Woven vinyl tubing

Copper tubing

If you have been putting off making the connection to the ice maker and cold-water dispenser in your refrigerator, read on. It's easier than you might think.

 Stuff to Buy	Time Commitment	Tools You'll Need	Related Topics

ICE MAKER HOOKUP KIT
Hardware and home-improvement stores sell generic kits that should meet your needs; you can use ¼-inch copper, woven stainless, or woven vinyl tubing

Time Commitment
2 hours

Tools You'll Need
Adjustable wrench
Drill
Screwdriver

Related Topics
Adding shutoff valves, 36–37
Copper pipe & fittings, 30–31
Valves & transitions, 34–35

How to Do It

Attaching to the shutoff

- Turn off the house water supply
- Drain the water using a faucet at a lower level
- Remove the shutoff valve and attach a T-fitting
- Connect the cold-water shutoff for the sink to one outlet of the T and the shutoff valve for the refrigerator tubing to the other outlet
- Run ¼-inch tubing from the tubing shutoff to the refrigerator

Attaching with a saddle valve

- Turn off the house water supply
- Drain the cold-water line in question using a faucet at a lower level
- Drill a small hole, sized according to instructions, in the line
- Position a saddle valve on the line, seating the lance in the hole; tighten it in place
- Connect ¼-inch tubing to the valve outlet and run it to the refrigerator

Connecting to the refrigerator

- Measure an extra 4 to 5 feet of tubing to allow room to move the refrigerator
- Slip connectors onto the tubing as specified in the refrigerator instructions
- With the refrigerator unplugged, unscrew the cover plate from the back of the refrigerator; two typical configurations are shown above

- Attach the tubing to the solenoid valve, following the manufacturer's instructions, and restore the cover plate
- Turn on the water and check for leaks; restore power to the refrigerator
- Turn on the ice maker and allow time for it to make ice

When to Call a Pro

Connecting a refrigerator with a built-in ice maker to your home's water supply is a relatively common do-it-yourself task. Adding a new ice maker to a refrigerator that doesn't have one is much more ambitious, as it requires both wiring and plumbing skills. You may prefer to hire a professional to tackle the job, or simply upgrade your refrigerator to a newer model.

5

Other Plumbing Projects

In this chapter, we cover a number of other common plumbing projects, including hooking up a clothes washer and a whole-house water softener. You'll also learn a lot about water heaters, from the various types of new ones on the market to trouble-shooting. To help you save money and energy, we show you how to lower the heater's temperature, perform routine maintenance, and replace basic parts.

Chapter Contents

Sinks for All Uses

Bathroom and kitchen sinks are the workhorses of home plumbing, designed with special features for their specific jobs. But there are plenty of sinks suitable for use elsewhere in the house, from rugged utility sinks to dazzling entertainment sinks in striking designs.

Entertainment Sinks

Traditionally known as bar sinks, entertainment sinks may indeed find a home in the classic downstairs bar, but designers now offer sinks for any home-entertainment area. A sink for entertaining may be designed to fit into a corner or another small space, or as a handy spot to keep bottles or glasses on ice. Alternatively, they may be striking conversation starters intended as design accents.

In this entertainment area, a Kohler cast-iron sink with a basalt finish serves as an ice bucket.

The sink in this studio is versatile enough for cleaning up after craft projects while remaining appealing to weekend guests.

Sometimes entertainment sinks are themselves entertaining, like this irregularly shaped Fete sink from Kohler.

Utility Sinks

The classic utility sink or laundry tub can serve as a discharge location for a clothes washer and a place to wash up after especially dirty projects. If you use one for the washer's discharge, make sure the sink is deep enough for the job, and make sure never to leave the drain blocked or plugged. It's also a good idea to keep any nearby floor drain fully uncovered in case the sink somehow does become blocked. A laundry sink is likely to hold far more water than a shallower kitchen or bathroom model, so make sure it has sturdy supports to handle the weight.

Green ceramic tiles like these can overpower an interior kitchen, but they look right at home outdoors.

This utility sink has been transformed into an ice basin for a serious fisherman.

Hooking Up a Washer

Clothes washers consume a lot of energy and water, so pick one that fits your lifestyle and living space. For an older washer, new supply tubes may be a smart, inexpensive way to avoid a flood.

An energy-efficient front-loading washer and dryer bookend a utility sink and a sturdy vanity.

Horizontal or Vertical?

There are two styles of washers: top-loading models, which are still the most common in the United States, and front-loading versions. Front loaders, also called horizontal-axis washers, use less energy and water, typically from a third to half the amount of water as a top loader. This also means less heating. And because a front loader spins faster, clothes come out needing less time in the dryer.

But if you have trouble leaning over, a top loader, or vertical-axis machine, may be a back-friendly choice. Top loaders usually cost less initially, though they are more expensive to operate. Also, front loaders may require a special detergent, whereas top loaders normally do not.

Choosing a New Washer

If you wash clothes often, buy a machine with a stainless-steel tub. People who wash less frequently may be fine with porcelain-coated steel or high-grade plastic. For different fabrics and different levels of dirtiness, choose a machine that offers specialty cycles and an optional second rinse. Multiple water-level settings supply the most efficient wash for loads of different sizes. Some machines can also boost water temperature to sanitize a load.

The size of your washer should match your dryer's capacity. Another item to consider is an automatic temperature regulator. A must in cold climates, this feature ensures that wash water comes in at a constant temperature. Also look for additional insulation and reinforced frames, both of which reduce noise. If you have limited space, there are stacking washer-dryer units in either full-size or apartment-size capacities. Stacking washers are front loaders, while top-loading washers must be installed beside the dryer.

How to Do It

When you buy a new clothes washer, you can usually pay a small fee to have it delivered and hooked up. But you can also undertake installation yourself. The job is simple if the laundry area is already set up for a washer. If you are installing a washer in a new location, you will need to run hot- and cold-water supply pipes to the connection point. You'll also need to terminate each line with a shutoff valve and, if necessary, a water-hammer arrester.

If there is an existing laundry sink or tub, you can hook the washer's drain hose over the sink's edge. Otherwise, the washer will need to drain into a standpipe, which is a 2-inch-diameter pipe with a built-in trap that leads into the nearest drainpipe. The top of the standpipe should rise between 18 and 30 inches above the trap (some codes allow a range of up to 42 inches). The trap should be 6 to 18 inches above the floor. Standpipes are available with built-in traps, or they can be assembled from scratch with standard drainpipe and elbow fittings.

How the Pros Do It

"Your major water use in a house is in the shower or bath, the toilets, and the washing machine. If you're concerned about saving water, I wouldn't get too excited about investing in a high-end dishwasher. Put the money into a horizontal-axis washing machine."

Doug Kirk,
GreenPlumbersUSA.com

1 Attach tubes to the washer

- Thread supply tubes onto the connections at the back of the washer
- Note which connection is for hot water and which is for cold water

2 Attach to the valves

- Connect the supply tubes to the correct valves
- Move the appliance into place
- Level the machine by adjusting the front feet

3 Route the drain hose

- Put the drain hose in the standpipe or laundry sink
- Make sure that nothing is blocking the sink drain and that the sink empties quickly with no clogging
- Turn on the water supply valves and check for leaks

Single-Lever Valve

The hoses that connect a washer can leak or burst, causing a potentially destructive flood. To prevent this, trade old supply hoses, or tubes, for high-quality, steel-jacketed replacements (below). Also consider a single-lever valve like this in place of conventional shutoff valves, with which you just flip the lever to shut off the water supply when the machine is not in use.

Replacing Old Supply Tubes

If the rubber hoses that came with your current washing machine are more than five years old, you should replace them with steel-jacketed flexible hoses that won't burst.

1 Remove old hoses

- Unplug the washer and turn off the water at the shutoff valves
- Pull the drain hose out of the drainpipe or utility sink and let it drain into a bucket
- Move the washer so you can reach the back
- Lay down a towel or place a bucket to catch spills
- Use slip-joint pliers to remove each hose; if the connections are too corroded to move, call a repairman
- Remove the other ends of the hoses from the shutoff valves

2 Clean the filters

- Check the washer connections for small filters designed to keep out sediment; if they aren't there, look in the old hoses and put the filters back in place
- Clean off any buildup with a small brush
- Connect steel-jacketed flexible supply tubes to the washing machine
- Attach them by hand, then tighten gently with a wrench or pliers; avoid overtightening

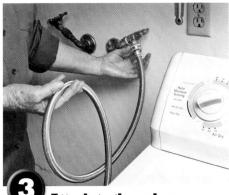

3 Attach to the valves

- Attach the other ends of the tubes to the shutoffs
- Make sure the hot-water line connects to the hot-water shutoff and the cold-water line to the cold-water shutoff
- Slowly open the valves and check for leaks
- If there are leaks, try using pipe-thread tape at the connections
- If you are replacing a cracked, brittle drain hose, do so now
- Move the washer back into place and return the drain hose to the standpipe or sink
- Plug the washer back in

About Water Heaters

Problems with traditional, storage-type water heaters are usually announced with noises, leaks, or water that's too hot, not hot enough, or ice cold. Often you can correct the problem yourself. Problems with on-demand (tankless) heaters require professional repair.

How Water Heaters Work

Most American homes have a storage-type water heater, which may be powered by electricity or gas. To a large extent, both work the same way. When a hot-water faucet is turned on, heated water is drawn from the top of the tank and is replaced by cold water that is delivered to the bottom of the tank via the dip tube. As the water temperature in the tank drops, a thermostat activates the heat source: a burner in a gas heater, heating elements in an electric unit.

A gas heater has a flue running up the center and out the top to vent gases. An electric heater needs no venting. In both types, an anode attracts corrosion that might attack the tank's walls.

Some homes combine a storage-tank water heater with a hot-water baseboard heating system. Combination space- and water-heating systems are good choices for small, well-insulated homes.

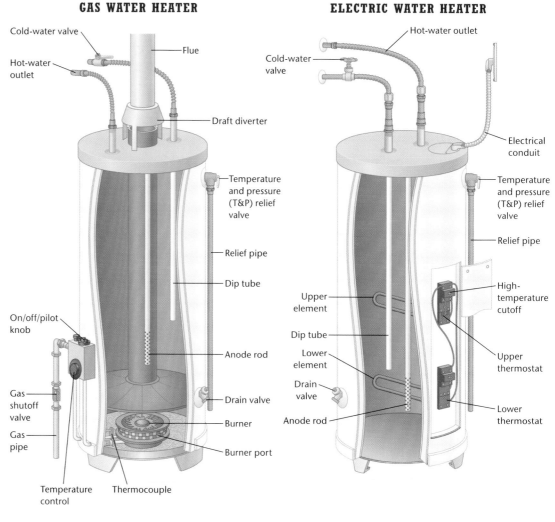

GAS WATER HEATER

Cold-water valve · Flue · Hot-water outlet · Draft diverter · Temperature and pressure (T&P) relief valve · Relief pipe · Dip tube · On/off/pilot knob · Anode rod · Gas shutoff valve · Gas pipe · Drain valve · Burner · Burner port · Temperature control · Thermocouple

ELECTRIC WATER HEATER

Hot-water outlet · Cold-water valve · Electrical conduit · Temperature and pressure (T&P) relief valve · Relief pipe · High-temperature cutoff · Upper element · Dip tube · Lower element · Drain valve · Upper thermostat · Anode rod · Lower thermostat

Assessing a Problem

Modern heaters sometimes have electronic controls that may help pinpoint what's wrong, or the controls themselves may cause a problem if they fail. Check the heater manual to learn whether blinking lights or similar signals are conveying information you can use.

GAS HEATERS

With a gas heater, knowing how to relight the pilot is very important. Directions vary, so follow the instructions on the tank. A gas heater has a thermocouple, a thermoelectric device that senses whether the pilot is on and shuts the gas off if the pilot light goes out.

ELECTRIC HEATERS

If there's no hot water, make sure there is power to the heater and any electronic controls have not failed. Next, check the high-temperature cutoff, the heating elements (upper and lower), or the thermostats that control them.

The high-temperature cutoff, elements, and thermostats are concealed behind one or more access panels on the side of the water heater. If the high-temperature cutoff has tripped because of water that's too hot, try pushing the reset button in the access panel. Because of the potential danger in working with high-voltage power, other repairs to the thermostats or high-temperature cutoff warrant a service call.

Related Topics
Water heater alternatives, 98–99
Water heater care, 96–97

Maintenance

If you have a gas heater, inspect the flue assembly twice a year to make sure that it is properly aligned and that its joints are sealed. Also check for obstructions in the flue itself. With the burner on, place your hand near the draft diverter. Air flowing out indicates an obstruction that should be removed.

For either type of heater, prevent sediment accumulation by draining the heater every six months, as explained in the following pages. Also, annually test the relief valve, which guards against hazardous pressure buildup, by lifting or depressing its handle. If the valve is working, water should drain from the overflow pipe.

Setting the Temperature

Water heaters are often set to heat water to 150 to 160 degrees Fahrenheit. By lowering the setting to about 120 degrees, you can increase safety and save on your fuel bills without affecting laundry or bathing. Dishwashers require higher temperatures to clean properly, but many models today are equipped with their own heating devices. Check your dishwasher manual to be sure.

When to Replace

Water heaters are such quiet and seemingly changeless parts of the plumbing system that it may be surprising to learn that they do not last forever. Although heaters vary and maintenance has an effect, heaters typically last 10 to 15 years. If your heater is in that age range, or older, consider replacing it. Always replace a heater that leaks around the bottom or shows other signs of wear. If a water heater rusts through, it can cause a serious flood.

If you get a new storage-style heater to replace your old one, look for the right size of tank for your family's needs and check for insulation and energy efficiency. A heater's energy factor (EF) indicates the overall unit efficiency based on the amount of hot water produced per unit of fuel consumed on a typical day. Also consider the first-hour rating (FHR), which tells you the amount of hot water the heater can supply per hour if the tank is full of hot water. To determine your needs, figure out the amount of water used in the household at the peak usage hour. Finally, compare the recovery rates on the units you consider. Water heaters with higher recovery rates heat the water faster. Gas heaters have higher rates than electric ones and, in most parts of the country, are far less expensive to operate.

Symptoms & Solutions

Symptoms	Solutions
No hot water	• *For a gas heater,* is the pilot light out? If so, relight it, then check for floor drafts or check the thermocouple. Ask the gas company to check the heater if the problem persists. • *For an electric heater,* is the power out? Check the fuse or circuit breaker. If the heater has a control panel, has it failed? If so, contact the manufacturer for a replacement. Has the high-temperature cutoff (found inside the access panel) tripped? If none of these questions can isolate the problem, call an electrician.
Not enough hot water	• If this is a sudden change and you have an electric heater, this may mean that one of the two elements has failed. Consult the following pages. • For a long-term problem, insulate the hot-water pipes, regularly drain the tank to remove sediment, manage household use of hot water, and consider buying a larger water heater.
Water is too hot	• Adjust the temperature setting at the water heater.
Leaks from the discharge pipe	• Try lowering the temperature setting. • Check the relief valve and replace it if it's failing. • For an electric heater, have an electrician check the thermostats and cutoff.

Warning Signs

If steam or boiling water comes out of a hot-water faucet or a valve, shut off the water heater at once. If you ever hear a rumbling sound, assume the heater is overheating and turn it off. If you smell a slight odor of gas near a gas water heater, turn off the gas inlet valve and ventilate the area. If the odor is strong, or if it persists, leave the house immediately and call the gas company.

Water Heater Care

When all goes well, water heaters don't play a prominent role in the daily life of a household, but it's smart to take care of the one you have and to replace it once it gets old. For a storage heater, the basic maintenance step is to drain it every six months to a year.

STOP!
Turn off the power and wait several hours to let the water in the tank cool before you drain it.

Replacing the Relief Valve

If your temperature and pressure relief valve either drips or operates with too much difficulty, replace it right away. You want a valve that stays closed when it's not needed but that will open when the need arises.

1 Remove the discharge pipe

- Turn off power to the water heater
- Wait a few hours, if possible, to let the water cool
- Drain part of the tank using a hose at the drain valve at the base
- Steady the valve with a wrench in one hand and remove the discharge pipe from the valve with another wrench
- It should be possible to remove the pipe; however, if necessary, you can cut the pipe near the old valve, leaving a stub in the valve

2 Remove the valve

- Once the discharge pipe is gone, use a pipe wrench to remove the valve
- Work carefully to avoid damaging the water heater

3 Add the new valve

- Wrap the base of the new valve with pipe-thread tape; insert it into the heater and tighten it by hand
- Finish tightening with a wrench, but do not overtighten; make sure the opening is pointed straight down
- Wrap the end of the discharge pipe with pipe-thread tape and screw it into the valve outlet; confirm that the pipe leads straight down
- Close the drain valve and refill the tank, then restore the power
- Check for leaks, and test the valve after the water reheats

Replacing the Drain Valve

1 Drain the tank

- Turn off power to the heater; wait several hours, if you can, for the water to cool
- Attach a hose to the existing drain valve and drain the entire tank

2 Remove the drain valve

- Take the hose off the drain valve, then use slip-joint pliers to turn the entire valve
- Keep turning until it is removed; you can probably make the last turns by hand

3 Insert the new valve

- Prepare the new drain valve with pipe-thread tape; insert it and begin tightening
- Finish tightening with a wrench, but do not overtighten; make sure the valve is pointing down
- Close the valve and refill the tank; test the valve (with a bucket or towel at hand) and check for leaks, then re-close it
- Restore power to the heater

 **Stuff to Buy**

BASIC SUPPLIES Pipe-thread tape, pipe-joint compound
REPLACEMENT ITEMS Drain valves, relief valves, discharge pipes, anode rods

 **Time Commitment**

Varies by task

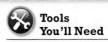 **Tools You'll Need**

Adjustable wrench (large)
Breaker bar
Element wrench
Hose
Pipe wrench
Screwdriver
Socket wrench (large)

 **Related Topics**

About water heaters, 94–95
Water heater alternatives, 98–99

Replacing an Anode Rod

Anode rods are designed to sacrifice themselves to corrosion, thus protecting the tank from rust. By intent, therefore, they do not last forever. Anode rods may wear out in about the same period as the original tank warranty (often five years). Replacing an anode rod at that time is a good idea.

1 Loosen the top nut

- Turn off power to the water heater; if possible, let the water cool for a few hours
- Turn off the water supply, but do not drain the heater
- Loosen the nut at the top of the anode rod with a breaker bar on a wrench
- Unfasten the nut and pull out the rod

2 Insert a new rod

- Apply a small amount of pipe-joint compound to the new anode rod
- Slip the rod into place
- Tighten it by hand, then with a wrench, but do not overtighten
- Restore water and power to the heater

Replacing an Electric Element

If you have warm but not hot water, the upper element may need to be replaced. If you have hot water for only a short time, the lower element may have failed. Always make sure to turn off the power and drain the tank before you replace an element.

1 Remove the cover

- Turn off the power at your home's electrical panel and double-check that it is off at the heater
- Wait a few hours for the water to cool
- Drain the tank so the water is well below the level of the element in question; you don't need to drain as much for an upper element
- Unfasten the access cover

2 Remove the screws

- Undo the screws or bolts securing the element in place

3 Remove the element

- Use an element wrench to turn and remove the element
- Element wrenches are also called shower sockets or bonnet wrenches
- Turn the wrench with a shaft, such as a screwdriver, through the holes at the end
- Inspect the old element for mineral deposits or other problems for future reference

4 Install the replacement

- Apply pipe-joint compound to the element and its washer
- Insert the element and tighten it by hand, then with the element wrench
- Reattach the screws or bolts and close the access panel
- With the drain valve closed, refill the tank, then restore the power

Water Heater Alternatives

Although traditional storage-tank water heaters remain common, they have been joined by some alternatives in recent years, from tankless gas or electric on-demand heaters to systems relying on solar energy.

This roof-mounted water heater, shown in mid-installation, is designed for flat roofs or ones with only a gentle slope.

Pros & Cons of Storage Heaters

There's something to be said for a classic storage heater, the kind with a large tank full of heated water. It's a proven technology, cheap to repair, and familiar to any plumber. There are numerous models available to accommodate families with different requirements. Energy-efficient, well-insulated heaters with electronic controls and insulated hot-water pipes reduce energy waste and even let you limit energy use during vacations or other absences.

Still, the essential fact is that the water in the tank—often 50 gallons or so—is kept heated and ready for use around the clock. Inevitably, this means some energy is wasted in raising and maintaining the temperature of all that hot water, even when none is needed. Water heaters can account for between 15 percent and 25 percent of a home's total monthly energy demand. It makes sense to determine whether less power-hungry options are available.

This water heater features programmable controls so you can easily regulate the hot-water temperature to save energy and money.

Going Tankless

One alternative is the tankless heater, also called an on-demand or instantaneous heater. This system heats water only when hot water is called for, using an electric heating element or natural gas. No energy is wasted on a standby supply. Because these units produce hot water on demand, rather than storing it, they never run out of hot water. They do, however, have a limited output or flow rate, typically 2 to 5 gallons of hot water per minute.

Depending on the heater you choose, the flow rate of hot water may mean you may need to schedule major household uses of hot water at different times. One way around that is to install multiple heaters in series. Because tankless heaters are small, they can also be stationed in different parts of the house, such as near a washer or a remote sink. This not only assigns a specific heater to the need but shortens the amount of hot-water-filled pipe, saving more energy.

As with many products, it's simpler and less costly to install tankless heaters in new construction. A retrofit is more expensive because you'll need larger natural gas lines and flues (for gas units), or higher-gauge wires and circuit breakers (for electric units), and because you'll have to re-plumb the supply lines.

In deciding whether to get a tankless heater, consider how much hot water your household uses, including clothes washing. In a house that uses 40 gallons of hot water a day or less (a relatively low usage level), on-demand heaters are about 30 percent more energy-efficient than a conventional water heater. But for a house that uses much more hot water—86 gallons a day or more—the energy savings are only about 10 percent. Be sure to review the specifications for particular heaters, including the recommended range of temperatures for your incoming cold water. If you have an unusually cold water supply, that could affect your decision.

Solar Water Heaters

Solar water heaters are solar thermal systems. Unlike photovoltaic (PV) systems that convert sunlight to energy, they use the heat from the sun.

There are many solar water heaters on the market, suited to different regional climates. The system illustrated below is just one example. Some directly heat the water used in the house, while others circulate a mix of water and antifreeze, then transfer heat from that fluid to the household water via a heat exchanger. Some have large, glazed rooftop collectors fitted with copper or other metal pipes. Others, more typically used to heat pool water, use unglazed, lightweight heat-collector panels.

Solar water heaters avoid damage from freezing weather in different ways, depending on the part of the country and typical temperatures. The system shown here sends water to a drain-back tank inside the house when it's cold.

The basic principle for all solar water heaters is the same, however. Water or a transfer liquid passes through one or more solar thermal collectors on the roof. The collectors transfer the heat of the sun to the liquid, which flows back to the water heater area, where the heat is transferred to the water storage tank, either directly or indirectly.

Solar water heating systems supplement your traditional water heater, rather than replacing it, but they make a real difference. Depending on where you live and the system you use, a solar water heater may account for 40 percent to 80 percent of the energy used to heat your water. This percentage is called the solar fraction. Consult a solar fraction map, like the one shown here, to see how your region measures up and to calculate your potential savings over time.

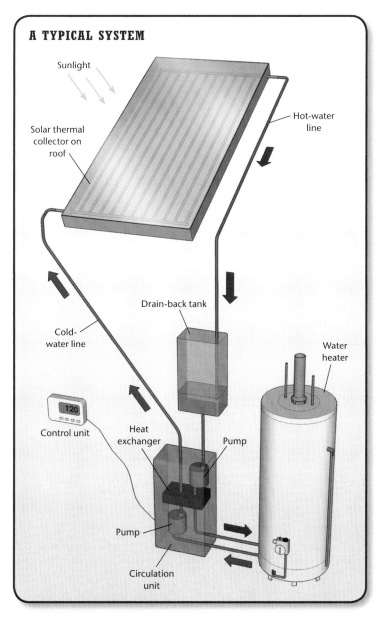

A TYPICAL SYSTEM

Sunlight

Solar thermal collector on roof

Hot-water line

Cold-water line

Drain-back tank

Water heater

120

Control unit

Heat exchanger

Pump

Pump

Circulation unit

How the Pros Do It

"Before you make the investment in a solar system, try other things first, like high-efficiency, low-flow showerheads and a horizontal-axis washing machine. You may be able to do almost as much with changes in your home and behavior. After that, look at a solar installation."

Doug Kirk, GreenPlumbersUSA.com

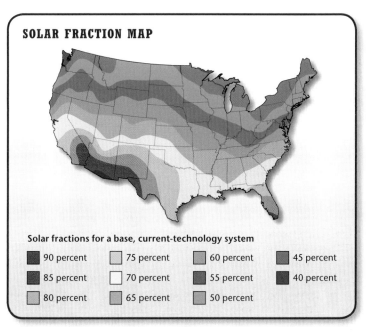

SOLAR FRACTION MAP

Solar fractions for a base, current-technology system

■ 90 percent	□ 75 percent	■ 60 percent	■ 45 percent
■ 85 percent	□ 70 percent	■ 55 percent	■ 40 percent
□ 80 percent	■ 65 percent	■ 50 percent	

TAX CREDITS

There are numerous tax incentives at federal, state, and local levels that may apply to a residential solar water heater. A good place to search for these online is DSIRE (Database of State Incentives for Renewables and Efficiency) at www.dsireusa.org.

When you find the tax credits that may apply, be sure to look for expiration dates, as not all credits last forever. And if tax credits are part of your plan (and why wouldn't they be?), make sure your project qualifies. Most credits require a product with the appropriate rating and certification, often by the Solar Ratings and Certification Corporation (SRCC). Some also require that it be professionally installed.

Whole-house Water Treatments

In some areas, the water supply may tend to be hard or may contain sediment. Provided the water is otherwise safe, hard water can often be remedied with a water softener, while sediment can be removed with a whole-house filter.

STOP!

Water softeners work by using sodium. If you have high blood pressure or any other condition that makes this a concern, research the information and possible settings for your softener and consider an untreated line for drinking water.

Here, a water heater, water softener, and whole-house water filter have been installed in convenient proximity to each other.

Installing a Water Filter

Sediment, usually consisting of fine clay or sand particles, can significantly affect your household plumbing, reducing the lifespan of your water heater and clogging the intake filters to your clothes washer, as well as other elements prone to clogging, such as aerators, sprayers, and showerheads. It can even collect visibly in toilet bowls and dishwashers or show up in standing water in a glass or pitcher. To sort out the sediment, install a water filter on the main cold-water supply line inside the house, before the water splits off to the water heater.

1 Choose a location

- Pick a spot on the main cold-water supply line, after the main shutoff valve but before it splits to go to the heater; avoid wasteful filtering of water for your outdoor lines
- Make sure you can easily reach the location to change the filter
- Mark the section of pipe to be removed

2 Install the filter head

- Shut off the water to the pipe and drain it at a nearby faucet
- Cut at the marks, using buckets and towels to catch remaining water
- Attach threaded fittings to the cut ends as specified in the instructions
- Position the filter with the "in" opening toward the incoming water supply
- Secure the filter to the fittings with an adjustable wrench, using pipe-thread tape at the connections

3 Install the filter

- For a metal pipe, use a jumper wire to ground from one side of the pipe to the other
- Insert the filter holder (also called the sump) with a filter in place; most holders come with a rubber washer for a watertight connection
- Slowly turn on the water, release trapped air as specified in the instructions, and check for leaks
- Flush water through the filter for several minutes, using the nearest house faucet
- Replace the filter material regularly

Stuff to Buy

BASIC SUPPLIES Electrical wire and jumper fittings; pipe-thread tape
REPLACEMENT FILTERS
SOFTENER SALT
WATER FILTER UNIT Look for one with an internal shutoff to simplify replacing filters
WATER SOFTENER

Time Commitment

Varies by task

Tools You'll Need

Adjustable wrenches
Broom
Pipe cutter

Related Topics

Assessing your water supply, 16–17
Filters at the sink, 74–75
Minor clogs & leaks, 218–219
Soldering a copper joint, 108–111
The supply system, 10–11

Maintaining Your Water Softener

As the name states, a water softener is designed to soften hard water that contains excessive minerals like calcium and magnesium. Hard water makes it impossible to get a good soap lather in the bath, shower, or sink, or when you're washing clothes or dishes. Even worse, it damages your plumbing with mineral deposits that clog aerators, showerheads, sprayers, and washing machine inlets, and it shortens the life of your water heater. If you suspect your water is too hard, have it tested.

A water softener can be installed as a do-it-yourself project, much like a whole-house water filter, or it can be installed by a company that offers a maintenance contract. You may also find yourself purchasing a house with a water softener already in place. Like a water filter, a softener may be installed at an accessible location in the cold-water supply line before it splits, so that the softener affects both the cold- and hot-water supplies. Alternatively, for people who don't like to drink treated water, a softener may be installed only on the line leading to the water heater. Avoid wasting the softener on water that will be used outside.

Water softeners work by passing cold water through a plastic resin imbued with salt (various salts are used in different units). Sodium is exchanged for the magnesium or calcium in the water, softening it. This exchange uses up the salty brine in the resin. Every few days, the unit recharges itself, purging the used water to a drain or disposal unit and taking in a fresh supply of saltwater from a storage tank. During the purge-and-refill process, the water in the house is temporarily hard again and water pressure may be reduced.

A typical water softener includes both the softener unit and a large storage container for the salt. You or your service provider must replace the salt in the storage tank regularly, which involves hoisting and emptying bags of salt. Make sure to use salt designed for use in the water softener.

If the salt solidifies a bit in parts of the resin, break up the crusting by stirring thoroughly with a broom handle, reaching throughout the resin from top to bottom. Crusts shouldn't form routinely, but they can develop in humid conditions or if you don't have the right salt.

Many modern softeners allow you to time the softener's recharge cycle so that it occurs at night, minimizing the inconvenience of reduced water that is momentarily hard. You may also be able to adjust how hard or soft your treated water will be.

Investing in the quality of the water in your home, from its purity to its softness, seems like a good deal when you consider how many members of your family will benefit.

6

Pipefitting

In this chapter, you'll learn how to work with a variety of pipe, from PVC and ABS to copper and galvanized steel. We show you how to cut it and join it, whether it's using glue on plastic to soldering copper. You'll also find out how to connect new plastic pipe to existing copper supply lines and cast iron drainpipes.

Chapter Contents

Working with Plastic Pipe

Make sure the variety of plastic you use is allowed by local code, and choose the right kind for the job. For example, PVC should be used only for cold water, but CPVC can handle hot and cold. Flexible PE tubing is often used for well water.

PVC pipe is perfect for improvements such as bringing water into a garage.

Calculating Makeup Distance

Fittings

Makeup distances

Face to face

Length needed

When you're measuring pipe lengths, first determine the face-to-face distance between new fittings. Then add the distance that the pipe will extend into the fittings, known as the makeup distance.

Cutting Plastic Pipe

Before you cut any pipe, make exact measurements, as rigid pipes will not give much if they are too long or too short. Flexible tubing, on the other hand, usually has enough play to make up for small differences, so minor measuring and cutting errors are rarely a problem.

To measure pipe or tubing, determine the distance between new fittings and then add the makeup distance, which is the length of pipe inside each fitting. This distance varies depending on the type of fittings. In push-on fittings, such as those used with PVC or ABS, pipe ends extend all the way to the shoulder (the interior stop). The pipes do not go quite as far in threaded fittings.

If you are cutting into existing supply lines in the house, turn off the main water supply and drain the lines through a nearby faucet. Have a bucket and rags or sponges ready to deal with any leftover water, and dry the existing pipe as much as possible.

Stuff to Buy

SOLVENT CEMENT Specified for your type of pipe

Tools You'll Need

File, knife, or reaming tool
Grease pencil
PVC scissors or handsaw and miter box
Utility knife or file

Related Topics

Adding a sprinkler system, 168–169
A home plumbing tool kit, 22–25
Plastic pipe varieties, 26–29

Cutting & Joining PVC Pipe

Use a solvent cement designed for PVC pipe. If the temperature is below 40 degrees Fahrenheit, use a low-temperature solvent cement instead.

1 Cut the pipe

- For fast, clean cuts, use PVC scissors for pipe up to 1 inch in diameter
- Alternatively, use a tubing cutter, a fine-toothed saw, or a power miter saw
- To use a saw on an installed pipe, brace the pipe with a free hand to avoid excess motion

2 Prepare the cut ends

- Use a file, knife, or reaming tool to remove burrs inside and outside the cut ends
- Check for cracks, gouges, and deep abrasions; if you find them, cut a replacement piece
- Test the fit of the pipe; it should enter the fitting but stop partway

3 Mark for alignment

- With the fitting temporarily in place, mark the pipe and fitting for proper alignment
- Make the marks long enough; when cement is used, the pipe will slip farther in, covering part of the marks

4 Apply primer

- Before gluing a pipe, spread PVC primer (often called purple primer) around the end of the pipe
- Also apply it inside the fitting down to the shoulder
- Allow the primer to dry

5 Apply solvent cement

- Solvent cement dries so fast that steps 5 and 6 must occur within seconds; review both ahead of time
- Work with solvent cement in a well-ventilated area, avoid breathing the fumes, and keep any flame source away from the fumes
- Apply the PVC solvent cement with the applicator brush if one is supplied; otherwise, use another soft brush
- Apply cement liberally to the pipe and lightly to the fitting socket

6 Connect the pipe

- Slip the fitting onto the pipe so the marks are offset by about ¼ inch, then immediately twist the fitting into alignment
- Hold the parts for a few seconds while the cement sets; there should be a narrow band of cement all around; wipe off any excess with a damp rag
- You can handle the joint gently after 60 seconds, but wait at least 2 hours before pressurizing the line with water; wait longer if it's cold and damp, before turning on the water to check for leaks

Cutting & Joining ABS Pipe & Fittings

1 Cut the pipe

- For clean, straight cuts through ABS, use a PVC saw and a miter box or a power miter saw
- If you don't have those, use a fine-tooth handsaw, making the cut as straight as possible

2 Smooth the cut end

- Use a utility knife or a file to remove rough edges around the interior that could snag waste and water
- Clean the outside of the pipe end with sandpaper or emery cloth

3 Dry-fit the connection

- Temporarily place the fitting on the pipe end and mark the alignment for later reference
- The pipe will slip farther into the fitting once cement is applied, so make long marks
- Use a marker you can see on black ABS, such as a white grease pencil

4 Apply cement

- You'll need to complete step 5 immediately after step 4, so read both ahead of time
- Work with solvent cement in a well-ventilated area, avoid breathing the fumes, and keep any flame sources away from the fumes
- Spread ABS solvent cement liberally around the outside of the pipe, then coat the interior of the fitting

5 Form the joint

- Slip the fitting all the way onto the pipe with the alignment slightly offset
- Immediately twist the fitting so the marks line up
- Hold the joint together for a few seconds
- Gently wipe away excess cement with a damp rag

Using Barbed Fittings on PE Flexible Pipe

1 Set up the connection

- Cut the PE tubing; you do not need to cut it perfectly straight
- Slide the stainless-steel ring clamp onto the PE
- Twist the barbed fitting into the PE tubing
- Line up the fitting with the new tubing run

2 Secure the clamp

- Slide the clamp over the PE tubing on the fitting
- Tighten the screw on the clamp
- If you must make changes later, you can usually loosen the clamps and pull the joint apart by hand; if you can't, pour hot water over the ends of the tubing to soften it, then pull it off

PE tubing is flexible, making it a good choice for drip systems in planting beds. It's also often used for well systems.

Soldering a Copper Joint

Copper pipe is lightweight, corrosion-resistant, and rugged, and it remains a popular choice for supply lines. It is fairly easy to join by sweat-soldering (usually just called soldering). Like any skill, however, soldering is best learned through practicing in advance.

Working with Copper Pipe

Sweat-soldering is the best way to join rigid copper pipe. If you want to be able to take apart a run of copper pipe in the future without unsoldering or cutting the run (to replace a water heater, for instance), fit two short lengths of the pipe together with a union.

You will need to use a small propane torch; very fine sandpaper, steel wool, or emery cloth; a can of soldering flux; a pipe brush to clean the pipes; a flux brush to spread the flux; and lead-free plumber's solder.

Flux

Lead-free solder

Flux brush

Pipe brush

Emery cloth

Measuring & Cutting

Before cutting a new length of copper pipe, be sure to consider the makeup distance, which is the length of the part that extends into the fittings. You can use a hacksaw, but a tubing cutter is much easier and makes a cleaner cut. To determine how much copper pipe you'll need, measure the distance between fittings, then add the makeup distance.

SOLDERED JOINT

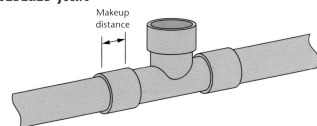

Makeup distance

COMPRESSION JOINT

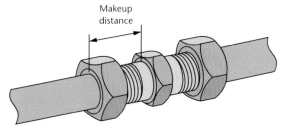

Makeup distance

UNION JOINT

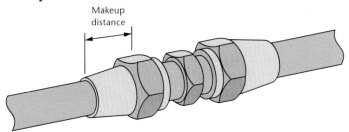

Makeup distance

FLARED JOINT (RARE)

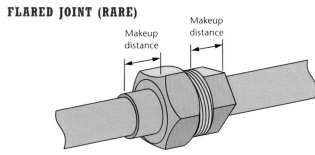

Makeup distance   Makeup distance

Removing Pipe

Drain water from the pipe by closing the supply valve and opening a faucet that is lower in the system. Brace and support the pipe to keep it from sagging. Cut copper pipe with a hacksaw or tubing cutter. Loosen a soldered joint with a propane torch (be sure to wear eye protection). To remove compression, flare, or union fittings, just unscrew them.

Related Topics

Copper pipe & fittings, 30–31
Other copper connections, 112–113

Tools You'll Need

Emery cloth
Flame guard
Pipe brush
Propane torch
Round file
Solder brush
Tubing cutter

Where to Use Copper Pipe

The copper intake pipes behind this claw-foot tub match the old-fashioned style of this handsome fixture.

In this loft kitchen, copper, galvanized, and cast-iron pipes are interconnected and left exposed as an architectural element rather than something that needs to be hidden from view.

In warm climates, copper is an excellent choice for amenities such as outdoor showers.

How To Do It

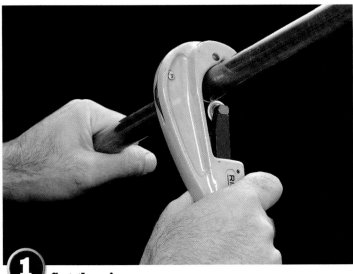

① Cut the pipe

- Cut new lengths of copper pipe with a tubing cutter designed for copper
- Put the cutter over the pipe, then twist the knob until the cutter wheel makes contact with the surface
- Rotate the cutter around the tube, tightening it after each revolution, until the pipe snaps in two

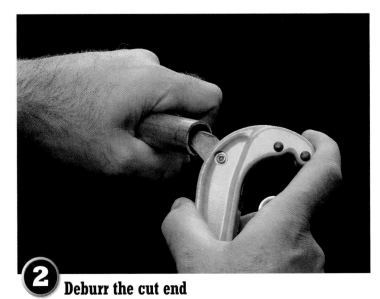

② Deburr the cut end

- At the cut end, clean off the inside burrs with a round file to ensure a smooth-flowing joint
- You can also use a retractable reamer if there is one on your tubing cutter

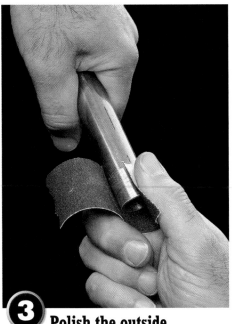

③ Polish the outside

- Smooth and polish the last inch of pipe on the outside
- Use emery cloth, steel wool, or sandpaper
- Stop once the surface is shiny, and do not overdo it; soft copper sands easily

④ Clean the fitting

- Clean the inside of the fitting from the end down to the shoulder (the point where it bends)
- Use a pipe brush if you have one, as demonstrated above on a piece of pipe
- Alternatively, use an emery cloth or steel wool

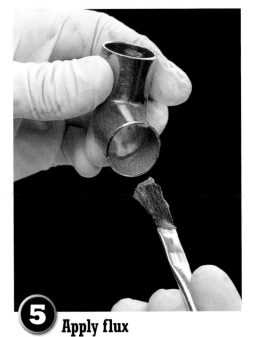

⑤ Apply flux

- Use a small, stiff brush to apply flux around the inside of the fitting and the outside of the pipe end
- Place the fitting on the pipe end; turn the pipe or fitting back and forth once or twice to spread the flux evenly
- Position the fitting correctly
- It's best to wear gloves, as the chemicals in flux can damage your skin

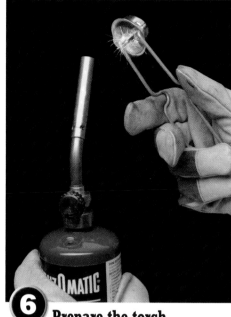

6 Prepare the torch

- Turn the gas torch's control valve on and then light the nozzle end with a striker tool
- Adjust the flame so it is steady and strong, making certain that it is not aimed at anything flammable
- If necessary, shield surrounding objects with a flame guard
- If you are not experienced at soldering, practice with scrap materials firs⁴

7 Heat the fitting

- Be careful where you hold the pipe, as it will get very hot
- With the fitting still in place on the pipe, position the torch nozzle about 4 inches from the fitting and move the flame back and forth to distribute the heat evenly
- Do not aim the torch at the joint itself
- Get the fitting hot but not too hot, as the flux will burn and vanish if it is overheated

8 Test the temperature

- Touch the solder wire to the joint occasionally as you heat the fitting; the joint is hot enough when the solder melts on contact
- Avoid directing the torch at the solder or the joint
- The instant the wire melts, the joint is ready for action

- ...ge of the fitting;
- ...o the joint
- ...olten solder shows all

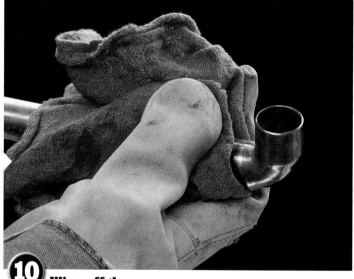

10 Wipe off the excess

- Once the solder cools (in just a few seconds), wipe off surplus flux with a damp rag
- Be careful, as the pipe can get quite hot up to a foot or two from the joint
- Do not bump or move the newly soldered joint for an hour or two, until the solder hardens

Other Copper Connections

Threaded unions are useful for connections you may need to take apart. Compression fittings are often used for supply lines to ice makers, water filters, and shutoff valves. Flared fittings are used for copper tubing, which can be bent as well as joined.

Making a Union Joint

A union is a joint that can be taken apart.
- Solder the male shoulder onto one pipe, then slip the nut onto the other pipe
- Solder the female shoulder onto the second pipe
- Bring the male and female shoulders together
- Slide the nut over the female shoulder and then screw it onto the male shoulder
- Tighten the joint with two wrenches, using one to hold the male shoulder and the other to turn the nut

Making a Compression Joint

 Add the nut & ring
- Slide the compression nut onto the tube, with the nut's broad shoulder facing away from the end
- Slip the compression ring on

Assemble the joint
- Push the tubing or pipe into the threaded body of the fitting
- Slide the compression ring down so that it is snug
- Screw the nut down onto the fitting

 **Tighten the joint**
- Tighten the joint using two wrenches, with one on the nut and one on the fitting
- Use either open-end or adjustable wrenches
- This should compress the ring around the tubing or pipe for a watertight seal

Tools You'll Need

Adjustable or open-end
  wrenches
Flaring tool
Tubing bender

Related Topics

Copper pipe & fittings, 30–31
Soldering a copper joint,
  108–111

Making a Flared Joint

1 Put the nut on the tubing

- Flared joints, used for soft-tempered copper tubing, are rarely needed today, since copper tubing is not used as commonly for plumbing
- Slide the flare nut onto the tube
- Make sure the tapered end of the nut faces away from the end of the tubing

2 Create a flared end

- Clamp the end of the tube into a flaring tool
- Screw the ram down hard into the opening
- Remove the flared tubing from the tool

3 Add the fitting

- Press the tapered end of the fitting into the flared end of the tubing
- Screw the flare nut onto the fitting

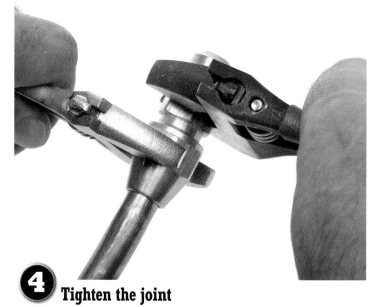

4 Tighten the joint

- Use two adjustable or open-end wrenches, one on the nut and one on the fitting, to secure the joint

Bending Copper Tubing

The best way to shape soft-temper copper tubing is with a tubing bender. Slip the bender over the pipe and then, with both hands, gently bend the tool and tubing into the desired curve. Go slowly. If you crimp the pipe, discard the piece and start again.

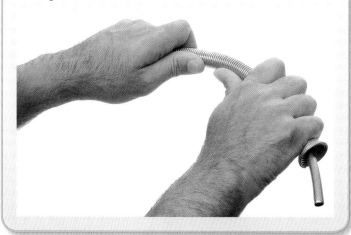

Working with Steel Pipe

Galvanized-steel pipe was once the standard choice for supply lines in American homes, but copper and plastic replaced it in new construction long ago. If your home has steel pipes, you may choose to repair it with the same material.

How to Thread Steel Pipe

Some stores offer to cut and thread galvanized steel pipe as part of your purchase. If this is an option, take advantage of it. The alternative is to rent the required equipment and do the job yourself, which takes more time and effort and may not yield as good a result. Also bear in mind that it's important to cut galvanized pipe perfectly straight so threads can be started accurately on the new end.

To cut and thread the pipe yourself, use a pipe cutter (below right) with a blade designed for steel pipe, and a pipe reamer (below left) to remove burrs from inside the cut pipe. Some cutters have a retractable reamer in the handle. You can rent the cutter and the reamer.

For threading, you will need a vise to hold the pipe steady, plus a threader (above right) fitted with a die and guide for the size of your pipe. These tools can also be rented.

To thread the pipe, first fit the head of the die into the threading handle. Then slide the head, guide first, over the end of the pipe. Exert force on the pipe while rotating the handle clockwise. When the head of the threader bites into the metal, stop pushing and simply continue the clockwise rotation.

Apply generous amounts of thread-cutting oil as you turn the threader. If the threader sticks, back it off slightly and blow or brush away metal chips.

Continue threading until the pipe extends about one thread beyond the end of the die. Remove the threader and then clean off the newly cut threads with a stiff wire brush.

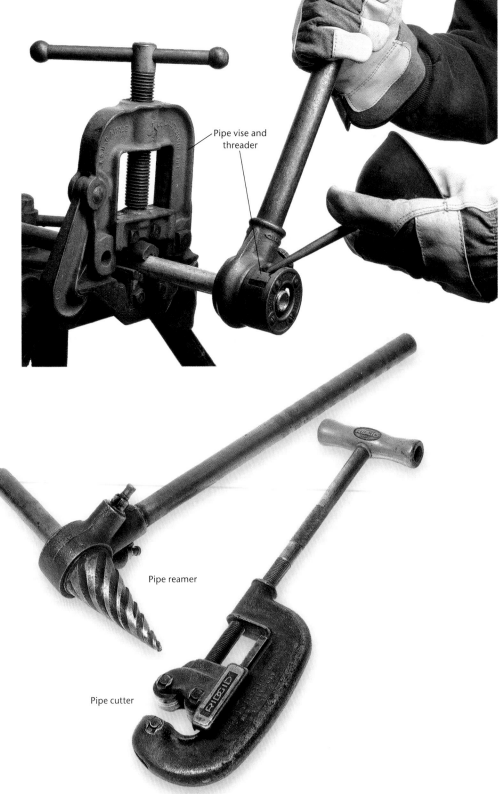

Pipe vise and threader

Pipe reamer

Pipe cutter

Stuff to Buy

Pipe-joint compound
Pipe-thread tape
Thread-cutting oil

Tools You'll Need

Pipe cutter and reamer (rented)
Pipe vise (rented)
Pipe wrenches
Small brush
Threader (rented)
Wire brush

Related Topics

Cracked or leaking pipes, 192–194
Galvanized steel pipe, 32–33
Making the connections, 120–121
Supply strategies, 144–145

Joining Galvanized Pipe & Fittings

Applying pipe-thread tape

- Wrap pipe-thread tape 1½ turns around the male pipe threads
- Pull the tape tight enough so that the threads show through
- Pipe-thread tape tears easily; if you prefer, use pipe-joint compound, but don't use both

Applying pipe-joint compound

- Instead of pipe-thread tape, you can apply pipe-joint compound
- Put it on the female threads, either directly from the tube or with a small brush
- Use just enough to fill the gaps between the threads

Tightening the connection

- Screw the pipe and fitting together by hand as far as you can
- Use two pipe wrenches for the final tightening
- Make sure the wrenches are turned the right way; if you have one or both backward, the wrenches tend to come off as you try to turn them

For simple projects like this spout near a child's sandbox, steel pipe has the advantage of being durable enough to withstand heavy use.

Working with Cast Iron

If your home was built before 1970, there is a good chance it has cast-iron piping in its drain-waste-vent (DWV) system. Cast-iron pipe is strong, dense, and corrosion-resistant enough to be the quietest of all piping materials.

Two Kinds of Fittings

There are two types of fittings for cast iron: bell-and-spigot and no-hub (or hubless). Bell-and-spigot joints, virtually obsolete, are found in older homes. They were joined with melted lead and oakum. Most codes no longer permit lead in DWV piping. The no-hub joint is used most commonly because it takes up minimal space inside wall cavities. This type of joint can also be used to modify existing bell-and-spigot systems.

Drainage fittings, unlike supply fittings, do not have interior shoulders, and each has a built-in fall or slope.

Cutting Options

Before cutting a drainpipe, turn off the water supply and alert other people in the house not to use toilets and other plumbing fixtures. Securely support the section to be removed and the pipe on each side of it. You can use plumber's tape (metal strapping) for this support. Pull it taut and nail it to nearby joists or studs. Cast iron should be supported every 4 feet in horizontal runs and within a few inches of joints.

To cut cast-iron pipe, the tool of choice for do-it-yourselfers is a reciprocating saw equipped with a metal-cutting blade; you can also use a snap cutter. Either can be rented.

In a pinch, you can cut the pipe with a hacksaw, a cold chisel, and a ball-peen hammer. Start by chalking a cutting line all around the pipe, then score the area to a depth of 1/16 inch with the hacksaw. Tap all around the section with the hammer and cold chisel until the pipe breaks.

No-hub coupling

Nut driver

Safety Tips

- When cutting cast-iron pipe, wear safety glasses and work gloves. If you use a snap cutter, stay clear when the pipe snaps in two.
- When cutting into an existing drainpipe, protect against disease by wearing gloves and safety glasses. Wash your hands thoroughly with soap after your work is done. Clean your tools carefully and wash cleanup rags with hot water, or toss them.

No-hub fittings

Cast-iron pipe

Tools You'll Need

Ball-peen hammer
Chisel
Hacksaw
Nut driver
Pliers
Reciprocating saw
Snap cutter
Socket wrench

Related Topics

Tying old to new, 122–123

Joining No-hub Cast-iron Pipe

1 Cut the pipe

- Cut the pipe, using either a reciprocating saw with a metal-cutting blade or a snap cutter, shown here
- The ratchet action in a snap cutter tightens a chain with cutting wheels that encircles and constricts the pipe until it snaps
- The cut pipe sections tend to jump, so stay clear of them
- Cuts are rarely perfect; use pliers or a cold chisel and a ball-peen hammer to break off any large, uneven chips

2 Place the fitting on one pipe

- Slide the stainless-steel shield onto the pipe
- Push the neoprene gasket onto the end of the pipe; it has a built-in stop to help center it at the joint
- Fold back the gasket lip

3 Position the other pipe

- Butt the fitting against the gasket's stop to center it
- Roll the gasket lip back into place
- If needed, push and pull until the pipe, gasket, and fitting are aligned

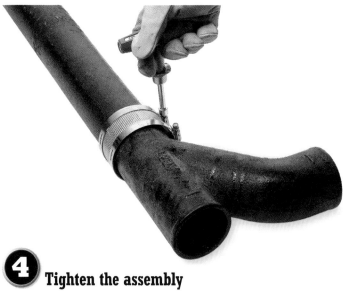

4 Tighten the assembly

- Slide the stainless-steel shield over the gasket
- Tighten the band screws with a socket wrench or a nut driver

Making the Connections

Tying into existing supply or drain lines entails cutting a section out of the pipe and adding the appropriate fitting. For supply lines, turn off the main house water supply and drain the pipes at a faucet. For drainpipes, make sure nobody uses the drains.

Tapping Supply Pipes

With rigid plastic or hard-temper copper supply lines, you'll need to cut out a section of pipe about 8 inches long and add one or two short lengths of pipe (depending on the play in the existing pipe), couplings, and a T-fitting. Make sure to dry the pipe after you cut it. If there's any remaining water in existing copper pipes, it will hinder a successful soldering job.

If you are tapping into a side-by-side pair of hot and cold supply lines, plan for the pipes you are adding to run parallel as well. Don't cut the gaps or assemble the joints until you have a plan.

Flexible supply pipes in a home could include polyethylene (PE) tubing for a well system or PEX tubing. For PE tubing, use the designated barbed connectors and hardware. For PEX tubing, it's probably best to have a professional make the connections with special tools and connectors.

If your supply lines are threaded galvanized steel pipes, you'll have to cut the pipe, then remove each cut section back to the nearest fitting. Install a union, the new pipe, and the T-fitting.

Installing a T in Copper

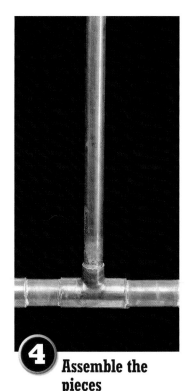

1 Cut the existing pipe

- Shut off the water supply and drain the pipes as much as possible
- Use a tubing cutter to remove about 8 inches of the existing pipe at the desired location
- Steady the existing pipe as you work
- Remove any remaining water with a pail and rags and dry the pipe

2 Slide on the couplings

- Ream and polish the newly cut ends
- Slide a slip or repair coupling all the way over each of the cut ends

3 Add the fitting and spacers

- Assemble a new T-fitting and two spacers (short lengths of pipe) to span the gap in the existing pipe
- Insert over-length spacers in the fitting, then hold them up to the gap and mark them for length
- Cut spacers to fit snugly

4 Assemble the pieces

- Hold the fitting and spacers in position
- Slide the slip couplings so they're centered over each joint
- Aim the T-fitting along the line of your new extension
- Solder each joint

Tapping into CPVC Lines

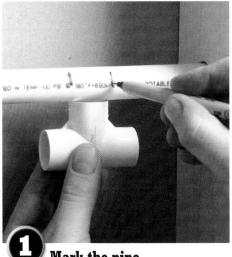

1 Mark the pipe

- Turn off the water at the main shutoff
- Drain the lines at a nearby, lower faucet
- Mark for the gap in the existing line

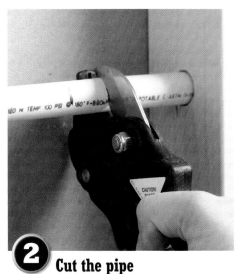

2 Cut the pipe

- Use PVC scissors
- Hold the pipe as you position the scissors so it does not move too much

3 Deburr the cut ends

- Use a reaming tool, file, or knife to deburr the cut pipe ends on the existing house line or lines

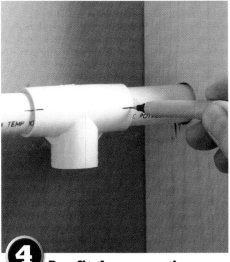

4 Dry-fit the connections

- Without using solvent cement, dry-fit the fitting in place
- Mark the fitting-to-pipe connections with alignment marks on both sides of each joint

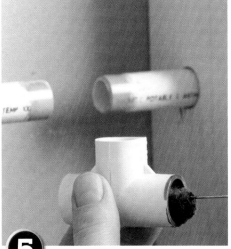

5 Prime the pipe & fitting

- Using purple primer, prime the fitting and pipe ends that will be connected

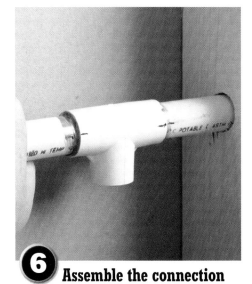

6 Assemble the connection

- Using solvent cement, attach the T fitting to one of the cut pipe ends, making sure to match the planned alignment
- Cement the other cut pipe end to the T fitting as well
- You will only be able to turn the first connection in the usual way as you cement it

Tying into Galvanized Pipe

❶ Cut the pipe

- Turn off the water at the main house shutoff and drain the pipe at a faucet
- For a repair, cut through the damaged area; for an extension, cut a gap in a pipe run between threaded fittings
- Make the cut with a hacksaw or with a power reciprocating saw
- Brace the existing run to prevent excess motion as you cut; for unsupported pipe, wrap plumber's tape (metal strapping) around the pipe every 3 feet and nail it to nearby framing
- Use a bucket and rags to catch any remaining water

❷ Remove the cut pieces

- Remove each of the two cut pipe pieces from its threaded fitting
- Use two pipe wrenches, twisting the pipe with one wrench and holding the nearby fitting with the other
- If the pipe won't budge, apply penetrating oil to the joint and wait 5 minutes

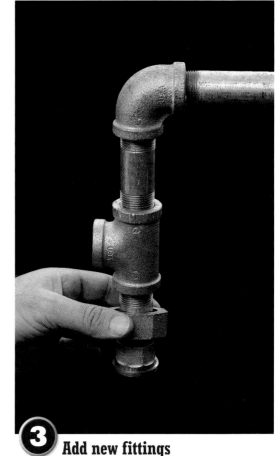

❸ Add new fittings

- Add a short threaded nipple, a T-fitting (in the case of an extension), a second nipple, and a union
- Tighten connections with the wrenches

❹ Secure the pipe to the union

- Thread the remaining pipe length onto the existing fitting; the other end butts against the union
- Slide the union's nut down across the pipe's threads
- Secure the joint with two wrenches

Extending a Plastic Drainpipe System

The steps shown here are for ABS plastic, commonly used in some parts of the country for drainpipe. In other areas, PVC plastic (which is off-white) is more common. Similar steps apply for PVC drainpipe. Make sure that the primer and solvent cement are suitable for the type of plastic and that the fittings are the same type of plastic as the pipe. For drainpipe fittings that change in size (reducer fittings), always direct the flow from the smaller diameter to the larger one.

① Cut the pipe

- Make sure nobody (and no appliance, such as a dishwasher or clothes washer) will use the drainpipe; you can post signs as a reminder
- Cut into the existing pipe with a PVC saw or a fine-tooth handsaw
- Cut off the ends squarely

② Assemble the pieces

- Depending on the amount of play and the type of couplings, you may need one or two spacers, plus the new fitting
- Mark and cut the spacers to fit, allowing for the makeup distance inside the fitting
- Mark locations and alignment as needed, using a white grease pencil

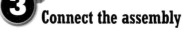

③ Connect the assembly

- Cement the spacers to the fitting
- Position the assembly in the gap and slip the spacers inside the couplings
- When you have aligned the new fitting, tighten the coupling bands

Tying Old to New

Your existing supply lines or drainpipes may use a pipe material that's different from your choice for new projects. Assuming the existing pipes are in good shape, it's usually fairly simple to transition from one to the other.

From Copper to Plastic Supply Lines

If you are planning a project, perhaps working on a whole room or building an addition, that will use rigid plastic supply lines, add a copper T-fitting to your existing copper supply line and then connect the copper-to-plastic transition fitting to that T. Remember to use CPVC, not PVC, for hot-water supply lines.

❶ Install the T

- Turn off the water to the pipe at the main house shut-off and drain the pipe with a faucet at a lower level
- Mark the pipe for a gap to accommodate the T-fitting; allow for makeup distances inside the fitting
- If you are tapping into parallel hot-water and cold-water lines, plan for how your new lines will be able to run parallel to each other and mark them accordingly
- Cut the pipe
- Use rags and a bucket for any remaining water and dry the pipe
- Prepare the cut ends and T-fitting for soldering
- Point the outlet in the direction of the new pipe
- Solder each side of the fitting to the pipe

❷ Install an adapter

- Solder a short length of pipe (a spacer) and a threaded female adapter to the outlet on the T-fitting

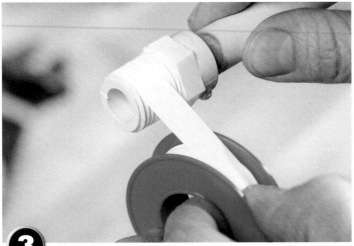

❸ Prepare the plastic pipe

- Cement a male threaded coupling to the plastic pipe, using the correct primer and solvent cement for the type of plastic
- Wait for the cement to set, following the directions on the container, then wrap the threads with pipe-thread tape

❹ Insert the pipe

- Screw the plastic pipe into place using the paired threaded couplings

Related Topics

Making the connections, 118–119
Running supply lines, 144–145
Working with plastic pipe, 104–107

From Cast-iron to Plastic Drainpipes

To add a plastic T-fitting to an existing cast-iron run, cut out a section of the cast-iron pipe, cement spacers to both ends of the plastic fitting, and then join the plastic spacers to the cast-iron pipe using no-hub couplings.

Not all couplings are alike. If possible, opt for repair couplings that don't have interior shoulders. This will allow you to slide them almost completely over the cut ends. Some codes may require you to use a Mission coupling. It's similar to the no-hub, except that half of the neoprene sleeve is made narrower to fit more snugly over cast-iron pipe, which is slightly smaller than plastic pipe.

❶ Cut the existing pipe

- Securely support the existing pipe, both the part to be removed and the adjacent sections
- Use plumber's tape (metal strapping) around the pipe, nailed to nearby framing
- Mark the section to be removed
- Cut the section with a reciprocating saw that has a metal-cutting blade, usually preferred by do-it-yourselfers, or a snap cutter like this one; rent these tools
- If you are using a snap cutter, note that the sections tend to jump when the cut occurs, and stay clear

❷ Add couplings

- Slip no-hub couplings over the cut ends of the cast-iron pipe
- Use couplings designed for transitioning from cast iron to plastic, if they are available

❸ Secure the fitting & spacers

- Cement spacers (short lengths of the plastic pipe) to the fitting
- Push the spacers firmly into the open coupling ends and tighten the stainless-steel bands

7 New Plumbing Lines

In this chapter, you'll learn how to map your system so you can get a new installation right the first time. We cover basic rules for supply- and drain-line sizes and lengths, venting requirements, and techniques for running pipe inside framing. The tools you'll need for rough-in work are identified, and we show you how to work with such tools safely and efficiently.

Chapter Contents

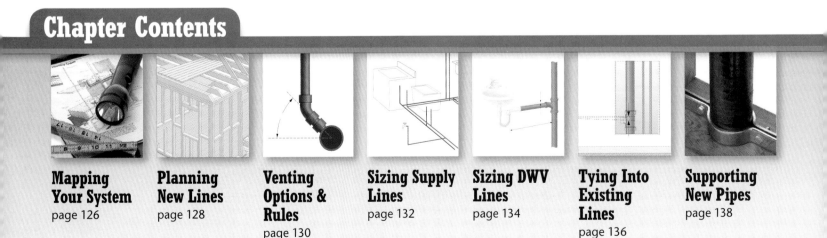

Pipes & Walls
page 140

Dealing with Floors
page 142

Running Supply Lines
page 144

DWV Planning
page 146

Roughing In
page 148

Finishing Up
page 154

page 144

Mapping Your System

A detailed map of your current plumbing system will give you a clear picture of where it's feasible to tie into supply and drain lines for extensions and whether the existing drains and vents are adequate for their intended use.

Creating Useful Maps

Using some simple lines and plumbing symbols, you can make good working drawings of your plumbing system. Such a drawing or map can save you a lot of time, whether you plan to add a fixture, plumb an addition to your house, or troubleshoot a problem.

ISOMETRIC DRAWING

Plumbing, like house framing, happens in three dimensions, so a two-dimensional riser drawing is often not enough. An isometric drawing, which is laid out on isometric graph paper or with a 30-60-90-degree triangle, can render more complex DWV systems.

Evaluating Your Options

Begin your investigation from an unfinished basement or crawl space or, if necessary, from the attic. Some handy mapping tools include a folding rule or a tape measure, a flashlight, a clipboard, and some graph paper.

Make a rough sketch of your findings as you go. Then, in cleaner, more comfortable surroundings, draw a detailed map of any area where you're considering making changes.

CHECKING THE DWV ROUTES

Locate the main soil stack, branch drains, and any secondary vent stacks. Note any accessible cleanouts. Determine the materials and, if possible, the diameters of all drain and vent pipes.

LOCATING SUPPLY LINES

Once you've tracked down the DWV system, it's time to trace the network of hot and cold supply pipes. Check the materials and sizes of all branch lines. Find the spots where vertical risers split off from horizontal branches and head up into a wall.

Isometric drawing

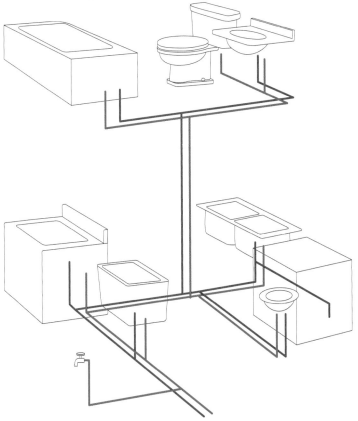

Time Commitment

Half a day

Tools You'll Need

Flashlight
Graph paper
Tape measure
Notepad

Related Topics

Home plumbing systems, 8–9
The DWV system, 12–13
The supply system, 10–11

PLAN DRAWING

Use a traditional plan drawing to place new or existing fixtures inside a room.

RISER DRAWING

The so-called riser drawing, a two-dimensional elevation, is adequate for sketching a small run of supply pipes.

Riser drawing

Plan drawing

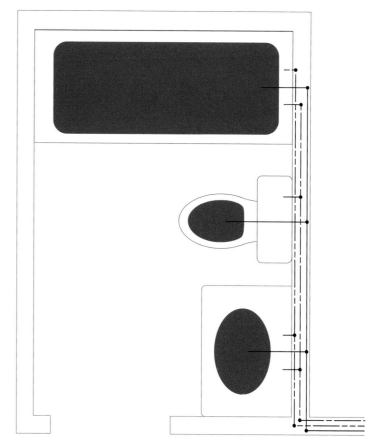

Plumbing Symbols

Simple, established plumbing symbols help you create drawings or sketches that clearly indicate key elements. Here are some of the most useful examples.

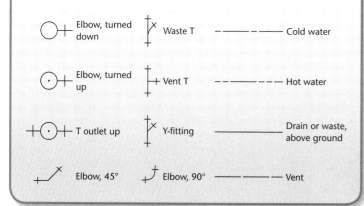

Elbow, turned down

Waste T

———— Cold water

Elbow, turned up

Vent T

– – – – Hot water

T outlet up

Y-fitting

———— Drain or waste, above ground

Elbow, 45°

Elbow, 90°

—— - —— Vent

Check Codes

Codes are a key part of the process, and you'll save time, money, and aggravation by learning about them ahead of time. Don't buy a pipe, a fitting, or a fixture until you've checked your local plumbing and building codes. Discuss your plans in detail with a local inspector, and be sure the methods and materials you're planning to use are acceptable. Take along a copy of your plumbing map.

The inspector will tell you whether you'll need a plumbing or building permit. Projects that involve changes or additions to your plumbing pipes usually require permits. You probably won't need a permit to install a replacement fixture or appliance, or for emergency repairs, as long as the work doesn't alter the plumbing system. Learn what work you're allowed to do yourself, as some codes require licensed plumbers to perform certain types of work.

Planning New Lines

For the most part, the feasibility of moving or adding a fixture depends on whether you can extend drainpipes and vents (the DWV system). You can almost always add supply lines, as long as you have enough water pressure for new fixtures.

Extending DWV & Supply Pipes

Plumbing codes specify several aspects of the drain-waste-vent (DWV) system in a home. Codes establish the size of the drainpipe or branch drain serving a new fixture or fixture group; the distance (called the critical distance) from the traps to the main stack, secondary stack, or other vent; and the point where a new drainpipe or branch drain ties into the existing branch drain or main stack.

If you have a cast-iron DWV system, you will probably want to make any additions to it with plastic drainpipe, which is considerably lighter and is easily joined with solvent cement. You can use either ABS or PVC pipe, depending on local codes and what's available.

Because supply pipes require no venting, extending them is a much easier task than extending a DWV system. First determine, however, whether your water heater and water pressure can handle the load of any additions.

The selection of correctly sized pipes, as outlined by local codes, depends on the type of fixture to be added, the volume of water it demands, and the length of the new pipe.

Your home's supply pipes are most likely rigid copper joined with soldered fittings, although old galvanized-steel systems still exist and some newer homes have plastic pipe. If you have old steel pipes, extend them with a more modern material, such as copper or plastic (make sure your code permits the latter). You can also extend a copper supply system with rigid plastic pipe, codes permitting, or with more copper. If your home lines are rigid plastic already, add any new lines using the same material. For homes with PEX flexible pipe, you may prefer to have a professional install new lines using special tools and fittings.

Placement Options

Broadly speaking, there are several options for tying into DWV pipes. The simplest, most cost-efficient approach is to connect a new fixture or group of fixtures to the existing main soil stack, either directly or through a branch drain. One way is to install them above or below existing fixtures on the stack (check codes for restrictions). Another is to place them back to back with an existing group attached to the stack.

If your planned addition is across the house from the existing plumbing, you'll likely need to run a new secondary vent stack up through the roof, and a new branch drain to the soil stack or to the main house drain via an existing cleanout.

If possible, tie a bathroom sink, tub, or shower stall (but not a toilet) directly into an existing branch drain instead, which will save on labor and demolition costs.

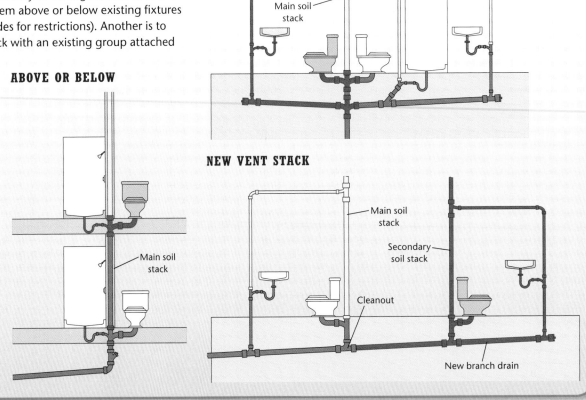

BACK TO BACK

New bath addition

Existing stack

Main soil stack

ABOVE OR BELOW

Main soil stack

NEW VENT STACK

Main soil stack

Secondary soil stack

Cleanout

New branch drain

Pipes & Framing

Once you've devised a strategy for tying into your DWV system, the next step is to study possible access routes for running pipes to the new fixtures or appliances.

Most wood-frame houses are built with 2 × 8 or larger floor joists, 2 × 6 or larger ceiling joists, and 2 × 4 wall studs, although interior wall studs may be 2 × 3 and exterior wall studs may be 2 × 6. Studs and joists are usually spaced 16 inches apart, center to center, but they are 24 inches apart in some homes and somewhat randomly spaced in roughly built older homes. In new construction, rough plumbing is added before wall, ceiling, and floor coverings. In a finished house, you will have to route pipes through existing walls, ceilings, and floors.

WHERE YOU HAVE ACCESS

It may be easy to install new pipes in unfinished basement ceilings and other areas, such as utility rooms, where framing is exposed.

You simply work from the uncovered side, drilling holes and threading pipes through the studs or joists. Avoid running supply lines in areas where pipes might freeze in winter.

WHERE ACCESS IS LIMITED

Getting pipes into walls, floors, or ceilings that have coverings on both sides involves cutting through the coverings, installing pipes, and patching the holes. Drywall, the most common wall and ceiling covering, is relatively easy to cut away and replace, though you'll need to match the paint or patch the wallpaper. Materials like ceramic tile, wood flooring, and plaster are more difficult to cut and patch and should be left alone when possible.

Related Topics

Dealing with floors, 142–143
DWV planning, 146–147
Pipes & walls, 140–141
Plumbing system basics, 8–9
The DWV system, 12–13
Tying into existing lines, 136–137
Venting options & rules, 130–131

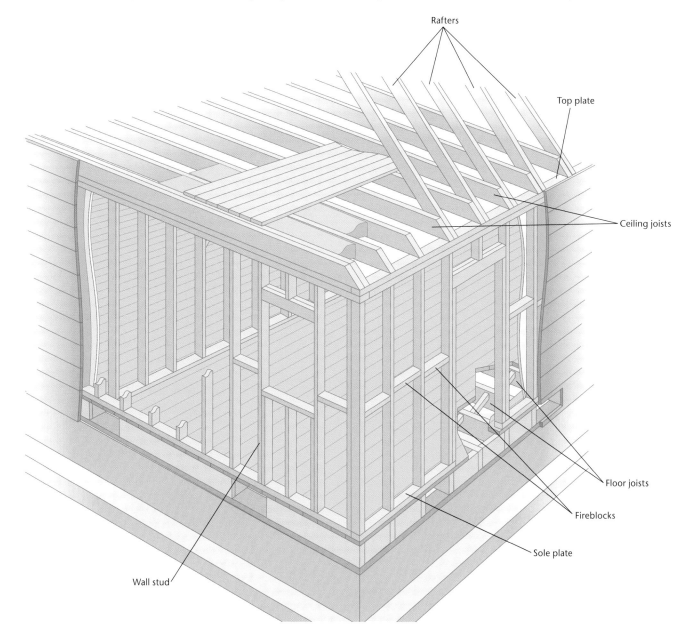

Rafters

Top plate

Ceiling joists

Floor joists

Fireblocks

Sole plate

Wall stud

Venting Options & Rules

Vent runs are normally installed either plumb (straight up) or level, with short diagonals to get around the occasional obstacle. Some codes require that horizontal vents be slightly sloped for drainage. Typical vent fittings have tighter bends than drain fittings.

Venting Configurations

The five basic venting options—subject to local codes—are wet venting, back venting, individual venting, indirect venting, and loop venting.

WET VENTING

Wet venting is the simplest option. The fixture is vented directly through the fixture drain to the soil stack.

BACK VENTING

Back venting is also called reventing. It involves running a vent loop up past the fixture to reconnect with the main stack or secondary vent above the fixture level.

INDIVIDUAL VENTING

Individual venting is also called secondary venting. It means running a secondary vent stack up through the roof for a new fixture or group of fixtures distant from the main stack.

INDIRECT VENTING

Indirect venting allows you to vent certain fixtures, such as a basement shower, into a laundry tub or into an existing floor drain without additional venting.

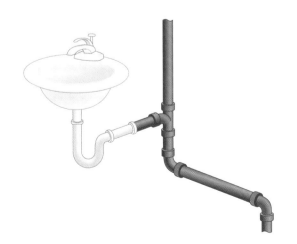

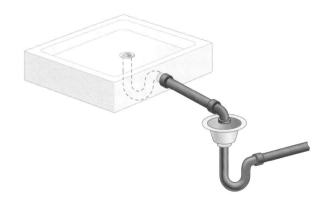

LOOP VENTING

Loop venting serves sinks in freestanding kitchen islands or in other spots where you can't vent within the critical distance. The loop, which runs up higher than the sink, allows proper air circulation for venting and drainage.

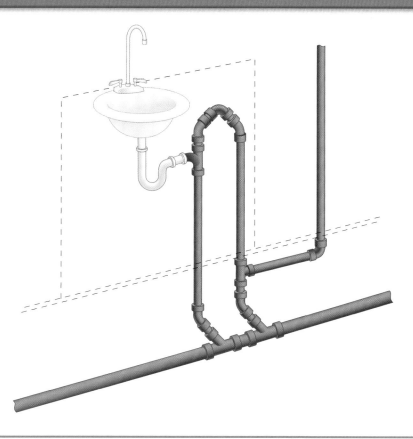

Keeping Vents High & Dry

Unlike supply lines and drainpipes, vents are intended to release waste gases, not carry water or waste. Some common code requirements are aimed at keeping such liquids out of the vent portion of the plumbing system.

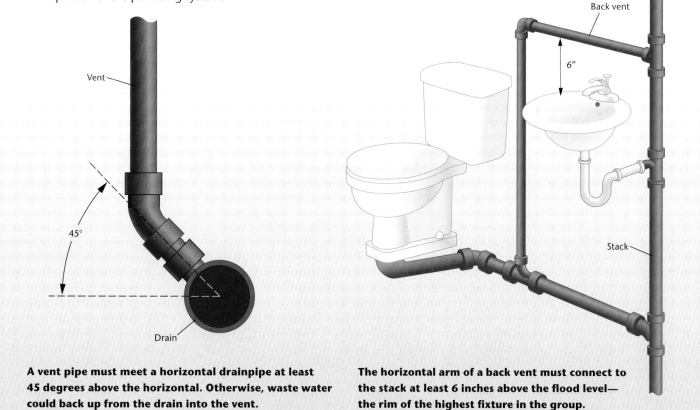

A vent pipe must meet a horizontal drainpipe at least 45 degrees above the horizontal. Otherwise, waste water could back up from the drain into the vent.

The horizontal arm of a back vent must connect to the stack at least 6 inches above the flood level—the rim of the highest fixture in the group.

Sizing Supply Lines

After you confirm that your water heater and water pressure can handle the planned fixtures, the next step is to determine the size of the pipes, as outlined by code. This depends on the fixture types, the volume of water required, and the pipe lengths.

STOP!
Sizing codes vary by region, so check all specs with your local inspector before finalizing your plans.

Calculating Fixture Units

Few code restrictions apply to simple extensions of hot and cold supply pipes, provided there is sufficient water pressure. The proper material and diameter for supply pipes serving a new fixture or appliance should be spelled out clearly in your local code, according to the number of "fixture units" that the type of installation typically uses. (One fixture unit represents 7.5 gallons, or 1 cubic foot, of water per minute.) In the illustration below, nine fixtures account for 17 fixture units.

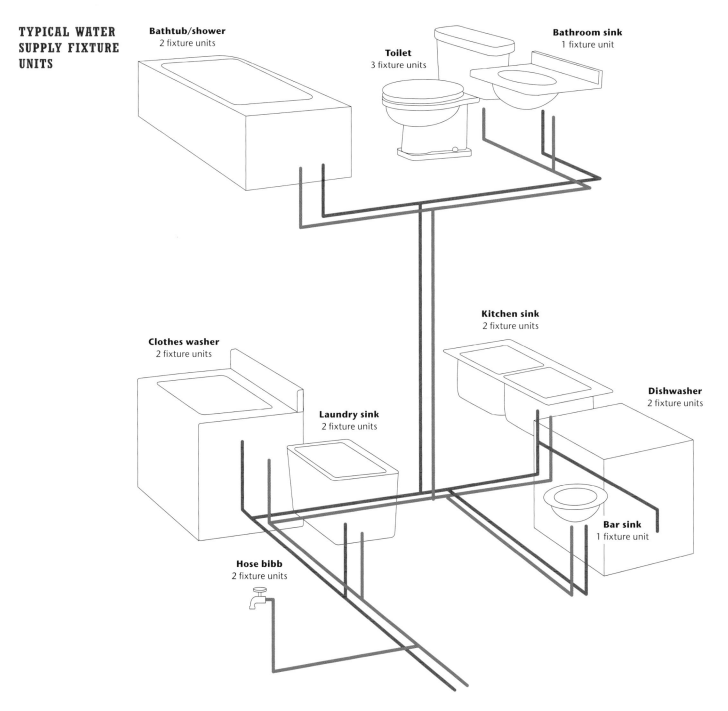

TYPICAL WATER SUPPLY FIXTURE UNITS

Bathtub/shower
2 fixture units

Toilet
3 fixture units

Bathroom sink
1 fixture unit

Kitchen sink
2 fixture units

Clothes washer
2 fixture units

Dishwasher
2 fixture units

Laundry sink
2 fixture units

Bar sink
1 fixture unit

Hose bibb
2 fixture units

Related Topics

Assessing your water supply, 16–17
Roughing in, 148–153
Running supply lines, 144–145
The supply system, 10–11

Choosing Pipe Sizes

Typically, the main supply pipe leading in from the street is ¾- or 1-inch pipe, supply branches are ¾-inch pipe, and risers feeding individual fixtures are ½-inch pipe.

To figure the pipe specs for a sizable remodel, you'll need to know how many total fixture units are used in your home. Add up the ratings of all the fixtures. Estimate, as best you can, the length of the distribution pipes and then see the chart below to determine pipe size. (Check your results against local codes; these chart figures are intended only as a starting point.)

Keep in mind that ideal pipe size may vary depending on the amount of delivered water pressure and the height of a proposed addition. Water pressure drops 0.5 pounds per square inch (psi) for every foot in elevation from the source—the water main or well. As a result, a second- or third-story addition might require a larger pipe. If you have higher or lower water pressure or a large elevation gain, consult local code for alternative pipe sizes.

For typical fixture riser sizes, see the chart at right.

Sizing Supply Risers

	Minimum pipe diameter	
	Cold water	Hot water
Toilet	⅜"	
Bathtub	½"	½"
Bathroom sink	⅜"	⅜"
Shower	½"	½"
Bar sink	⅜"	⅜"
Kitchen sink	½"	½"
Dishwasher		⅜" to ½"
Clothes washer	½"	½"
Laundry sink	½"	½"
Water heater	¾"	
Hose bibb	½" to ¾"	

Sizing Water Distribution Pipes

Meter & street service	Size of main supply pipe & branches	Maximum length for total fixture units (46 to 60 PSI)					
		40'	60'	80'	100'	150'	200'
¾"	½"*	7	7	6	5	4	3
¾"	¾"	20	20	19	17	14	11
¾"	1"	39	39	36	33	28	23
1"	1"	39	39	39	36	30	25
1"	1¼"	78	78	76	67	52	44

*¾" minimum for main supply

Sizing DWV Lines

Plumbing codes specify minimum diameters for drains and vents in the vertical main stack, horizontal branch drains, and separate vent systems. The diameters are related to numbers of fixture units, which are specified in the code for different plumbing fixtures.

STOP!
Sizing codes vary by region, so check all specs with your local inspector before finalizing your plans.

Calculating Fixture Units

To determine drainpipe diameter, check the code's fixture-unit chart for the new fixtures you're considering. Add up the total fixture units (in the illustration below, nine fixtures account for 17 fixture units). Then look up the drain diameter specified for that number of units in the chart on the opposite page.

TYPICAL DWV FIXTURE UNITS

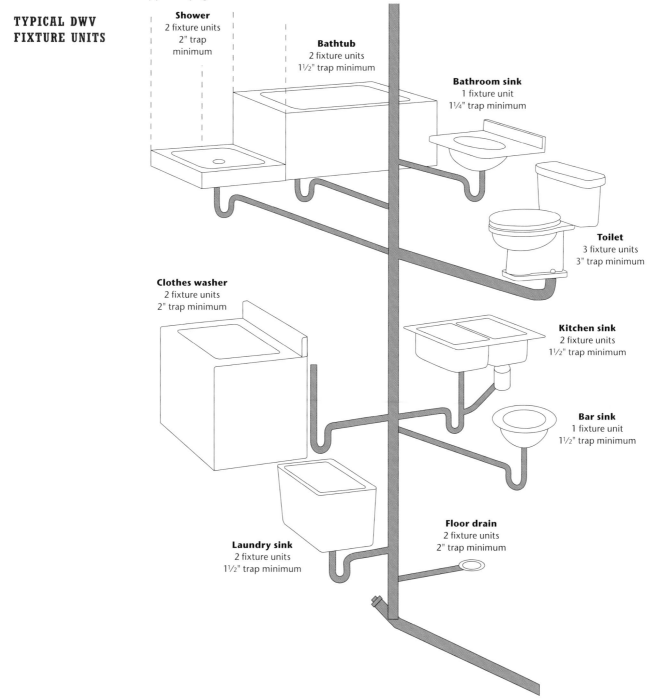

Shower
2 fixture units
2" trap minimum

Bathtub
2 fixture units
1½" trap minimum

Bathroom sink
1 fixture unit
1¼" trap minimum

Toilet
3 fixture units
3" trap minimum

Clothes washer
2 fixture units
2" trap minimum

Kitchen sink
2 fixture units
1½" trap minimum

Bar sink
1 fixture unit
1½" trap minimum

Floor drain
2 fixture units
2" trap minimum

Laundry sink
2 fixture units
1½" trap minimum

Related Topics

DWV planning, 144–145
Roughing in, 148–153
The DWV system, 12–13
Tying into existing lines, 136–137
Venting options & rules, 130–131

Sizing for Drainpipes

Pipe size	Maximum fixture units for horizontal drain	Maximum fixture units for vertical drain
1¼"	1	1
1½"	1*	2
2"	8	16
2½"	14	32
3"	35	48
4"	216	256
*Except for sinks		

Critical Distances for Vent Pipes

Size of fixture drain	Minimum vent size	Critical distance
1¼"	1¼"	2 ½'
1½"	1¼"	3 ½'
2"	1½"	5'
3"	2"	6'
4"	3"	10'

Checking Critical Distances

Plumbing codes also specify the maximum allowable distance between fixtures and vents. This distance—from a fixture's trap to the main stack, a secondary stack, or another vent—is called the critical distance. The code lists critical distances by size of fixture drain.

The height of the fixture drain is also regulated by code. No fixture drain may be completely below the level of the trap's crown weir (as shown below), or the drain would act as a siphon and empty the trap.

If you figure in the ideal drainpipe slope of ¼ inch per foot, the length of that drainpipe quickly becomes limited. But if the fixture is vented properly within the critical distance, the drainpipe's run to the actual stack or drain may be any length.

If your fixture is too far from the vent, you have several choices: increase the size of the drainpipe, move the fixture closer to the existing vent, or add a vent closer to the fixture location.

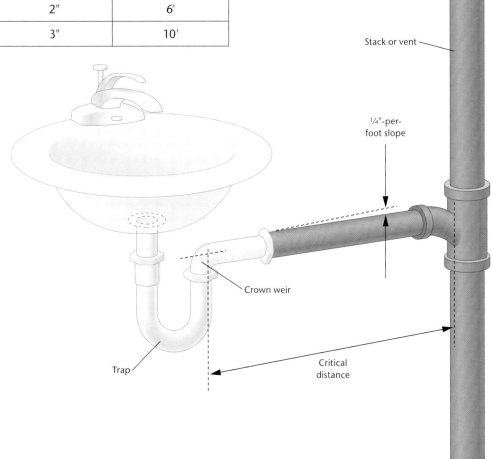

Stack or vent

¼"-per-foot slope

Crown weir

Trap

Critical distance

Tying Into Existing Lines

Before you install new fixtures or appliances, you have to tie into the existing supply and DWV lines. First you'll need to pinpoint the pipes' locations inside the wall, ceiling, or floor. Then carefully remove materials in the immediate area to access them.

To cut into drywall, drill small pilot holes at the corners of your planned cutout, then cut from hole to hole with a drywall saw or jab saw along the marked lines.

Locating Pipes

If you've drawn a plumbing map for your house, you already know roughly where the pipes are. (If you haven't prepared a map yet, it's a good idea to create one now.) Starting from the map, locate the pipes related to this project as precisely as possible from above or below. You may have to drill or cut exploratory holes to find the exact positions of stacks, branch drains, or water supply risers inside a wall or ceiling. Once you find one riser, the other is normally about 6 inches away.

Decorating Tip

Save a small piece of the drywall you remove. At the end of the project, have a local paint store match the color so you can hide the patch seamlessly.

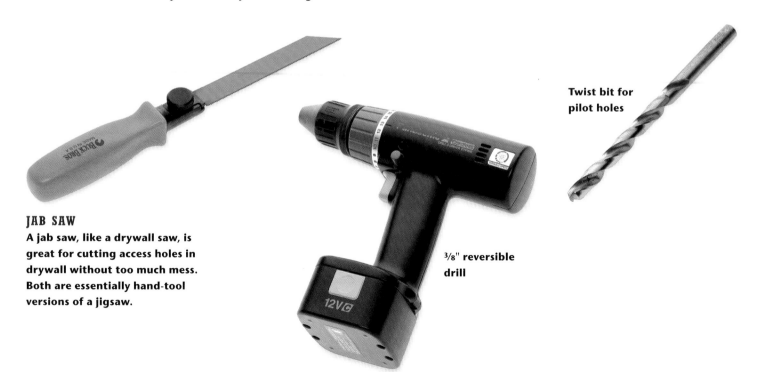

JAB SAW
A jab saw, like a drywall saw, is great for cutting access holes in drywall without too much mess. Both are essentially hand-tool versions of a jigsaw.

³/₈" reversible drill

Twist bit for pilot holes

Exposing Pipes in a Wall

To open a wall, you will need to cut a rectangle about 3 feet high between adjacent studs. First insert a tape measure into an exploratory hole near the pipes you're tying into. Extend the tape to the left until you hit a stud. Note the measurement, then mark that point on the wall. Do the same to the right.

Using a carpenter's level that also shows plumb, draw vertical lines about 3 feet long through the marks to show the stud edges. With level horizontal lines, connect the vertical lines above and below where you plan to access the pipes. Cut through the lines as shown on page 136 (top). Be careful to avoid electrical wiring.

Exposing Pipes in Floors & Ceilings

Cutting into floors can be a messy job, as it requires tearing out and repairing the floor covering and the subfloor. To open a wood subfloor, drill pilot holes, then make the cutout with a jigsaw or handsaw. If you're skilled with a portable circular saw, you can also carefully make a series of pocket cuts.

If you're tying into a branch drain, try to gain access from below—from the crawl space or basement for a first-floor drain or through ceiling materials to reach an upper floor. To open a ceiling between joists, follow the procedure for opening a wall.

Plotting Pipe Routes

Many new fixtures include a fixture template or roughing-in measurements for correctly positioning the supply stubouts and the trap exit—the spot where the drainpipe enters the wall or floor. Transfer these measurements carefully to the wall or floor at the fixture's planned location.

The length of the drainpipe, combined with the height of the trap exit on the wall, or its distance below the floor, will determine where the connection to the stack or branch drain will be made.

For a sink, as shown below, plot the ¼-inch-per-foot slope for the drainpipe by running a tape measure from the center of the

trap exit mark on the wall to a point at the same height on the stack. Then multiply the number of feet in this distance by ¼ inch and lower the mark on the stack by that amount.

For a toilet, shower, or bathtub, figure the slope from a closet bend (for a toilet) or a trap (for a shower or bathtub) below the subfloor. Mark it with a chalk line snapped on a parallel joist or a string pulled taut along the proposed run.

Supply pipes are not required to slope in the same way that drainpipes are, but figuring in at least a slight downward slope will allow you to drain the pipes later. Run the hot and cold supply pipes parallel to each other, about 6 inches apart.

PLOTTING SLOPE FOR A DRAINPIPE

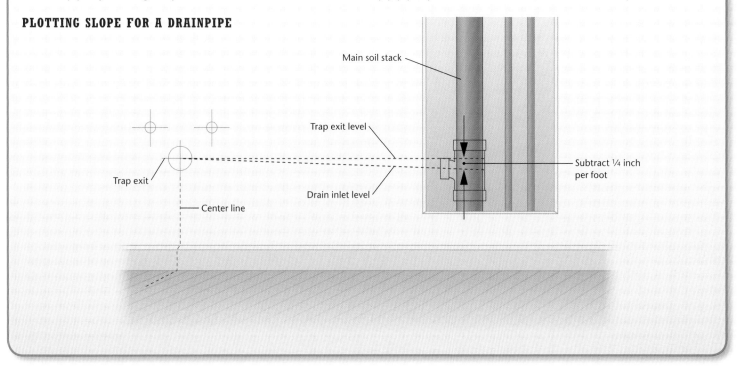

Supporting New Pipes

Your new pipes will need solid support at intervals no greater than those shown in the chart below. The type of support is also vital. Most important to remember: Don't use one type of metal hanger to support pipe made of another type of metal.

The Right Hardware for the Job

Always purchase the correct kind of supports for the pipe you are installing. When you're using metal pipe or tubing, it's essential to use hangers made of the same kind of metal to avoid corrosion.

Supply-pipe hangers are made of metal or plastic and are used to hang copper or plastic supply pipe. Some have integral nails, while others must be nailed or screwed to a wall stud or floor joist. Copper supply straps allow you to anchor hot- and cold-water

stubouts to studs. Pipe bushings cushion pipes that run through drilled holes in studs or joists.

DWV hangers are bigger than supply supports and are designed for large-diameter drain-waste and vent pipes. Plumber's tape (metal strapping) also works. It comes in both galvanized and plastic versions. Friction clamps are needed for heavy vertical runs of cast-iron pipe.

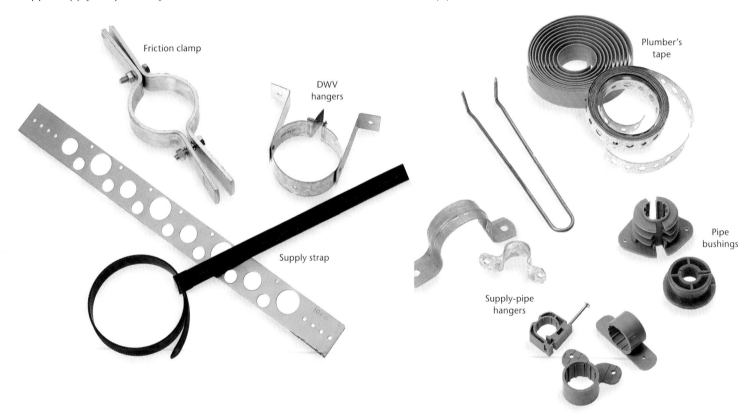

Friction clamp

DWV hangers

Plumber's tape

Supply strap

Pipe bushings

Supply-pipe hangers

Distances Between Supports

The maximum distances, or intervals, between pipe supports are set by code. The distances listed here are typical, but you should ask your inspector about requirements in your area. By the same token, the numbers are maximums. There is no harm in supporting pipes at somewhat shorter intervals, and there may be a benefit.

Most vertical intervals are listed here as 10 feet. In fact, codes generally state that these vertical runs should be supported at every story or every 10 feet. Galvanized steel needs to be supported only every other story.

The 10-foot horizontal spec for cast iron is for modern no-hub pipe. (Traditional bell-and-spigot cast iron needs support every 5 feet.) Any cast-iron pipe needs support within 18 inches of a joint.

Maximum Support Distances

Type of pipe	Horizontal support interval	Vertical support interval
Copper	6'	10'
CPVC	3'	10'
PVC	4'	10'
ABS	4'	10'
Galvanized steel	12'	15'
Cast iron	10'	10'

Connecting to Framing

In a typical wood-frame home, the supports for supply lines and drainpipes are designed to secure the pipes to parts of the framing. The scenarios shown here are common examples.

Floor joist

Plumber's tape

Supply-pipe hanger

Ceiling joist (unfinished ceiling)

Pipe bushings

Friction clamp

Pipes & Walls

Ideally, new pipes should run between and parallel to framing members, though some may have to go through the framing, using methods permitted by local code. There are several ways to deal with wall studs.

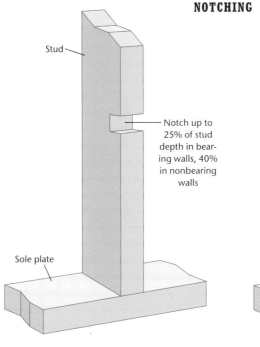
STOP!
Avoid cutting through electrical wiring, plumbing lines, or other utilities inside of walls as you work.

Cutting into Wall Studs

Check local code for approved methods to pass pipe through studs. The rules are different, and more restrictive, for bearing walls, those that support joists or framing above them.

An alternative to running pipe through holes is to cut notches in the sides of studs. You may notch up to 25 percent of the stud depth in bearing walls and up to 40 percent in nonbearing walls. Notches should be braced with steel plates, which will also help to shield pipes from a stray nail or screw in later years.

1/16" steel plate

NOTCHING

Stud

Notch up to 25% of stud depth in bearing walls, 40% in nonbearing walls

Sole plate

Steel plate across notch

Drilling Holes

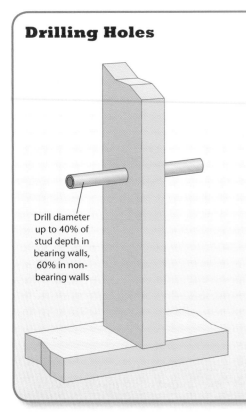

Drill diameter up to 40% of stud depth in bearing walls, 60% in non-bearing walls

In general, you may drill a hole with a diameter up to 40 percent of the stud depth in bearing walls and up to 60 percent in nonbearing walls. You may drill a hole up to 60 percent of the stud depth in a bearing wall if you nail another stud to the first stud for strength. Holes should be centered.

Most drills work in a straight line, but in tight quarters, such as between studs, you may not be able to get a drill body, your hand, and your line of sight into the space you need to drill in. That's where a right-angle drill shines. Be careful, though, as these powerful tools have a lot of torque and can twist your wrist and arm, so you'll need an experienced hand and extra caution. Cordless right-angle drills are usually a bit smaller than corded versions.

A cordless right-angle drill bores a string of 3/4-inch holes through a run of studs, preparing the way for a run of pipe. Drill through the centers of framing members, well away from the edges.

Right-angle drill

Tools You'll Need

Reciprocating saw
Right-angle drill and bits

Related Topics

Dealing with floors, 142–143
DWV planning, 146–147
Running supply lines, 144–145
Supporting new pipes, 138–139

Reciprocating Saw

The primary power tool for roughing-in or demolition work, the reciprocating saw is a good choice when it's necessary to notch existing studs (or joists). With the right blade, it can also handle lath and plaster, steel pipe, and even nails. Use high speeds for making cuts in wood, low speeds for fine work and for cutting metal. Saw blades are flexible, which helps when you're making tricky cuts, but they can snap if you're not careful. Have extra blades on hand.

Alternative Strategies

Running pipes outside a wall requires no notching and less wall patching. Use blocks of wood to support pipes temporarily, then fasten pipe supports to the studs. You can hide the pipes by building cabinets, a closet, a vanity, or shelves over them, or by thickening the wall to accommodate them. To thicken a wall, build out the entire wall, erecting new studs and wall coverings, or thicken only the lower portion where the pipes are, topping it off with a storage ledge or shelf.

If you're building a wall from scratch, you can also hide bulky pipes inside an oversized wet wall, in which studs run along the two sides of the sole plate, leaving room in the center for drainpipes or supply lines.

Reciprocating saw

ANATOMY OF A WET WALL

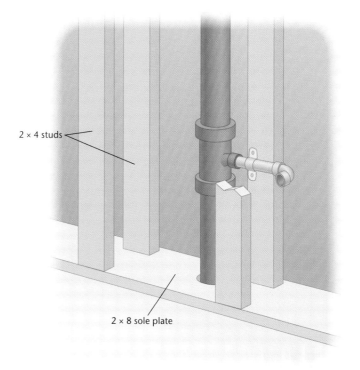

2 × 4 studs

2 × 8 sole plate

The supply pipes to this bathroom sink are hidden behind the cabinets, which means there was no need to run pipes inside the wall.

Dealing with Floors

Just as with wall framing, it's best to run pipes between and parallel to floor or ceiling joists (many techniques for floor joists apply to ceiling joists as well). If a project requires going through some joists, consider these methods, if they are permitted by code.

STOP! Look before you cut, to avoid slicing wiring and pipes.

Cutting into Floor Joists

Cutting into framing members, although it's necessary in many plumbing projects, is a serious step because it affects the structure of your house. The methods shown here are common, but check with your local inspector to verify the codes in your area.

Generally, if a pipe run hits a joist near its center, you may drill a hole through the joist as long as the hole's diameter is no greater than one-third the depth of the joist.

If a pipe run hits a joist near the top or bottom, a notch may accommodate it. The depth of the notch must be no greater than one-sixth the depth of the joist, and the notch cannot be placed in the middle third of the span. Top-notched joists should have lengths of 2 × 2 wooden cleats nailed in place under the notch on both sides of the joist for added support. Joists notched at the bottom should have either a steel brace or a 2 × 2 cleat nailed on.

When you're roughing-in plumbing, you need not worry about minor cosmetic damage to a floor if you plan to cover everything up with tile, as in this bathroom.

Safety Tip

As always, wear the appropriate safety gear. For demolition tools like reciprocating saws and circular saws with masonry blades, this means ear protection, a dust mask, long-sleeved shirt and pants, shoes, and safety glasses.

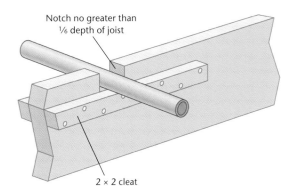

Notch no greater than 1/6 depth of joist

2 × 2 cleat

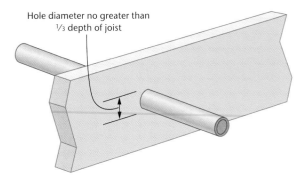

Hole diameter no greater than 1/3 depth of joist

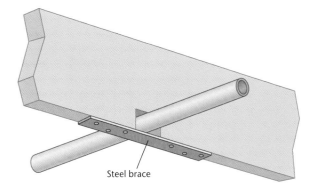

Steel brace

Tools You'll Need

Reciprocating saw
Right-angle drill and bits

Related Topics

DWV planning, 146–147
Pipes & walls, 140–141
Supply strategies, 144–145
Supporting new pipes, 138–139

Alternative Strategies

Building up the floor will cover a new branch drain. Either build a platform over the pipes for the fixture or appliance or raise the floor over the entire room with furring strips around the new pipes. Remember, however, that a raised floor will affect the fit of doors and transitions to the floors in other rooms.

Sometimes you might need to cut an entire section out of a joist to accommodate a DWV section. Reinforce that section by using doubled headers on both sides of the cut. Check local code for details.

BUILDING UP A FLOOR

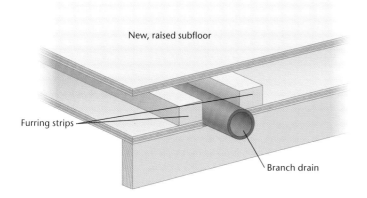

New, raised subfloor

Furring strips

Branch drain

FRAMING A FLOOR OPENING

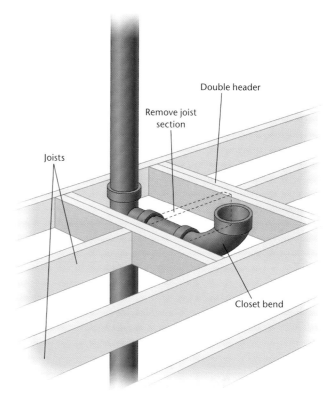

Double header

Remove joist section

Joists

Closet bend

Cutting into Concrete

For many homeowners, a new bathroom is an important part of a basement conversion. Drainage is usually the greatest concern. If your main drain runs above floor level, you'll probably need to pump water or waste uphill to meet it, which can be challenging. If the main drain runs beneath the concrete slab, you may be able to tie into it directly with new drain lines from a fixture, such as a toilet, sink, or shower. Tying in requires removing part of the slab, which is a messy but not particularly difficult job.

MAKING CUTS IN CONCRETE
To cut through concrete, use a heavy-duty circular saw with a masonry or diamond blade to score lines along the planned opening. Mark the location of the main drain with chalk or tape and use the same method to mark for the new drain lines. Then make two or more slow cuts along your lines, increasing the depth of each pass. You'll make a lot of noise and kick up a lot of dust—and

even some sparks. Break up the concrete with a sledgehammer or a rented electric jackhammer. (If you use a jackhammer, take care not to cut into the drain line.) Remove the concrete and dig out the dirt around the drainpipe.

ABOUT SHOWER DRAINS
The area around a shower drain must remain accessible after the concrete is patched, so that the trap can be connected. Your local plumbing supplier may sell plastic tub boxes for this purpose, or you could build a 12-inch-square wood frame around the drain. You should also wrap the stub for a toilet drain with a cardboard sleeve, available at plumbing supply stores. This will keep concrete far enough away to allow the floor flange to fit around it. After the new plumbing has been inspected, plan to return dirt and gravel to surround the pipes, then add a 3-inch layer of concrete to patch the hole.

Running Supply Lines

Supply lines are smaller and a bit easier to install than drainpipes, although most supply lines come in hot and cold pairs, doubling some parts of the job (cold lines to toilets are among the exceptions). Use the methods here to streamline the installation.

Assembling Long Runs

Whenever possible, lay out and assemble new supply runs in large sections. For example, if copper pipe is going into a cramped crawl space, plan to cut the pipe and solder the joints outside. Remember to consider the makeup distance—the amount the pipe extends inside each fitting. You can often find a little slack, or room to fudge, along a run of supply pipe, but don't count on much.

Slide long pipe runs through drilled or notched holes, or use appropriate hangers to secure the runs. If possible, install the new runs with a slight pitch and add a shutoff or stop-and-waste valve at the lowest point.

Switching Pipe Materials

If you wish to change pipe type—say, from galvanized steel to copper or plastic—you'll need to insert the appropriate adapters at the pipe ends.

STOP-AND-WASTE VALVE

When you're extending your supply system, it's a good idea to slope each new pipe for drainage, then add a shutoff valve. The shutoff variety known as a stop-and-waste valve includes a bleeder screw on one side. With the valve turned off, open the screw to drain the pipe.

GALVANIZED STEEL TO COPPER

GALVANIZED STEEL TO PLASTIC

COPPER TO PLASTIC

Related Topics

Dealing with floors, 142–143
Making the connections, 118–121
Pipes & walls, 140–141
Roughing in, 148–153
Sizing supply lines, 132–133
The supply system, 10–11
Tying old to new, 122–123

Changing Directions

Negotiate turns and obstacles with the appropriate fittings. Couplings join straight lengths of pipe. Street fittings have ends that slip right into another fitting's interior shoulder, eliminating the need for a spacer (a short length of pipe) to make the joint. Use 45-degree fittings to "leapfrog" one parallel pipe over another. Fittings can also be rotated in opposition to each other to create subtle directional changes.

Some change of direction is good because long, straight runs lead to noisy water-hammer problems. However, unnecessary bends, especially 90-degree fittings, create friction. If your run calls for more than four 90-degree elbows, the rule is to replace some or all of them with gentler 45-degree fittings.

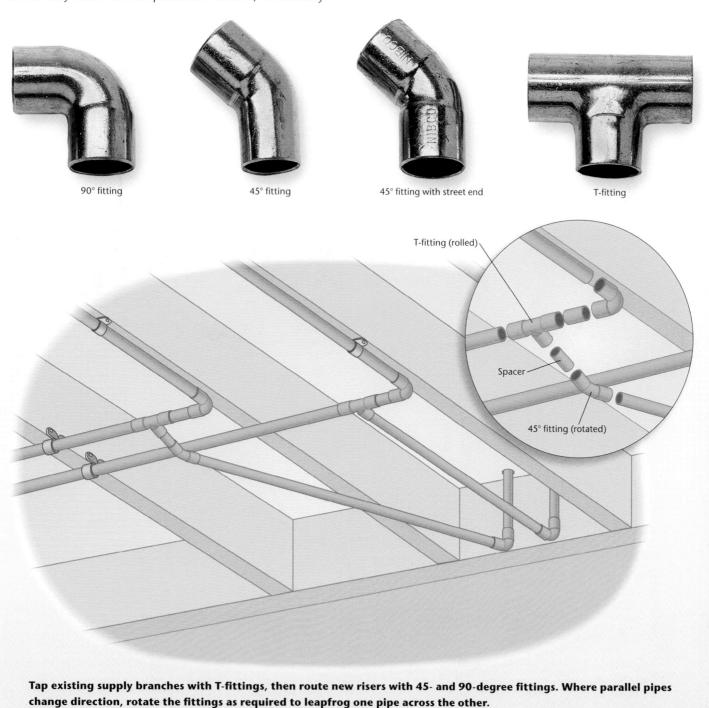

90° fitting   45° fitting   45° fitting with street end   T-fitting

T-fitting (rolled)

Spacer

45° fitting (rotated)

Tap existing supply branches with T-fittings, then route new risers with 45- and 90-degree fittings. Where parallel pipes change direction, rotate the fittings as required to leapfrog one pipe across the other.

DWV Planning

Drainpipe logistics often depend on altitude—the vertical space you have to work in. An unfinished basement may offer plenty of headroom, while a second-story drain needs to fit within the confines of the ceiling below.

Changes of Direction

DWV connections are largely a game of piecing together horizontals, verticals, and changes in direction. Codes specify fittings for horizontal-to-horizontal, vertical-to-horizontal, and horizontal-to-vertical connections. A fixture drain to a branch drain is a typical vertical-to-horizontal intersection, while a branch drain's connection to the main soil stack is a good example of a horizontal-to-vertical junction.

As with supply connections, you can gain a lot of play by rotating one DWV fitting in opposition to another. If you have the altitude or horizontal headroom, use spacers (short pipe pieces) to join opposing fittings. If you're cramped for space, you can slip a street fitting inside an adjacent fitting's shoulder without using the spacer.

Vertical Requirements

Because of a drainpipe's slope requirements, the altitude that you need depends in part on how far a pipe must extend horizontally. The longer the run, the greater the required altitude. In addition, some fittings take up more vertical space than others. Plastic fittings tend to require less headroom than older cast iron.

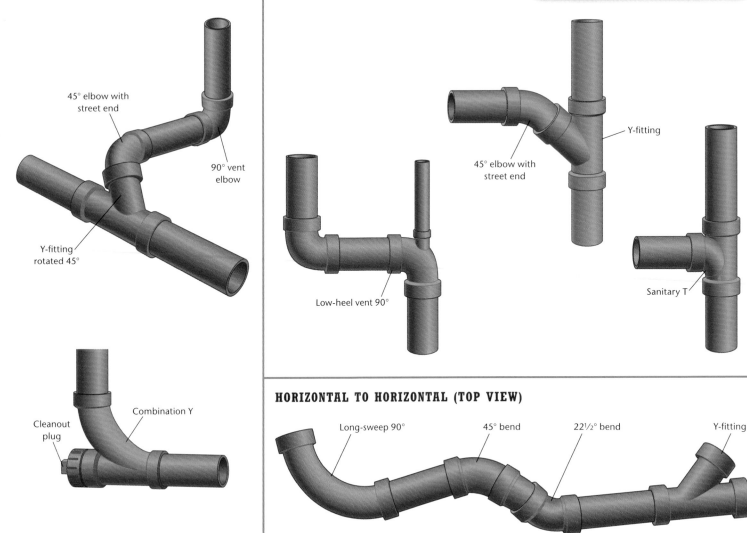

VERTICAL TO HORIZONTAL

- 45° elbow with street end
- 90° vent elbow
- Y-fitting rotated 45°
- Cleanout plug
- Combination Y

HORIZONTAL TO VERTICAL

- Y-fitting
- 45° elbow with street end
- Low-heel vent 90°
- Sanitary T

HORIZONTAL TO HORIZONTAL (TOP VIEW)

- Long-sweep 90°
- 45° bend
- 22½° bend
- Y-fitting

Fitting Choices & Restrictions

As you select the drain fittings for your system, find out what's permitted in your area. For example, a sanitary T on its side is approved in some areas but not in others, where you'd need a combination Y instead. A sanitary cross may be fine for some uses, but only if the top and bottom are two pipe sizes larger than the side inlets (for example, 2-inch sides and a 4-inch top). You might be required to install a cleanout wherever a vertical drop meets a horizontal drainpipe.

Combination Y

Sanitary T

Sanitary cross

Cleanout fitting

Cleanout plug

VENTING LOGISTICS

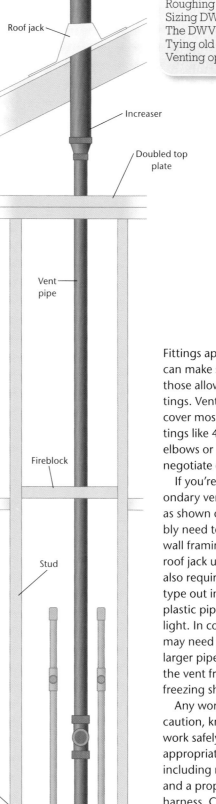

Roof jack

Increaser

Doubled top plate

Vent pipe

Fireblock

Stud

Sole plate

Related Topics

Dealing with floors, 142–143
Making the connections, 118–121
Pipes & walls, 140–141
Roughing in, 148–153
Sizing DWV lines, 134–135
The DWV system, 12–13
Tying old to new, 122–123
Venting options & rules, 130–131

Fittings approved for vent use can make sharper turns than those allowed for drainage fittings. Vent elbows and vent T's cover most vent uses. Drain fittings like 45- and 22½-degree elbows or long-sweep 90s help negotiate obstacles.

If you're running a new secondary vent through the roof, as shown on left, you'll probably need to bore holes through wall framing, then install a roof jack up top. Code may also require a switch in pipe type out in the open, since plastic pipe corrodes in sunlight. In cold regions, you may need an increaser (a larger pipe size) to keep the vent from icing up and freezing shut.

Any work on a roof requires caution, knowledge of how to work safely at heights, and appropriate safety precautions, including nonslip footwear and a properly anchored safety harness. Consider having a professional do at least the roof part of the task.

Roughing In

Here and on the following pages, you will find notes for roughing-in lines for new fixtures and appliances that require tying into or extending your plumbing. Refer to local codes for specific requirements. Measurements may vary in a bathroom designed for universal access.

Toilet

A new toilet is the most troublesome fixture to install in a house because it requires its own vent (2 inches minimum) and a drain that is at least 3 inches in diameter. If the toilet is on a branch drain, away from the main soil stack, it cannot be upstream from a sink or a shower. Another difficulty is that the closet bend and the floor flange must be roughed in first, requiring that you carefully calculate their positions so that the flange will be at the level of the eventual finished floor.

One thing, however, is a little simpler for a toilet. Unlike with most fixtures, only one supply line, for cold water, is needed—a ½-inch riser with a stubout and cap. You may require a water-hammer arrester like the ones illustrated to the right for a bathroom sink.

Securing Pipes

There are plenty of ways to secure pipes to the wall framing, from 1 × 4 bracing boards to copper supply straps or plastic pipe bushings where supply risers pass through the sole plate. The method is up to you. What matters is that pipes remain rigid when pushed or pulled.

Bathroom Fixture Clearances

Building and plumbing codes also specify clearances between bathroom fixtures. These distances are minimums, and they are getting larger, reflecting the move toward barrier-free design. Clearances vary, but those shown here are typical. Always check your local codes, and any additional requirements for your chosen fixtures, before you plan the bathroom layout.

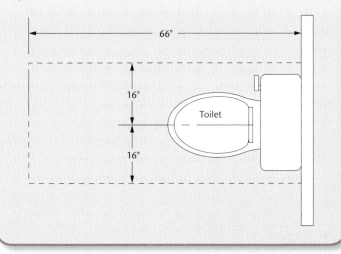

ROUGHING IN A TOILET

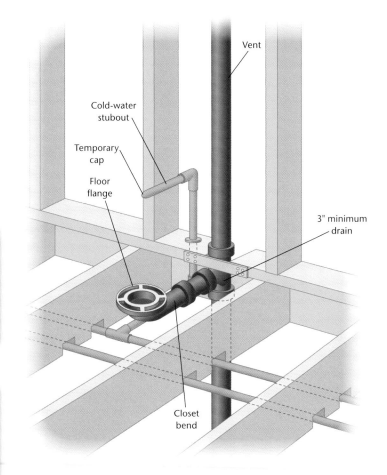

TOILET ROUGH-IN DIMENSIONS

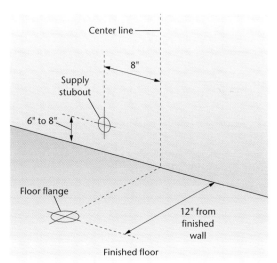

For a toilet rough-in, the distance from the finished wall to the floor flange is critical. Most toilets call for 12 inches, but this can vary. Check the installation instructions before proceeding.

Bathroom Sink Clearances

SIDE-BY-SIDE BATHROOM SINKS

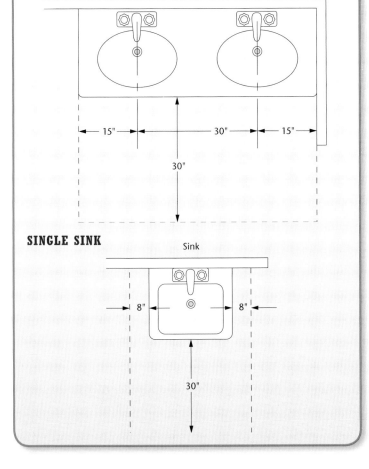

SINGLE SINK

Bathroom Sink

A bathroom sink requires hot- and cold-water supplies, a drain, and a vent line. If these pipes already exist close to where the sink will go, the job of roughing-in is fairly easy. A bathroom sink can normally be wet-vented (vented directly through its drain to the soil stack) if the drainpipe is large enough and the distance it travels is short enough, two factors that are determined by codes. Otherwise, the sink must be back-vented, which means connecting to the main stack above the fixture.

You will need ½-inch hot and cold supply risers, stubouts, and caps. Prefabricated or homemade water-hammer arresters may be required on the hot and cold supply pipes. The illustration shows a typical arrangement.

BATHROOM SINK ROUGH-IN DIMENSIONS

ROUGHING IN A BATHROOM SINK

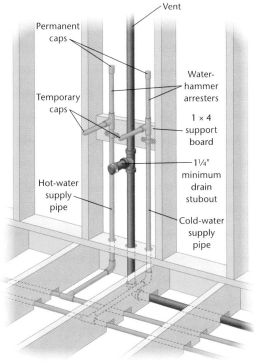

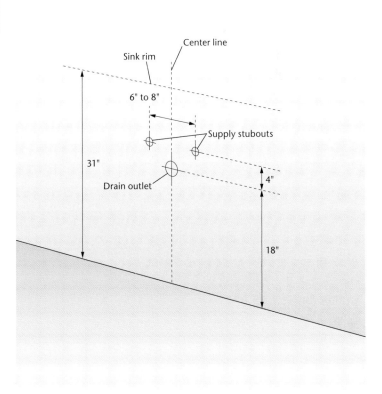

Rough-in dimensions for a bathroom sink typically place the rim at 31 inches.

Bathtub & Shower

Bathtubs and showers are often positioned on branch drains and vented the same way sinks are. Both enter the main soil stack at or below floor level because of their below-floor traps. Bathtubs can be installed on their own, with no shower, but the work required to add a shower is so modest that it's usually worth it to give family members the extra option. A shower's faucet body (called a diverter valve for a tub-and-shower combination) and shower pipe assembly are both installed while the wall is open.

Supply pipes required include 1/2-inch hot and cold supply lines and 1/2-inch pipes to the showerhead and the tub spout. Some large tubs and high-flow showers, particularly those with multiple sprayers, use 3/4-inch supply pipes. Increasingly, showers are plumbed with their own supply branches to help maintain water pressure and temperature when nearby fixtures are turned on. If possible, place gate or ball valves on these risers where they can be accessed, such as from below the floor or behind the wall. In addition, you may want to cut a small opening and add a door below, behind, or beside the tub to allow later access to the trap and drainpipe.

Tub Clearances

TUB & SHOWER ROUGH-IN DIMENSIONS

ROUGHING IN A TUB & SHOWER

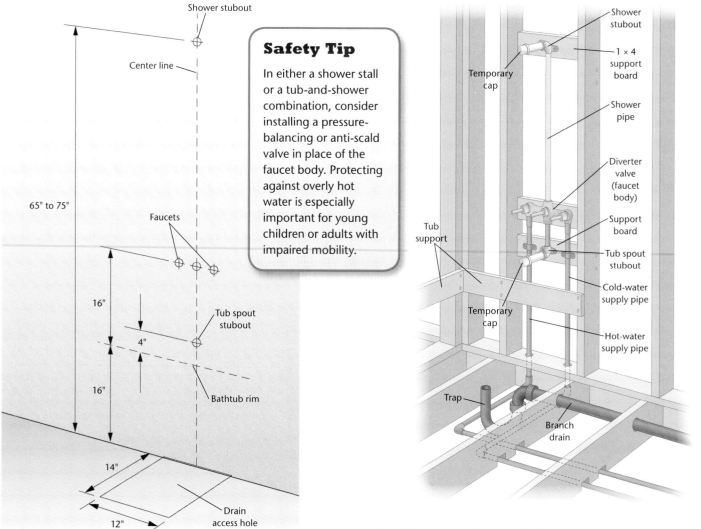

Safety Tip

In either a shower stall or a tub-and-shower combination, consider installing a pressure-balancing or anti-scald valve in place of the faucet body. Protecting against overly hot water is especially important for young children or adults with impaired mobility.

Roughing in a combination bathtub and shower calls for installing a diverter valve in the wall with the supply piping.

Shower Stall

A shower stall is roughed in much like a tub-and-shower combination, but the job is simpler because there are no tub faucet handles and no tub spout. The drainpipe arrangement is the same, and you'll need to run ½-inch hot and cold supply lines to the faucet body, which leads to the shower stubout via the shower pipe. The framing is also simpler, with no need for horizontal tub supports or for a tub-spout support board.

SHOWER STALL ROUGH-IN DIMENSIONS

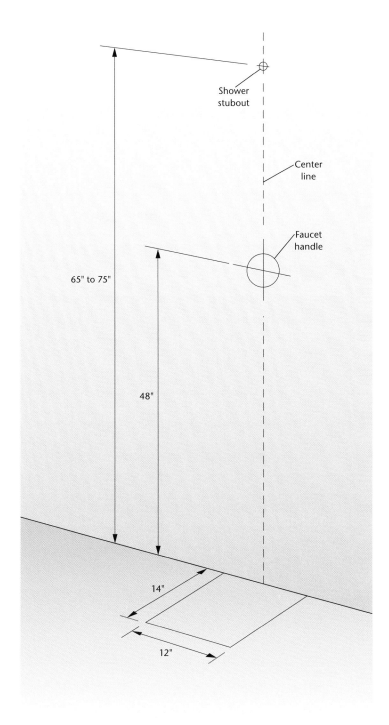

ROUGHING IN A SHOWER STALL

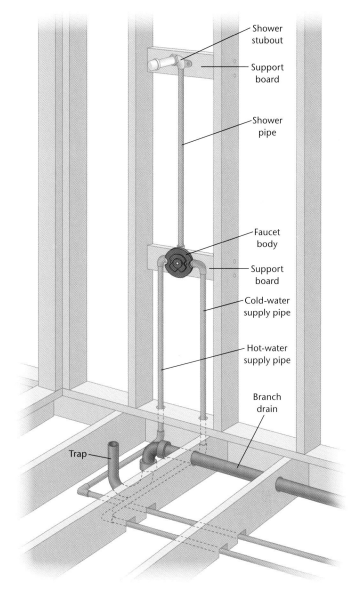

Shower Clearances

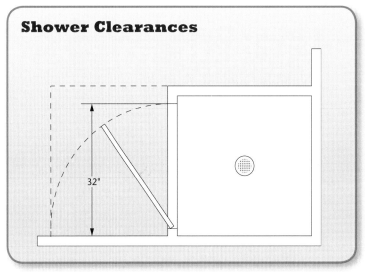

Kitchen Sink

For convenience and economy, most kitchen fixtures and plumbed appliances are adjacent to the sink. Because of this, a single set of vertical supply pipes and one drainpipe generally serve the entire kitchen. Supply pipes or tubing for a dishwasher, hot-water dispenser, automatic ice maker, and chilled-water dispenser often branch off the hot and cold supply lines leading to the sink faucet. Similarly, the dishwasher and garbage disposer share the sink's trap and drainpipe.

Pipes you'll need include $1/2$-inch hot and cold supply risers, stubouts, and caps. Water-hammer arresters, either prefabricated or homemade, may be required on both hot and cold supply pipes.

This arrangement shows one possible setup for supplying an ice maker, which, like other kitchen fixtures, is usually supplied by the same lines as the kitchen sink. Some plumbers also recommend installing water-hammer arresters on the sink's supply lines.

In most kitchens, all fixtures requiring plumbing are grouped into one area. Here, plumbing lines run under the right counter only. The left counter requires only power and a gas line.

ROUGHING IN A KITCHEN SINK

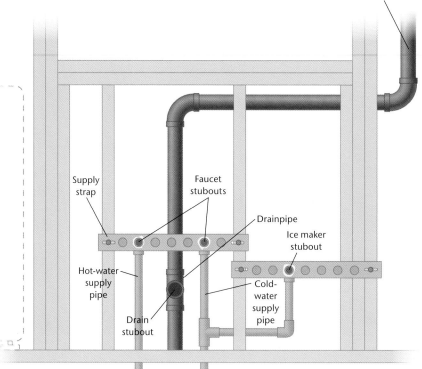

Vent

Supply strap

Faucet stubouts

Drainpipe

Ice maker stubout

Hot-water supply pipe

Cold-water supply pipe

Drain stubout

Clothes Washer

The hot and cold supply pipes for a clothes washer are usually ½ inch in diameter. Plan to employ either a pair of washing machine shutoff valves or a single-lever or twin-lever washing machine valve to make the supply hookups. A washing machine valve sits inside the wall, and risers run directly to it.

When installing a pair of shutoff valves, as shown here, put T-fittings on the risers inside the wall, water-hammer arresters vertically above them, and supply stubouts toward the machine. Because the stop and start cycles of washing machines are particularly hard on valves, hoses, and the machines themselves, some manufacturers recommend that water-hammer arresters be one size larger than the supply pipes and as long as 24 inches.

If a laundry tub or sink is nearby, the drain hose can hook over the edge of it. (You'll need to be vigilant, though, to make sure the tub drain is always left open and unobstructed.) Otherwise, drain the washer into a standpipe—a vertical 2-inch pipe that connects to a 1½-inch trap. The top of the standpipe should be between 18 and 30 inches above the trap (some codes allow for a height of up to 42 inches). The trap itself, as shown here, should be 6 to 18 inches above the floor.

ROUGHING IN A CLOTHES WASHER

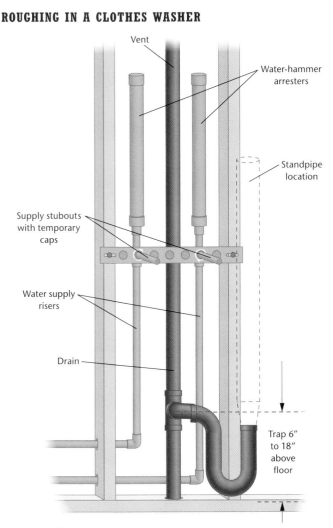

It's a good idea to install water-hammer arresters when you're roughing-in a washing machine.

Water Heater

A classic storage-type water heater, still the most common style in the United States, requires a cold-water supply pipe, typically ¾ inch. In addition, a pipe of the same size carries hot water to all the fixtures that require it. A gas water heater requires a gas supply pipe and a flue for venting combustion gases (have a professional handle the natural gas connections; the flue is normally installed after the rough-in).

Install a shutoff valve (either a ball or gate valve) on incoming and outgoing pipes. If you are moving a water heater, pick a location as close as possible to the main areas of hot-water use in the house. Keep in mind that you must provide adequate clearance between a gas water heater and any combustible materials. Some codes require a floor drain within 6 inches of your heater's pressure-relief valve. Even if code does not specify this, it's a good idea to have a drain nearby. You'll appreciate it when you drain the heater for maintenance, and even more in the event of a major leak.

ROUGHING IN A WATER HEATER

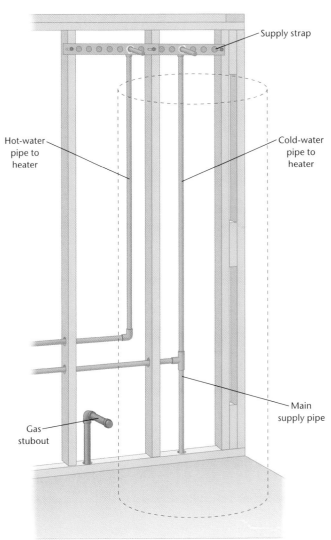

A water heater receives cold water from the main supply pipe. Then, through a similar pipe that often runs next to it, it delivers hot water to the house's plumbing system.

Finishing Up

Before you add those highly anticipated new fixtures and appliances, a few final steps are required, from testing and inspecting to closing up the walls, ceilings, and floors and repairing (or redoing) the paint, wallpaper, or other finishes.

Testing Your Work

Once you've roughed-in your new pipes, you'll need to test your extensions for leaks using the methods described below. A building inspector will probably want to run these tests also, but you can increase your odds of approval by first running them yourself. The testing devices described here are available at many rental centers, or you can buy them.

SUPPLY TESTING

Cap all of the new supply pipes, turn on the water, and look closely for leaks. Usually this visual test is all you need.

If a leak might spray water where it could do damage during the test, you can install a test gauge on the supply line instead to test the lines with air instead of water. The test gauge has a small capped nipple. Screw an air pump (even a bicycle pump) to this nipple and inflate the line with 50 pounds of air pressure, then watch the gauge. If the pressure drops, you have a leak. To trace it, brush soapy water onto the connections and look for bubbles.

If you find a leak, try tightening the connections. Disassemble and replace fittings if necessary.

Pressure gauge

Test caps

Air pump

Test balloon

DWV TESTING

There are two methods for testing drain-waste and vent pipes. In new construction, there's the water test. All new drainpipes are capped off, water is poured in from a roof vent, and then the pipes are inspected for leaks. This test is rarely done in remodeling work, though, because a leak could do a lot of damage in a finished house. If this test has to be done, leave it to the inspector, both to protect your house and to avoid working on the roof.

The pressure test, which the inspector may run or have you run, is used most often for testing extensions of existing lines, as in a remodel. First, the pipes are capped or sealed with test plugs. Then either an inflatable ball (called a weenie) or a test cap (called a Jim cap) is inserted into a cleanout and the sealed pipes are pumped with 5 pounds of pressure. If the pressure drops within 15 minutes, you have a leak. To find the leak, brush the connections with soapy water, as for a supply line, and watch for bubbles.

$ Stuff to Buy

DRYWALL Match the thickness of existing drywall
DRYWALL SUPPLIES Drywall screws, self-adhesive mesh tape, joint compound
PAINT AND PRIMER

Tools You'll Need

Cordless driver
Drywall knives in varying widths
Painting tools
Sandpaper (400-grit)
Test equipment as needed
Utility knife

Related Topics

Dealing with floors, 142–143
Pipes & walls, 140–141
Tying into existing lines, 136–137

Making Repairs

In running new lines, you may have drilled small exploratory holes, which are usually fairly easy to patch. Similarly, there may be some holes around stubouts that you'll need to patch. More significant are the large openings created where you've tied into existing pipes. Though you're almost done, it's worth taking the time and care as you repair these, so that your walls, ceilings, or floors look like new again, with no sign of a patch.

FLOORS

Begin repairing floors by securely closing the opening in the sub-floor according to code. Patching or replacing the floor covering is a task that varies by material. For vinyl floors, which tend to wear out over time, it may make more sense to put in a new vinyl floor instead of patching the old one.

WALLS & CEILINGS

For walls and ceilings, you will most likely patch drywall. For small repairs, simply use a drywall knife and some joint compound.

To replace a large section, you'll need to install a piece of new drywall to fill the hole, as shown in Step 1 below. If there are no studs or joists underneath to attach the replacement piece to, add some wood blocks for support. After the patch is completed, prime and seal the surface with a good interior primer. Then paint or wallpaper the patch to match the surrounding wall.

PATCHING PLASTER

For ornamental, patterned plaster, hire an expert plasterer to make repairs. Plain, featureless plaster, however, is not much harder to repair than drywall. Patching around trap outlets and supply stubouts is simple. Use a wide-blade knife to apply commercial plaster compound. Try to match the texture of the surrounding wall. For larger holes, you'll have to nail on some backing (such as lath), clean and moisten the edges of the hole, and in some cases apply more than one coat of plaster compound. Finish with primer and then paint or paper to match the wall.

How to Do It

1 Install new drywall

- Touch up the opening, if necessary, to make sure it is cut squarely and cleanly
- Check for studs and fireblocks to which the patch can be anchored; add blocking if required
- Measure and cut new drywall; use a piece that's the same thickness as the existing drywall
- Fit the piece into place, then attach it to the wood framing with drywall screws

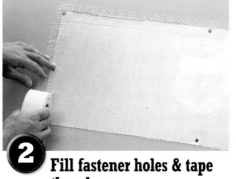

2 Fill fastener holes & tape the edges

- Spread joint compound to fill the dimples around the screw heads
- Don't apply excess compound; it will shrink as it dries, and additional coats will do more filling
- Apply self-adhesive mesh tape over the edge joints

3 Finish with joint compound

- Sand excess dried compound at the screw-head dimples, then apply joint compound again
- Apply joint compound over the edge joints with a wide-blade drywall knife
- Let it dry, then sand the compound smooth and flat
- Apply a second coat, feathering the edges of the first coat; let it dry, then sand again
- Apply, dry, and sand a third coat as needed
- Use a scrap of drywall from the old wall to match the paint color
- Prime the patched area, let it dry, then paint it

Outdoor Projects

In this chapter, we take you outside to learn how to install sprinklers and drip systems, as well as how to make sure your irrigation systems are delivering water only to the plants that need it. We show you the materials you'll need to build a small garden pool and fountain, and help pool and spa owners choose the filters and heaters that are best for them.

Chapter Contents

Outdoor Plumbing Basics

Outdoor plumbing installations use many of the same techniques as indoor jobs, but there are a few differences in the materials and methods. They also pose issues such as potential sun damage to certain plastics and the need to avoid underground utility lines.

Making the Connection

Some outdoor plumbing projects, like most sprinkler and drip systems, draw on your house's water supply whenever they operate. Others, such as fountains, garden ponds, hot tubs, and swimming pools, largely recirculate the same water, with new water added occasionally from the house supply. Still others use alternative water sources, including wells, ponds, rain barrels, and water storage tanks.

For projects connected to the house's plumbing, you'll tap into the existing system and then run pipe to a new location. Whenever you extend a supply pipe outdoors, you need to add a backflow preventer (bottom, next page) to block outdoor wastewater from heading back inside.

Outdoor projects don't connect to the house drains, though. Any runoff or used water must go elsewhere.

A hot tub is a great example of an attainable outdoor plumbing project. The barrel hot tub (top left) sits on a wooden deck that has been braced from below to bear the weight. The fiberglass hot tub (below left) is ringed by a stone bench to make it a garden focal point.

Safety Tips

KEEPING KIDS SAFE

Outdoor water projects such as swimming pools, spas, garden pools, and similar elements pose a drowning risk. Install and operate such features in a fenced yard. Do not leave young children or pets unattended near them, and do provide covers and other safety components as appropriate. Check local codes for other requirements.

PROTECTING EXISTING SYSTEMS

Before you start digging for an outdoor project, ask utility companies where gas, water, sewer, electrical, and other lines are so you can stay away from them. If your home has a septic tank, also locate and avoid the tank and drainage field.

Materials to Use

Plastic PVC pipe is the workhorse for outdoor extensions, sprinkler installations, and other irrigation projects. But standard white PVC does not stand up well to sunlight. For aboveground use—for example, where supply lines for a sprinkler system travel from house to ground, or for vertical sprinkler risers—use threaded, precut pieces of charcoal-colored Schedule 80 PVC pipe, which is also stronger. Since sunlight is not an issue for underground lines, you can use white Schedule 40 PVC for those, or substitute slightly thinner, slightly less-expensive schedules.

In some regions, flexible PE may be used for outdoor systems carrying potable water. It's often used for drip irrigation as well. Join sections as necessary with barbed couplings, elbows, and T's.

Flexible copper tubing, Type L, may be used for extending the supply system from the house to an outbuilding, such as a detached garage or studio.

For outdoor drainage, many landscapers use PVC—usually either Schedule 40 in diameters up to 2 inches, or thinner and less expensive schedules in sizes up to 8 inches. Flexible, corrugated drainpipe, either perforated or solid, comes in coiled lengths of 10, 50, and 100 feet.

Smart Steps for Bigger Projects

For a wide-ranging project like a sprinkler or drip system, it's a good idea to make a scale drawing of your property on graph paper. Mark the areas to be watered or drained; the locations and types of plants; any obstacles like fences, walkways, and patios; and slopes or elevation changes. The more detailed your map, the easier it will be to select the right components when you're ready to shop. Now is also the time to check with your building department for any necessary permits.

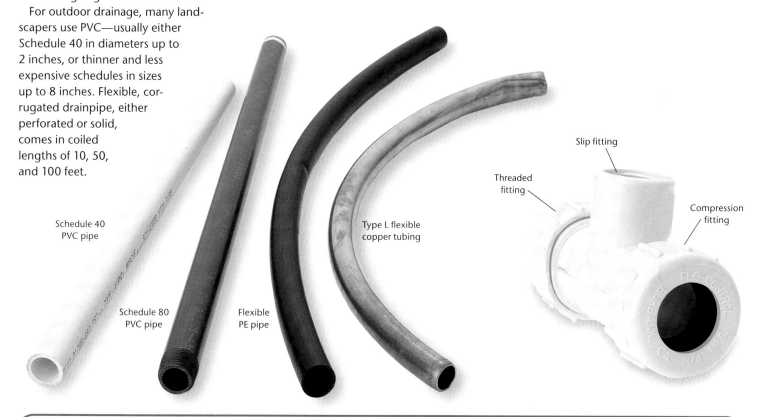

Schedule 40 PVC pipe

Schedule 80 PVC pipe

Flexible PE pipe

Type L flexible copper tubing

Threaded fitting

Slip fitting

Compression fitting

Backflow Preventers

Whenever you extend an indoor plumbing system outdoors, you need to install either a vacuum breaker (bottom left) or an antisiphon valve (top right). Both are designed to prevent the backflow of used outdoor water into the house's water system, which could occur if pressure in the interior system suddenly dropped.

The vacuum breaker screws onto the end of an outdoor hose bibb, and a garden hose screws onto the breaker. An antisiphon valve is required on sprinkler and drip systems or whenever an interior pipe system is extended to a location in the garden or to another building.

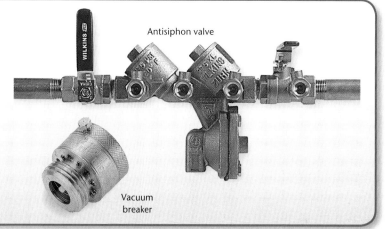

Antisiphon valve

Vacuum breaker

Installing New Hose Bibbs

Outdoor faucets, known as hose bibbs, come in several models, most with threaded spouts for attaching hoses. Make sure the hose will be convenient to use, but also consider how easy it will be to tap into an existing indoor supply line.

Choosing a Faucet

Some hose bibbs have bodies with female threads and are screwed onto a pipe, while others have male threads and are screwed into a threaded T-fitting or elbow. Some hose bibbs have an escutcheon, or notched flange, which allows the faucet to be mounted on an exterior wall (this type is often called a sillcock). The no-kink model (below right) has an outlet that points out as well as down, making the path of a garden hose that much smoother. You can also get plastic hose bibbs, but check the rated temperature range and water pressure as well as the plastic's resistance to sunlight.

Hiding a Hose

This ceramic container is designed to hide a hose. The hose runs from the outdoor water supply through a hole on the lower side of the container. It stays neatly coiled when not in use.

SILLCOCK

GARDEN VALVE

DECORATIVE 90° HOSE BIBB

NO-KINK HOSE BIBB

$ Stuff to Buy	🕐 Time Commitment	⚒ Tools You'll Need	◎ Related Topics
Caulk Hose bibb Pipe and fittings Silicone or foam sealant Stop-and-waste valve Vacuum breaker	Half a day	Drill with appropriate bits Pipefitting tools	Basin choices, 44–45 Connecting to water, 164–165 Conserving water, 14–15 Outdoor plumbing basics, 158–159 Running supply lines, 144–145

Adding the Hose Bibb

When installing a new faucet, first decide where you want it. The location should be convenient for outdoor watering and, if possible, high enough to clear a bucket. Also consider the location of the indoor cold-water pipe you'll tap into; it's probably in your basement or crawl space. Plan the entire installation and acquire the pipes and fittings before you start.

CONNECTING THE FAUCET

Turn off the water at the main house shutoff and drain the pipes. Tap into the water supply pipe with a T-fitting and connect the new pipe and fittings. Unless you're using a freeze-resistant faucet, plan to add a stop-and-waste valve to the supply pipe that will feed the new hose bibb.

A stop-and-waste valve is an indoor shutoff valve with a drain. It allows you to turn off the outside water inside a warm basement or crawl space and to drain the water beyond it so it won't freeze and cause the pipes to burst. Just remember to take those winterizing steps.

Run the new pipe through the wall and connect the faucet to it. Connecting pipes must be anchored to the house's framing near the

Freeze-resistant Faucets

If you live in an area where winter temperatures often dip below freezing, it makes sense to install a freeze-resistant faucet. This type of faucet has an elongated body that extends well into a basement or crawl space, plus a valve seat placed far back in the body. When you turn off the faucet, the water flow stops inside the house so the water won't be exposed to the cold.

Freeze-resistant faucets come in multiple lengths. Purchase the right length for your local climate and for the thickness of your wall.

Freeze-resistant faucets are self-draining. You install the unit at a slight tilt toward the ground outside, which allows any remaining water to run out after the faucet is turned off and the hose or any other attachment is removed. Check the manufacturer's instructions or the packaging to make sure no other steps are required to drain it fully.

Never leave a hose attached to any hose bibb during cold months.

EXTENDING NEW PIPES OUTDOORS

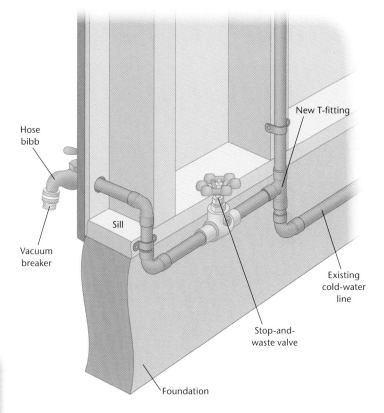

Hose bibb

New T-fitting

Vacuum breaker

Sill

Stop-and-waste valve

Existing cold-water line

Foundation

wall and all along the pipe run. Fill any gaps around the pipe with silicone or foam sealant. When installing a flanged faucet, you can caulk the space around the pipe before screwing the flange into place.

Many codes require that you install a vacuum breaker or backflow preventer, and it's a good idea anyway. This device, screwed on between the faucet spout and the hose, prevents the backflow of possibly polluted water into your supply system.

DRILLING THROUGH THE WALL

Check indoors before you drill through the wall, to make sure you won't hit drainpipes, electrical lines, heating ductwork, studs, or floor joists.

Avoid the foundation. If the water supply pipe is below the foundation's top surface, plan to drill above the foundation and route the new pipes down to the supply pipe.

If possible, drill a small pilot hole from the inside out to mark the location. Select the right bit for the job: a spade bit for wood, a masonry bit for brick or stucco. Then, using an extension bit if necessary, drill through the wall from the outside, boring a hole large enough to fit the pipe that will be attached to the faucet.

Spade bit

Sprinklers & Drip Systems

For years, underground sprinkler systems were the last word in home irrigation. A common water-saving alternative is drip irrigation, which uses above-ground tubing. The two types of systems are not mutually exclusive, so you can use both in one garden.

A drip emitter (left) delivers water to plants one drop at a time. Many emitters can be set to dispense from ½ to 2 gallons per hour (gph). A sprinkler (right) is less efficient, but you can at least purchase a sprinkler head to put water where you want it, as with this quarter-circle head.

Sprinklers, Drip, or Both?

In a region with heavy summer rainfall, an installed system may be overkill. If you have just a few plants to water during short dry spells, you can automate a portable sprinkler or soaker hose by connecting it to a hose bibb with a manual timer. The timer prevents overwatering.

Although homeowners and professional landscapers often weigh the pros and cons of drip and sprinkler systems, you may find that your landscape benefits from a combination of both, with each deployed in different areas. It is often easier to irrigate a lawn with sprinklers, whereas water-saving drip irrigation may be better for shrubs, trees, and other plants, getting water to the roots without wetting the stems and leaves. If you already have a sprinkler system, you can also convert all or part of it to drip irrigation with a kit.

It's increasingly common to use both sprinkler and drip irrigation in one garden, sending sprinkler circuits out to a lawn or a large area of ground cover, for example, and drip lines to flower and vegetable beds, containers, shrubs, and trees.

If you decide to combine sprinklers and drip irrigation, install enough control valves to operate all the circuits. Put the sprinkler system in first, since it requires trenching. Then run your drip circuits. The same timer can control both circuits.

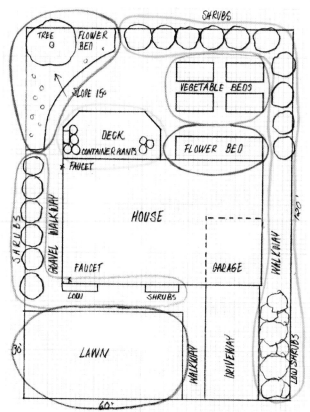

Before you make irrigation choices, create a garden plan—a scale drawing of your property, including your house and property lines, the plantings to be watered, significant slopes, existing outdoor faucets, and obstructions like driveways and decks. Mark the hydrozones, circled here in different colors, that have different water requirements.

Sprinkler Systems

An underground sprinkler system is best suited to watering large, thirsty areas such as lawns or big sections of uniform ground cover. You can also use sprinklers to irrigate flower or vegetable beds, as long as you have a multi-circuit system to water each area separately. (You'll also need to be careful placing the heads so the spray is not blocked by the plants as they grow.)

A sprinkler system is almost invisible, with most of the heads flush with the ground when they're not in use. This makes it an attractive system that's also easy to maintain, as buried parts are less likely to be damaged. Old-fashioned sprinkler systems tended to be major water wasters, but newer sprinkler heads apply water more precisely.

Sprinkler systems must be planned carefully. They need adequate water pressure and flow rates, and installing one requires digging trenches throughout your landscape.

Drip Irrigation

Water conservation is the most common reason people select a drip system. Because drip emitters and sprayers apply water much more slowly than conventional sprinklers do, a drip system largely eliminates water runoff and reduces water loss through evaporation and overspray. The water also won't be blown off course by wind.

Drip is also the best way to ensure consistent moisture to the roots of individual plants. Drip emitters don't irrigate the surrounding soil (which would encourage weeds), and they don't spray leaves, petals, and trunks, where excess moisture can encourage fungal diseases. Drip is usually preferable on hills because the water is less likely to run off. Drip systems are also more accepting of low water pressure or flow rates.

Installation is easy, but unlike sprinklers, drip systems are not an "out of sight, out of mind" solution. All the tubing and components are exposed, so drip systems may need more adjustments or repairs after encounters with children, pets, visitors, and lawn mowers or other tools. Their components also tend to clog more easily than sprinkler heads.

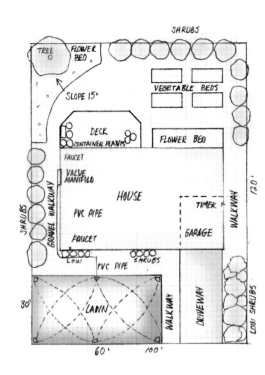

A single sprinkler circuit leads from a valve manifold beside the house to six strategically spaced sprinklers on a 30-by-60-foot lawn. Dashed lines show the area covered by each rotating sprinkler head, with deliberate overlap of the spray areas for uniform watering.

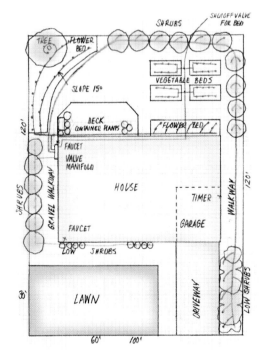

Multiple drip lines, each color-coded in this scale drawing, serve the watering needs of shrubs, trees, flowers, vegetable beds, and container plants. On this property, only the lawn is irrigated by sprinklers, which are better suited to its size and water needs than drip lines would be.

The Slow Approach

Multi-stream rotating sprinklers are increasingly popular for reducing water use, because they put out up to 30 percent less water than traditional sprinklers. The secret is the slow and even distribution of water, an approach that also reduces runoff.

Connecting to Water

To supply a new sprinkler or drip irrigation system for your property, you'll have to tap into your existing cold-water supply system. First make sure you have the pressure and flow rate you need, then proceed to planning and completing the connection.

Pressure & Flow Rate

You'll save yourself a world of frustration if you check ahead of time whether your system's water pressure and flow rate are suited to your planned irrigation project. Sprinklers and drip systems require a certain pressure to operate well—30 to 50 psi (pounds per square inch) for most sprinkler heads and 20 to 40 psi for drip emitters. Overly high pressure can cause drip systems to malfunction or drip lines to burst.

Flow rate, measured in gpm (gallons per minute) or gph (gallons per hour), is simply the amount of water that moves through pipes in a given period. Sprinkler heads and drip emitters have designated flow rates. Add up these ratings for each planned circuit to be sure your system's flow rate can supply the circuit. If it cannot, divide the system into smaller, separate circuits.

Effects of Elevation on Water Pressure

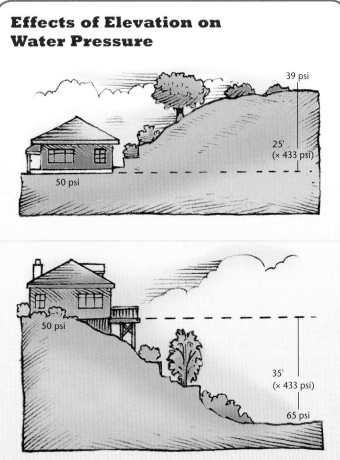

Water is delivered to both of the houses at 50 psi. But water traveling through irrigation pipes to their backyard gardens will lose pressure in the upslope garden and gain pressure in the downslope garden.

To check flow rate, fill a bucket to the 1-gallon or 5-gallon level, then empty it. A 5-gallon test takes longer but is more accurate. Stop-watch in hand, record how long it takes to fill to the mark, then do the math to determine the flow rate of gallons per minute or per hour. For a 5-gallon test, remember to divide by five.

CHECKING THE NUMBERS

You can determine water pressure by threading a standard pressure gauge onto an outdoor faucet. Stop all use of water in the house, then turn on the faucet and read the gauge. To get a realistic figure, take readings at different times of day, and check all outdoor faucets, not just one. Once you have a number at the house, keep in mind that a steep slope, or the friction from very long pipe runs, will affect the pressure at the delivery end of the irrigation system.

Avoiding Backflow

Whenever you attach to a potable-water system, always install a backflow preventer to keep used water from flowing back into the water supply. For a single-circuit system that runs directly off the hose bibb, you can screw a vacuum breaker onto the end of the faucet.

If you are using antisiphon control valves for your irrigation circuits, a preventer is built into each valve.

Inline valves need a pressure vacuum breaker at the start of the system, as long as the breaker is placed higher than the highest sprinkler head. Otherwise, you'll need to install a reduced-pressure (RP) principle backflow preventer on the main line before the valves at least 12 inches above the ground.

Vacuum breaker

 **Stuff to Buy**
Pipe, nipples, and fittings
Shutoff valve
Vacuum breaker or other
 backflow-prevention device

 **Time Commitment**
Several hours

 **Tools You'll Need**
Bucket
Pipefitting tools
Pressure gauge

Related Topics
Automating the system, 166–167
Conserving water, 14–15
Outdoor plumbing basics,
 158–159
Running supply lines, 144–145
Sprinklers & drip systems,
 162–163

Where to Start a System

In mild climates, you may tap into an outdoor faucet. In cold-winter climates, or if you don't have adequate water flow at the faucet, you can cut into your main supply line. Typically, the control valves for the irrigation system may be some distance from the tap-in point. In the illustrations here, a line runs underground to the valves.

For a plastic-pipe installation, use charcoal-gray Schedule 80 PVC, or another material suited to direct sunlight, for the above-ground part of the project. Sun can damage standard white Schedule 40 PVC.

CUTTING IN AT AN EXISTING HOSE BIBB

Often the easiest course of action is to make the connection at the pipe serving the faucet. With this method, you avoid cutting the pipe. Turn off the house's water supply and drain the faucet, then remove the faucet and install a T. Match the outlet sizes to the faucet pipe and the irrigation

At an Existing Hose Bibb

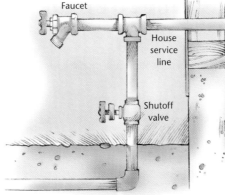

To irrigation control valves

At the Service Line

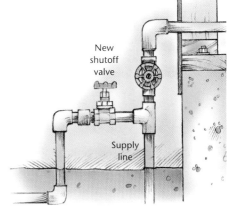

To irrigation control valves

pipe you plan to use. Reattach the faucet, then install a short length of pipe in the stem of the T-fitting and connect a shutoff valve to that.

CUTTING IN AT THE SERVICE LINE

To attach to your main supply line before it enters the house, first shut off the water

before the point where you will be cutting. For an aboveground connection, as illustrated here, remove a short section of the supply pipe, leaving just enough of a gap to slide on a slip T. Install a short piece of pipe in the stem of the T and attach a shutoff valve to it.

Wells & Other Water Sources

Homes with well water can also be connected to sprinkler or drip irrigation systems. You can also try alternative sources like pond water, although their use may be regulated by code and can involve more complications than you might expect, like thorough filtering for particles.

WELL WATER

If you don't have records of your well's flow rate, measure it at an outdoor faucet. Run the water long enough for the pump to come on and stay on before you measure. If the flow rate is below 10 gpm, you might be limited to a drip system. Measure the water pressure with a pressure gauge on the wellhead pipe. If it's too low, you might need to get a more powerful well pump or install a booster pump.

SURFACE WATER

If you have water rights to a pond, river, or stream on your property, you might be able to use it for irrigation. Unless the water is elevated above your garden, you'll need a pump to move it. Make sure that the water is appropriate for plants and that it poses no health threat to humans. Use a suitable heavy-duty filter to remove algae, sand, and other materials that would clog irrigation components.

GRAY WATER

Gray water is lightly soiled water, such as that from a clothes washer. Irrigating with it is increasingly permitted in some Western states, but the process is strictly regulated by code. Work closely with your inspector in preparing a gray-water irrigation system and consider having a professional design and install it. Typically, the gray water runs through a parallel drainpipe system within

the house, with a means of switching it back to the main drains. It is usually released underground in perforated pipes.

Automating the System

Any irrigation system can be turned on manually or with a timer. Timers, which often operate multiple circuits, are the more dependable choice to avoid overwatering and underwatering. Smart timers adjust for factors like humidity and heat, saving water while serving plants' needs.

Basic Timers

Timers ensure that plants get the water they need while also preventing overwatering—a real possibility if you operate a system manually and have to remember to turn it off.

In the simplest case, perhaps in a small garden that rarely needs additional water, use a mechanical timer. It attaches to a single hose bibb (or a hose Y) and to the hose that feeds a sprinkler or drip system. As with a kitchen timer, you set it each time you run the system.

Battery-operated timers also fit between the hose bibb and the drip or sprinkler system, but they can be set to turn the system on and off at designated times—perhaps on certain days of the week or every few days. Some can operate several circuits independently. Look for a model that indicates when the battery is low, and check the indicator often.

Wall-mounted Electronic Timers

Programmable wall-mounted electronic timers permit the most flexibility in scheduling your watering. They plug into a 110-volt power receptacle. Some models are designed for outdoor installation, while others must be installed indoors. Low-voltage insulated cable connects a timer to the irrigation system's control valves, which operate each sprinkler or drip system circuit.

Programming features vary by model. Think about the functions you will likely need, and make sure the timer supplies them. For example, you may want to set one circuit to water a lawn three days a week for two short intervals, and another to water a hedge once a week for a longer duration. If you have sufficient water pressure and flow, you can also get a timer that can operate two valves with separate programs at once.

Look for timers with battery backup, so the clock and program information is retained if the power fails, and expandability, so you can add circuits as your landscape grows or changes. A very valuable addition is a rain sensor, a small device that attaches to the outside of your house and shuts off the irrigation system if it detects too much rain. Some controllers also come with remote controls.

TIMER TYPES

Mechanical timer

Battery-operated timer

In a typical wall-mounted setup, irrigation wires run to the timer through a protective pipe leading from the control valves for the sprinkler or drip circuits. Color-coded wires like these are much easier to connect correctly to the timer.

How the Pros Do It

"A lot of the water agencies in the West are encouraging the use of smart controllers, which adjust for factors like rainfall, outdoor temperatures, and the types and needs of plants. They save water, and the plants look better too."

Tom Bressan,
www.urbanfarmerstore.com

Control Valves

To automate a multi-circuit system, you will need a control valve for each circuit. The best place for the control valves is in a manifold near the house. This facilitates wiring the valves to the timer. For a sprayer system, choose a spot out of the line of spray, in case you have to reach a valve while the system is operating. If your water supply has a flow rate of more than 8 gpm, use a 1-inch pipe from the point of connection with the water supply to the control valves and circuits. If the flow rate is lower, you can use ¾-inch pipe.

Control valves come in two varieties: antisiphon valves, which provide backflow prevention, and inline valves. If you're using inline valves, install a vacuum breaker or reduced-pressure backflow preventer at the start of the system. Antisiphon valves are placed at least 12 inches above the highest sprinkler head, while inline valves are typically installed in a valve box in the ground, with a top that's even with the ground surface.

Low-voltage insulated wire (typically AWG-14 or 18) that is approved for direct burial is used to connect the control valves to the timer. Use color-coded multi-strand cable. A different color wire joins each valve to the timer, and another color (usually white) links all the valves to the timer. Thus, if you have four valves, you'll need five-strand cable. If you might expand your system, get cable with extra strands so you won't have to rewire the whole system later. Run the cable underground to the timer location.

Related Topics

MANIFOLD SYSTEMS

Antisiphon valves

Inline valves

Head Assemblies

In addition to control valves, drip systems require one head assembly per circuit. A head assembly always includes a filter and a pressure regulator and might include a fertilizer injector. You assemble it yourself from separate pieces. Place a head assembly at the hose bibb for a single drip circuit, or just after each control valve on a multi-circuit system. If you connect at the hose bibb, use components with hose threads. To connect to a control valve, you'll need components with pipe threads.

A head assembly includes only a few pieces, but some are bulky enough to be in danger of being knocked into and harmed. Add suitable bracing if you feel it's necessary.

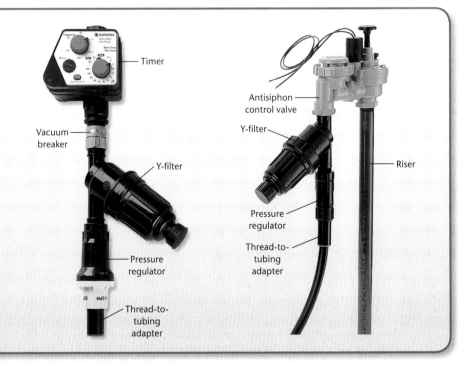

Timer

Vacuum breaker

Y-filter

Pressure regulator

Thread-to-tubing adapter

Antisiphon control valve

Y-filter

Riser

Pressure regulator

Thread-to-tubing adapter

Adding a Sprinkler System

After you've planned the circuits and installed the control valves, you'll need to measure and mark for trenches, dig the trenches, install pipes and risers, and restore the soil and sod. After all that, your final step may be sitting down with a cold drink.

Digging Trenches

Once your timer and control valves are in place, the next step is to install the circuits, which consist of pipes, risers, and sprinkler heads. You'll need to dig trenches for each one. In mild climates, trenches 8 to 12 inches deep are adequate. In most areas where hard frosts occur, 18 inches is sufficient. For very cold climates, consult a local irrigation supplier. Trenches should be as straight and flat as possible.

A sturdy, flat shovel and a pick are all you need to dig trenches by hand, but a rented trenching machine will make the job easier. Soften up hard ground by watering it with a portable sprinkler a few days ahead of time. Set aside sod on a tarp for use after the trenches are refilled.

STOP!
Before you dig, ask utility companies for the location of gas, water, sewer, electrical, and other lines. If your home has a septic tank, locate and avoid the tank and drainage field.

Installing risers

- Mark the locations of sprinkler heads with flags or colored stakes. The distance between the locations should be equal to the radius of the heads you will use.

Using a shovel

- The simplest way to dig a trench is with a sturdy, flat-headed shovel.

Using a tarp

- Set sod and soil on a tarp to make easy work of refilling your trenches.

Using a machine

- A trenching machine digs through undeveloped areas or existing lawns quickly and efficiently.

Stuff to Buy

Flags or marker stakes
Pipe-thread tape
PVC pipe, fittings, primer, and
    cement
Risers
Tarp

Time Commitment

One or two weekends

Tools You'll Need

PVC cutters
Shovel and pick, or a rented
    trenching machine
Tape measure

Related Topics

Laying Pipe

From the control valves, run the pipes for each circuit in the trenches. For long, straight runs, you can use pipes with straight and flared ends instead of connecting the lengths with couplers. If you live in a cold-winter climate, install drain valves along the pipe at the lowest points in the run. Install the valves pointing downward, and line the area below and around them with gravel. The valves will open when the line pressure drops below about 3 psi.

You can lay out all the pipe lengths and fittings first and then go back to make the connections, or you can connect as you go. Pipe should be laid as flat as possible at the bottom of the trench, though a little unevenness won't be a problem. When carrying lengths of PVC pipe, don't knock them together or drop them. The pipe can break or, worse, develop a hairline crack that you won't notice until the pipe bursts under normal water pressure when the system is running.

1 Cut pipe

- Measure and mark the pipe
- Make straight cuts with PVC ratcheting cutters (a hacksaw leaves shards that can clog the system)

2 Position pipes

- Prop the pipe ends on spare lengths of PVC set across the trench, making sure both ends stay clean
- Here, a cut end is being attached to a flared end; to attach two cut ends, use a coupling

3 Apply primer

- Spread PVC primer around the cut end and inside the flared end down to the shoulder
- Let the primer dry for a minute or so

4 Apply solvent cement

- Read Steps 4 and 5 together; you'll need to work quickly
- After the primer dries, apply PVC solvent cement
- With a soft brush, apply cement liberally to the pipe, lightly to the flared end

5 Secure the connection

- Immediately slip the pieces together and twist them partway around to secure the connection
- Hold the pipes for a few seconds while the cement sets, then wipe off any excess with a damp rag

6 Install risers

- Determine the desired height of each sprinkler head
- Make a pop-up sprinkler even with the ground and a stationary sprinkler high enough to clear the foliage
- If you use a cut-off threaded riser, cut it to height
- Wrap the riser threads with pipe-thread tape and screw the riser into the T-fitting

7 Flushing the system

- Wait at least six hours before running water through the pipes—longer under cold, damp conditions
- To flush the system, open the shutoff control valves by hand briefly
- Don't run water for too long; don't flood the trenches

8 Attach sprinkler heads

- Screw rotors and spray-head bodies to the risers
- Most spray-head bodies come with flushing caps
- Flush the system again and then replace the caps with nozzles
- Refill trenches with the soil and sod you set aside

Sprinkler System Repairs

While sprinkler system damage is relatively rare, it does happen. Check your system regularly as described below. Fixing sprinkler heads is easy. Replacing a broken riser requires a little more work, as does repairing pipes, if one breaks underground.

Inspection & Maintenance

At the start of planting season, turn on the water for each circuit and check for leaks, blockages, or broken parts. At least once a year, flush the lines to minimize clogging from loose debris. Remove the spray nozzle or rotor at the end of each line of pipe and turn the water on for several minutes until it runs clear from the risers.

The small filters below spray nozzles should be cleaned frequently. (Brass spray heads may need cleaning more often because they lack filters.) If you have a clean municipal water supply, once a year may suffice.

COMMON PROBLEMS

Inspect your system at regular intervals, at the hour when it is normally in use. Turn each circuit on in sequence to check whether the spray of any sprinkler head is off center and requires adjustment. If water shoots straight up from a riser, it is likely that the riser has been damaged or that the spray head or rotor has broken off.

If all the sprinklers on a circuit are underperforming, the water pressure may have dropped. Check for a partially closed valve, a maladjustment to the main pressure regulator, a sprinkler valve that is not opening fully, or an underground pipe leak.

If spray or rotor nozzles fail to put out a steady spray or stream, they may be clogged and require clearing.

Often the only sign of a leak in an underground pipe is an unexpected rise in your water bill. Another sign may be a swampy area of ground that won't dry out. If you suspect an underground leak, cap off all the sprinkler heads in each circuit, turn the water on, and wait for a puddle to appear. Dig carefully to expose the break or crack in the pipe, then repair it.

The flow rate of many spray heads can be adjusted easily with a small screwdriver. Others heads require a special tool provided by the manufacturer.

ADJUSTING SPRAYS

A misdirected spray head or rotor is easy to adjust. With some spray nozzles, you simply turn the head or nozzle to point in the correct direction. With others, you'll need to turn a flow-adjustment screw on the top of the nozzle with a small screwdriver. Most gear-driven rotors come with a set of nozzles to allow easy adjustment of the throw distance and precipitation rate. If the spray arc is too high or too low, change it with a special tool provided by the manufacturer, following the manufacturer's directions.

Cleaning Clogged Sprinklers

A clogged sprinkler head will usually force water out at an odd angle, or the spray may be greatly reduced. Any head can become clogged if soil, mineral deposits, insects, or other debris collects in the slits or holes from which the water emerges.

Clean the slits or holes with a piece of thin, stiff wire, such as a straightened paper clip. A dental pick also does the job nicely. With spray heads, if necessary, remove each nozzle according to the manufacturer's directions and hold the nozzle under running water to blast out the debris. Also rinse out the filter basket below the nozzle.

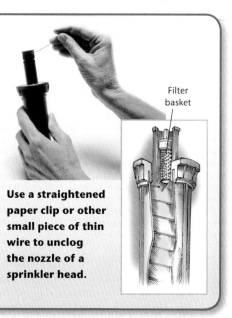

Filter basket

Use a straightened paper clip or other small piece of thin wire to unclog the nozzle of a sprinkler head.

Tool for Threaded Risers

If a threaded riser breaks, you can replace it by digging around it down to the PVC pipe, unscrewing it from its T-fitting, and screwing in a new one. A broken riser may be difficult to extract; use a stub wrench for additional leverage. Put the stub wrench into the riser and twist it counterclockwise.

Stub wrench

Repairing a Leak in PVC Pipe

A minor leak in an underground system can usually be traced to one crack or break in a pipe. Once exposed, the broken section can be cut out and replaced with a slip-fix coupling.

Before installing the coupling, make sure the water supply is off. Digging carefully to avoid further damage to the pipe, make a trench wide enough and deep enough to work with the pipe easily without getting soil into the system. Clean the pipe next to the area to be mended. Cut out the damaged section with PVC ratcheting cutters, then install the coupling. Adjust it to fit the space as necessary. Flush the system thoroughly and test for leaks before reburying the pipe.

A cracked underground pipe can be repaired with a slip-fix coupling.

Once it's attached to the old pipe, the coupling is adjusted to fit the space.

Repairing Unthreaded Risers

If an unthreaded riser is damaged, replace all or part of it with a threaded riser. If the bottom portion is intact, cut the riser pipe off cleanly a few inches above the T. Cement a slip-threaded coupling to the end of the cut riser. Cut a new threaded riser to length. Wait half an hour, then wrap the riser threads with pipe-thread tape and screw the riser into the T.

If an entire unthreaded riser is broken, dig a trench around the T below it, cut out the old T, and replace it with a new threaded T. Wait half an hour, wrap the riser threads with pipe-thread tape, and screw in the new riser. As you work, be careful not to let soil spill into the pipes. After completing the repair, remove all downstream sprinkler heads on the circuit and flush the system until the water runs clear. Then replace the sprinkler heads.

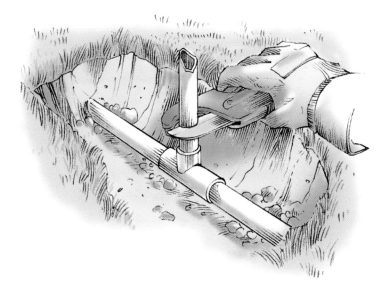

Remove the damaged part of the riser with PVC cutters.

Glue on a slip-threaded coupling, then add a threaded riser cut to length.

Installing a Drip System

Drip irrigation is much easier to install than an underground sprinkler system, for one big reason: There's no digging involved. But you plan the circuits in much the same way, and you need to place the tubing and emitters with care.

A vegetable garden is usually well suited to a drip system because edibles like to be watered slowly, which keeps the soil moist longer.

Before You Begin

Drip irrigation can include many pieces—fittings, drip emitters, sprayers, mini-sprinklers, misters, bubblers, goof plugs, and stakes. Buy those you need and sort them into marked containers or bags. Organize them by size and type so that when you start the installation you can find the ones you need.

For a new, stand-alone drip system, identify where you will connect it to your water supply, then make the connection. Drip circuits that are being added to a sprinkler system simply require their own control valves. Once you have a place to connect to, prepare a head assembly for each circuit.

Laying Drip Tubing

Drip tubing is easy to install. Start by inserting the drip tubing for a given circuit into the thread-to-tubing adapter at the end of the head assembly. Lay the tubing for the whole circuit, following your irrigation layout. To avoid kinking the tubing, unroll it as you lay it out, rather than pulling it out of a coil lying on the ground. Leave a little slack and anchor it to the ground with stakes at intervals. Try to keep dirt out of the tubing as you work.

To make acute turns, cut the tubing with pruning shears and rejoin the ends with an elbow. To branch the line, cut it and rejoin the pieces in a T-fitting. Emitter line (tubing with emitters installed at intervals) can be laid either at the same time as the tubing or when you install the emitters and sprayers.

Polyethylene tubing can be stiff when cold. In a warm climate, take it outdoors early and leave it in the sun to soften. If you have trouble inserting the tubing into a fitting, dip the end into hot water to soften it more. Do not use soap or any lubricant, such as grease or oil, to force the tubing in. Never force the tubing too far into a compression fitting, or it may interfere with the water flow. An inch into the fitting should be enough.

To keep drip line from kinking, unroll it as you lay it out.

How to Do It

Before you add watering devices to the tubing, flush it free of dirt and debris. Once the water runs clear from the ends of the lines, turn off the water and close the lines with end caps or figure-eight closures. Use your irrigation layout as a guide in placing the various watering devices, but rely on your own judgment in repositioning them as needed.

To install a drip emitter directly into ½- or ⅜-inch drip tubing, punch a hole in the tubing and then insert the barbed end of the emitter. You can also install an emitter on microtubing run from the main drip line. Connect one end of the microtubing to a hole in the drip line with a barbed ¼-inch connector. Then insert an emitter into the other end and position it at the plant. You can hold the emitter in place with a stake. On slopes, place emitters on the uphill side of the plant.

To install emitters and barbed fittings, use a punch designed to make holes in drip tubing. Hold the punch at a right angle to the tubing to ensure a round hole that will seal tightly.

A run of microtubing is attached to the larger drip tubing.

Staking a drip emitter on the end of a run of microtubing keeps it where you want it.

Sprayers, Mini-Sprinklers & Misters

To install a spray device, run microtubing from a hole in the main drip line, attaching it with a barbed connector. Extend the microtubing to a plastic stake at the desired location. Some devices screw directly to the stake; otherwise, the stake merely supports the microtubing. Pop-up sprayers and mini-sprinklers go into the ground. Some mister heads come with built-in spikes.

EMITTER LINE

Larger, ½-inch emitter line can be connected to the main drip line with a compression fitting such as a T-fitting, an elbow, or a coupling. Plug the end with an end cap. Attach ¼-inch emitter line to the drip line with a barbed connector and seal the end with a goof plug or, if you want extra flushing action, a drip emitter.

FINISHING THE JOB

The last step in installing drip irrigation is to test the system. If you haven't connected your drip-control valves to the timer, do so now. Open the shutoff valve and then manually switch each circuit on at the timer. If no circuits come on, make sure the valves are installed in the right direction. Then check the wiring. If only one circuit fails, check its flow-control setting.

Once the water is flowing, look for leaks. Fill any open holes with goof plugs, and repair any gashes by replacing the damaged part with a compression coupling.

Check for clogged emitters and sprayers and clean them out. Make sure all the watering devices are positioned near plants. If necessary, move them and plug holes in the tubing. Adjust the direction or throw of the sprayers and mini-sprinklers as required.

Mini-sprinklers deliver the wide water distribution of sprinklers in a simple drip system.

During your final check, look for any water spraying from a hole that was placed incorrectly or is no longer meant to be used. You can seal a hole easily with a goof plug.

Drip System Remedies

Once you've installed your drip system, maintaining it is a snap. Keep a compression coupler and some goof plugs on hand, but wait to purchase replacement emitters and sprayers until you've done a complete inspection of the system.

Your goal is a drip system that is working perfectly to bring just enough water to plants and not one wasteful drop more.

Easy Repairs

Drip systems are subject to more damage than sprinkler systems because all the parts are aboveground. The devices clog more easily and tubing can be cut or chewed by animals, but most of the damage is easy to repair and requires no special tools.

CLOGGED OR BROKEN DRIP DEVICES

If water is dribbling out at an erratic rate, chances are the device is clogged with debris. Insert a thin piece of wire, such as a straightened paper clip, in the opening of the emitter or spray nozzle and run it gently around the inside. If you can't clear the clog, just replace the device with a new one. Drip devices are inexpensive, so you can keep an assortment of them handy for such quick fixes.

SEALING HOLES

If you punch a hole in a drip tube by mistake, or just need to move an emitter from one location along the tubing to another, fill the hole with a goof plug. Simply push the barbed goof plug into the hole. Keep a bag of extra goof plugs handy for such repairs.

Related Topics

Automating the system, 166–167
Connecting to water, 164–165
Installing a drip system, 172–173
Sprinklers & drip systems, 162–163

Repairing a Cut Tube

To fix a gash in a run of drip tubing, make clean cuts on each side of the gash, then connect the two cut ends with a coupler.

To join two ends of ½-inch tubing, push each end into a compression coupler. If working with compression fittings is difficult for you, use a locking fitting that requires no force. Insert the tubing into the fitting and turn a locking mechanism at the end of the fitting.

For microtubing, connect the two ends with a barbed coupler.

Whenever you repair a cut in drip tubing, remove the end caps from the line and flush the system of any dirt or debris that may have gotten inside. Secure any tubing that has come loose from its stake.

To join two sections of drip tubing, first push one end of tubing into a compression coupler, then insert the other end.

Basic Maintenance

Run and check your circuits at the start of the watering season to spot leaks, blockages, or broken parts. Puddles, miniature geysers, and eroded soil are clues. If you see those, inspect the tubing around them until you find the damage. Small leaks in drip tubing will appear as spraying or bubbling along the line. Dead plants are obvious signs of trouble, but dry soil may not be.

Every six months or so, flush the lines to minimize clogging from loose debris. Open all end caps and run the water for two to five

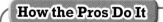

How the Pros Do It

"When people see the ground looking dry near a drip line, there's a common misconception that there is a problem. The whole point, though, is not to have surface water but to deliver the water so slowly that it spreads out underground. You are really watering the roots and not oversaturating the soil. It worries people, though, because they're so used to seeing the nice moist soil."

John Stokes, www.urbanfarmerstore.com

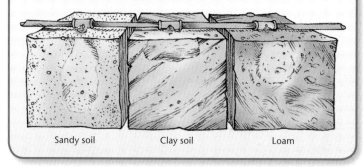

Sandy soil   Clay soil   Loam

minutes. If you are using water that may contain sediment, flush more frequently.

Clean the filters regularly. To clean an inline filter, remove its screen and wash it under running water. Replace any screen that is damaged. You can clean out a Y-filter or T-filter by unscrewing the cap and removing the filter. Some have flush valves that allow you to clean the screen in place.

Just because the surface soil in a container looks dry does not mean the drip emitter is failing to work properly.

If a tree appears to be underwatered, reposition the irrigation line so that it forms a ring around the tree's drip line.

You can flush most filters by opening a flush valve or by removing an end cap from the bottom of the filter.

Garden Pools

Water features such as garden pools can lend tranquility and focus to any backyard. Provided you obey the law and follow safety guidelines, installing a garden pool is not as difficult as you might think. The following pages offer a guide to some of the key components, including pumps, valves, and filters.

Safety Tip

Garden ponds, even shallow ones, pose a drowning risk to unattended young children and even some pets. Install and operate garden pools only in a fenced yard, and don't leave children or pets unattended near them. Check local codes for other requirements.

Water lilies provide shelter for fish. The shallow-water grasses are planted in containers set on a shelf within the pool.

Pipes & Drains

Whenever possible, opt for plastic pipe and fittings for both water supply and drain lines. Plastic is easy to cut, straightforward to assemble, and won't corrode like copper or galvanized steel. Small water features that are powered by submersible pumps may require only flexible PE tubing. But for larger pools, rigid Schedule 40 PVC pipe and fittings are the standard. Make sure any aboveground runs are a different type of plastic that can withstand sunlight—perhaps dark gray Schedule 80 PVC.

ABS plastic may be used for larger drain lines. A small pool or fountain may not need a drain, but larger pools should have a main drain so the pool can be emptied for maintenance or emergency repairs. Drains come in a variety of shapes and sizes. Swimming pool and spa suppliers are good places to find them.

Choosing the Right Pump

Electric pumps are used in garden pools to recirculate water, as well as to deliver a steady stream of water to the head of a waterfall or to operate a fountain. Pumps are useful for filtering pool water, and they provide the aeration required to support fish. A pump also allows you to drain a pool quickly in the event of a leak or for cleaning or maintenance.

Use only pumps made specifically for garden pools, and choose one based on the size of your pool. You can use the same pump to serve more than one pool feature by adding a T-fitting to the supply line, provided you use a suitably powerful pump. Garden pool suppliers offer a wide variety of pumps for most needs.

All manufacturers give electrical specifications—amperage, wattage, and horsepower—for their products to indicate how much power they consume and put out. But the practical measure of a pump's performance is its head, which determines the volume of water it can pump vertically. Fountain spray jets are usually designed for a specific water pressure, while pump requirements for waterfalls and streams vary depending on the desired effect.

PUMP CHOICES

Submersible pumps are the most popular choice for garden pools. They sit on the bottom of the pool and are usually quiet and unobtrusive. They also tend to be less expensive than comparable external pumps. Good submersible pumps have stainless-steel shafts and sealed plastic housings, use no oil, and are quite energy-efficient. Attached strainers or screens block debris from clogging the pump.

External pumps are used most often in swimming pools and very large garden pools. They can move large quantities of water (far more than required in most garden pools) and can be noisy. Because they are placed outside the pool, external pumps require their own housing, which can be difficult to hide.

PUMP KIT

Pump kits include a pump, filter, and fountainhead. This one is suitable for small pools.

SUBMERSIBLE WITH FILTER

This energy-efficient submersible pump has an attached foam filter to keep water clean.

SUBMERSIBLE PUMP

Submersible pumps are a popular choice for everything from container fountains to garden pools with small waterfalls. This powerful model can pump water at a rate of 4,000 gallons per hour.

EXTERNAL PUMP

External pumps can move large amounts of water quickly, making them ideal for waterfalls and large ponds.

VALVE CHOICES

Valves allow you to control the flow of water to a fountain or waterfall, divert water to a nearby drain, or shut down the entire system for repairs or maintenance. Well-placed valves can make your garden pool more enjoyable and easier to use.

BALL VALVE

A ball valve turns water on and off quickly, away from the supply source.

GATE VALVE

A gate valve is better than a ball valve for adjusting flow rate, but it's not as efficient at turning water on and off.

THREE-WAY VALVE

A three-way valve can shut off water flow to the pool, send a controlled flow to a fountainhead, or open a line for draining.

FLOAT VALVE

A float valve can automatically control the water level, replenishing water lost to evaporation and splash. You can hide it under rock edging or in an adjacent holding pool.

Koi are a beautiful addition to a backyard pond, but you need a good filter to keep the water clean.

A Choice of Filters

In theory, a pool properly stocked with plant and animal life should not require any filtering device. In practice, however, overfeeding fish, excessive sunlight, soil, and fish waste make a filter necessary. Filters help to maintain a clean, healthy pool by trapping dirt, algae, and fish waste. For a filter to work properly, all the water in the pool should pass through it every two hours.

Any filter requires intake and outlet plumbing. Always position the filter on the outlet side of the pump, unless you're using a separate pump and plumbing route just for the filter—a good idea in large pools. A separate ball valve on this line is handy.

The three basic types of garden pool filters are mechanical, biological, and chemical. For even better results, add an ultraviolet clarifier to supplement your main filter.

MECHANICAL FILTERS

Mechanical filters use a straining mechanism to trap debris in the water. The type at right circulates water through a box or cylinder containing granules of pulverized fuel ash or activated carbon, zeolite, brushes, foam, or fiber padding.

These devices are economical, but they tend to clog easily under heavy service (as in a fish pond), requiring frequent backwashing and replacement of the filter media. Most mechanical filters are powered with a submersible pump.

Another mechanical option is a pressurized swimming pool filter. These require regular backflushing and change of sand.

OTHER FILTERS

At their core, biological filters are similar to mechanical ones in that pumped water circulates through a filtering agent. The difference is the filter bed in a biological filter supports a colony of live bacteria. The bacteria consume ammonia and harmful pathogens, converting them into nitrites and then into nitrates for use again by plants and fish. This system depends on the constant movement of water, and thus oxygen, through the filter to keep bacteria alive. A reliable pump is a must.

MECHANICAL FILTER

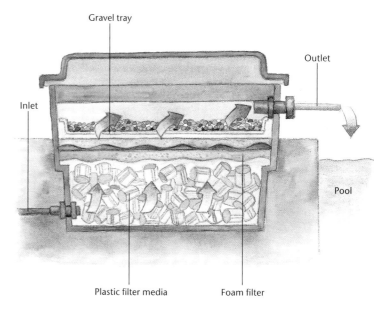

Gravel tray

Outlet

Inlet

Pool

Plastic filter media

Foam filter

How the Pros Do It

"Consider the ease and frequency of cleaning for the filtration system that you use. If you have to drag a messy, smelly intake filter out of the pond every few days to keep the pump flowing smoothly and the water clear, you're going to end up with an abandoned pond. Pick the right filter for your size of pond and its sun exposure, water treatments, types of plants, and presence or absence of fish."

John Stokes, www.urbanfarmerstore.com

BIOLOGICAL FILTER

The most popular and easy-to-use biological filters are installed outside the pool and can be disguised behind plants or rocks. Biological filters are also available with an attached fountainhead.

CHEMICAL FILTER

Chemical filtration simply means using algicides and other water-cleaning agents to attack particular impurities. This method is often used in small garden pools with no plants or fish.

ULTRAVIOLET CLARIFIER

For crystal-clear water, supplement your filtration system with an ultraviolet clarifier, which uses ultraviolet radiation to rid the pool of virtually all algae. Submersible and external units are available. The compact external ultraviolet clarifier shown above uses a replaceable bulb to control algae, which is the source of "green water" problems.

Garden Fountains

A flowing fountain is an attractive addition to a garden pool or a garden wall. Despite appearances, most modern fountains are not water hogs. A pump feeds water from the pool to the fountain, which returns the water to the pool to be cycled again and again.

Safety Tip

Garden ponds, even shallow ones, pose a drowning risk to unattended young children and even some pets. Install and operate garden pools only in a fenced yard, and don't leave children or pets unattended near them. Check local codes for other requirements.

A pump-mounted fountain is a simple addition to a garden pool. In a large enough pool, it is possible to accommodate a small fountain as well as fish and plants.

Spray Fountains

A flowing fountain can be a wonderful complement to your garden pool. Aesthetically, it makes water the center of attention in the garden, entertaining with sound and motion. Fountains also aerate pool water, providing oxygen to plants and fish. A large spray can turn your garden pool into a cool retreat on a hot day while screening out noise and other distractions with its soothing rhythm.

Spray fountains have heads that shoot water upward in patterns ranging from massive columns to delicate and nearly unnoticeable mists.

If your pool will include plants or fish, plan the installation very carefully. Many water plants, especially water lilies, do not like heavy turbulence. Fish tend to avoid the area near a fountain, although the aeration provided by the moving water is good for them.

As a general rule, the pool diameter should be at least twice the spray's height. The fountain jet is usually installed just above the water level.

The primary design rules for a spray fountain are:
- Use a short, heavy column of water in windy spots.
- Go for height and drama where the spray will not blow widely.
- Try to position a spray fountain against a background that dramatizes the movement of water. Dark backgrounds are great.
- Fine sprays look their best against a flat surface.

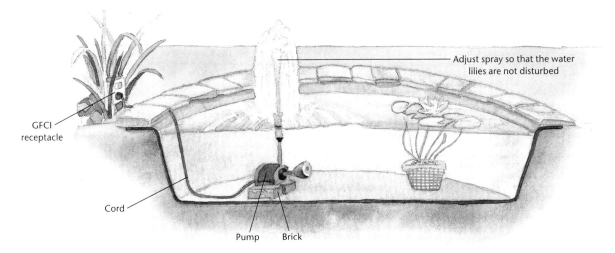

GFCI receptacle

Adjust spray so that the water lilies are not disturbed

Cord

Pump   Brick

Stuff to Buy

Electric drill
Fountain mask, cork, metal
  dowel (for a wall fountain)
Sealing agent for basin (for a
  wall fountain)
Spray or spill fountain kit
Tubing

**Time
Commitment**

A day or weekend

**Tools
You'll Need**

Electric drill
Masonry bit

**Related
Topics**

Garden pools, 176–179
Outdoor plumbing basics,
  158–159

Wall fountains, once used as practical water sources, are now primarily ornamental. Water can flow directly from a pipe, overflow from a basin, or exit from the mouth of a gargoyle, a lion, or a cheerful sun.

Wall Fountains

Although a wall fountain looks quite different from most other garden fountains, it operates much the same way. Water circulates from a pool or basin through plastic tubing to an outlet in the fountain mask, then falls back to the basin or pool.

Wall fountains are frequently installed on brick walls, but you can build one just about anywhere you like. You can use a wall vine to hide the tubing, but you can also attach lattice or place a trellis against a wall to serve the same purpose. Alternatively, run the tubing up the back of the wall through a drilled hole, then attach the mask to the wall with mortar.

Be sure to choose a watertight basin. If the basin isn't watertight, coat the interior with a sealing agent from a garden supply store.

How the Pros Do It

"Fountain and waterfall pumps are designed to provide high flows at relatively low pressures, so it's important to minimize pressure losses in the piping. Accomplish this by using large-diameter tubing that the water can flow through easily. The most common mistake we see is people installing small-diameter pipe—sometimes literally cast in stone—and then hoping for high flows."
John Stokes,
www.urbanfarmerstore.com

Installing a Wall Fountain

1 Prepare the fountain mask

- Place the fountain mask face-down on a soft surface
- Glue cork to the back to allow room to run tubing between the wall and the mask
- Mark a spot for a mounting hole on the back just above the spout hole
- Using an electric drill and a masonry bit, drill a 45-degree hole at the mark, stopping halfway through the mask

2 Insert the tubing

- Cut a piece of clear vinyl tubing long enough to wind down the wall to the basin
- Slide an elbow fitting into the tubing
- Connect a second piece of tubing to the elbow fitting
- Push the second tubing piece through the spout hole from the front of the mask to the back of it

3 Hang the mask

- Using the masonry bit, drill a 1½-inch-deep hole at a 45-degree angle into the brick wall
- Slide half of a 3-inch-long metal dowel into the hole
- Hang the mask on the wall by sliding it over the other half of the dowel.

4 Add the pump & fill the basin

- With the mask in place, wind the tubing through vines and down the wall
- Slide the other end of the tubing over the outlet of a small submersible pump
- Place the pump in the basin
- Fill the basin with water, then plug the pump into a suitable receptacle

Swimming Pool Basics

Swimming pool water needs to circulate in order to stay fresh. Circulation helps mix chemicals in the water and prevent warm spots and cold spots if you have a heater. Most important, it makes it possible to strain and filter out any debris or particulates in the water.

Pool Plumbing

Behind the walls and underneath an in-ground swimming pool—or attached to the outside walls of an aboveground pool—lies a network of pipes to circulate the water and keep it fresh.

The pool water flows in a continuous loop. Water drains from the pool, either through the main drains or through side drains called skimmers. It then passes through a pump that pressurizes it, forcing it through a filter and a heater (if the pool has one). From there, the water travels through return lines and sprays back into the pool through nozzles called inlets.

PVC or CPVC plastic pipes are typically used for pool plumbing. They're inexpensive, easy to work with, and, unlike copper or other metals, resistant to corrosion. Some plastics, like white Schedule 40 PVC, can be damaged by sunlight. For any aboveground lines, substitute dark gray Schedule 80 PVC or other sunlight-resistant plastic.

Skimmers

Skimmers help keep pools clean by skimming the water surface and capturing floating debris, such as leaves and grass clippings. This means you need to empty debris from the strainer baskets often—once a day is a good starting point. You can also attach a portable pool vacuum to a skimmer, allowing you to clean the pool bottom and walls. The vacuum's tube connects to the skimmer's suction line and is powered by the pool pump.

A well-placed skimmer can keep up to 500 square feet of pool surface clean. Skimmers must be installed with an equalizer line—a pipe that connects from the bottom of the skimmer basket through the pool wall and into the water. The equalizer prevents air from being sucked into the system if evaporation should cause the water level to drop below the level of the weir. If air were to enter the system, it would cause the pump to stall.

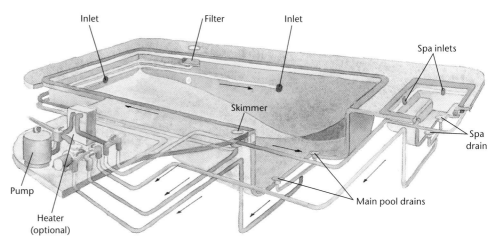

Inlet   Filter   Inlet   Spa inlets   Skimmer   Spa drain   Pump   Heater (optional)   Main pool drains

This pool and spa combination requires more complicated plumbing than a separate pool or spa, but the principle is the same: Water is continuously drawn away through the drains and skimmer, filtered and possibly heated, and then returned via the inlets.

BUILT-IN POOL SKIMMER

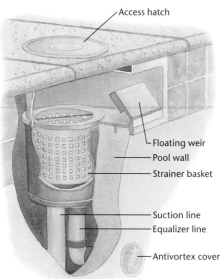

Access hatch   Floating weir   Pool wall   Strainer basket   Suction line   Equalizer line   Antivortex cover

In a typical skimmer, a self-adjusting piece of plastic called a weir regulates how much water enters the skimmer. Because the weir allows only a thin layer to spill over, water is pulled off the surface rapidly, keeping a large area clear. Debris is caught in the strainer basket.

Safety Tip

Swimming pools pose a drowning risk, especially for unattended young children and pets. Make sure your pool is in a fenced yard. Don't leave young children or pets unattended near it, and do provide covers and any other appropriate safety components, such as fencing, a self-closing gate, and antivortex drain covers. Check local codes for other requirements. Never leave young children and pets unattended by a pool.

FLOATING SKIMMER FOR ABOVEGROUND POOL

Instead of wall-mounted skimmers, some aboveground pools use collector units that hang on the side or float in the water.

Related Topics

Outdoor plumbing basics, 158–159
Pool filters & heaters, 184–185
Spas & hot tubs, 186–187

Drains

In addition to skimmers, most pools have a pair of main drains at the bottom, usually at the deepest point in the pool. Water and non-floating debris are sucked through the main drains toward the pump, then through the filter.

If you've ever placed your hand over the main drain in a swimming pool, you've felt the tug generated by the pump. Especially where there is only one drain, a blocked flow can create a hazardous form of suction known as a vortex. This strong pull can trap swimmers even in a shallow pool, posing a grave danger. Having multiple drains and skimmers reduces the risk but doesn't eliminate it.

For further safety, all drains—and all equalizers installed with skimmers—should be fitted with an antivortex cover. This slatted or perforated cover prevents people's hair and limbs from getting caught in the plumbing. If antivortex covers are in place and the pool is built and operated correctly, there is virtually no risk of suction pinning someone against a drain.

Hydrostatic Valves

Groundwater that lies beneath the swimming pool is not a problem as long as the pool is filled, because the sheer weight of the water keeps the pool structure in place. If the pool is emptied, however, groundwater exerts tremendous pressure against the bottom and sides. The pressure can crack concrete pools and lift fiberglass pools out of the ground.

Fitting each main drain with a hydrostatic relief valve prevents the problem. The valve consists of a floating ball that lies in a pipe between the drain and the groundwater. During normal operation, water in the pool presses down against the ball and seals off the drain from the groundwater. When the pool is empty, the ball floats up and unblocks the pipe if the pressure from the groundwater increases to dangerous levels. Then the pool simply fills with groundwater.

MAIN DRAIN

HYDROSTATIC VALVE ANATOMY

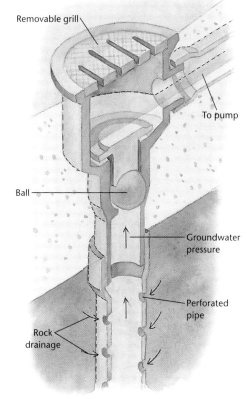

Removable grill

To pump

Ball

Groundwater pressure

Perforated pipe

Rock drainage

POOL PUMP

ANTIVORTEX COVER

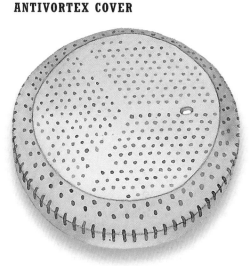

Pool Pumps

Pumps vary in size according to the amount of water they have to circulate. A properly sized pump should be able to turn over the entire volume of water once every 8 to 24 hours. (Check with your building department on the required circulation rate in your area, which is often governed by code.)

The volume of water flow depends on the pipe diameters as well as the pump. Pipes that drain the pool are commonly 2 inches in diameter. Return pipes typically start at $1\frac{1}{2}$ inches but connect to smaller pipes where they reach the inlets to produce pressurized jets.

Usually a 1.5-horsepower pump is sufficient. The flow of water is limited by the pipe size, so a larger pump will work in vain to force water out faster, seriously shortening the pump's life from the strain. A properly sized pump may last 10 years or longer, but an oversized pump being strained may burn out after only three or four years. It's also noisier. Matching the pump to the pool's plumbing requires careful calculation and is best left to a contractor.

Pool Filters & Heaters

Skimmers, drains, pumps, and inlets work together to circulate pool water. Treating the water as it flows by is a job for other components: the all-important filter and, in many areas, a heater. Pool chemicals are added in other ways, such as from a floating feeder.

Choosing the Right Filter

There are many types of filters, including high-rate sand filters, filters filled with pulverized material called diatomaceous earth, and cartridge filters, which are analogous to the air filter in a car. While sand filters were once the favorite, advances in cartridge filters have made them so over-whelmingly preferred that about 99 percent of home pool owners now use a cartridge filter. Although other filter types are still used for public or commercial pools, cartridge filters are the best choice for a residential pool. Here's why.

Pool water will stay this clean only if the pool filter is working properly and you clean it regularly.

HIGH-RATE SAND FILTERS

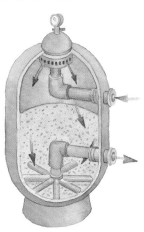

Until recently, the high-rate sand filter was the most popular option for swimming pools. The pressurized tank is filled with special grades of sand that can trap particles as small as 5 microns (a human hair follicle is between 40 and 120 microns thick). The flow of pressurized water drives particles deep into the sand bed. But the sand must be backwashed frequently in order to remove the particles and maintain the filter's efficiency. While not a difficult task, backwashing uses a lot of water—as much as 500 gallons per cleaning.

DIATOMACEOUS EARTH (D.E.) FILTERS

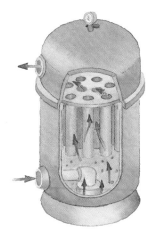

In a D.E. filter, water passes through filter grids coated with diatomaceous earth, a naturally occurring substance. Particles in the water catch on the edges of the D.E. and are held tight. D.E. filters are more compact than high-rate sand filters, because they do not contain a pressurized tank and they filter tinier particles—as small as 3 microns. Like sand filters, D.E. filters also require backwashing, which again means using as much as 500 gallons of water each time. Moreover, the diatomaceous earth itself is classified as a hazardous waste in many localities, and disposal is increasingly regulated.

CARTRIDGE FILTERS

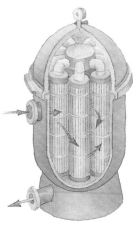

Modern cartridge filters are almost as effective as high-rate sand filters, trapping particles as small as 6 microns. They're also much easier and safer to maintain, and they require very little water for cleaning. In a cartridge filter, water from the pool passes through a filter made of polyester cloth or corrugated paper. Instead of backwashing, you simply remove the filter and hose it off. After a few years, the filter will need replacing, but this is a simple process explained in the manufacturer's instructions.

Related Topics

Outdoor plumbing basics, 158–159
Spas & hot tubs, 186–187
Swimming pool basics, 182–183

Heaters

The ideal temperature for pool water depends on your personal preference, but the range is usually between 78 and 82 degrees Fahrenheit. Even in summer, in most places the only way to guarantee that is with a heater.

Because a heater is connected to the plumbing outside the pool, it is very easy to add a heater after the pool is built. If you're thinking of adding a heater sometime in the future, however, have all the necessary plumbing installed ahead of time.

Pool heaters come in different styles based on the energy source—gas, electricity, or solar thermal. (Solar thermal systems use the heat of the sun directly, so no conversion to electrical energy is involved.) An experienced pool contractor will know which type of heater is the best value for your region.

GAS HEATERS

Gas heaters, which run on either propane or natural gas, are the most popular because of the relatively low cost of the fuel. In addition, they are convenient and tend to heat water quickly because they use a direct flame. They come in three distinct types.

CONVECTION HEATER

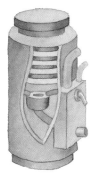

A large flame heats a steady stream of slow-moving water to a very high temperature. This type of heater is suitable for small pools and spas.

TANK HEATER

A small flame heats a large volume of water. It's cost-effective but not sufficient in cold climates.

COIL, OR FLASH, HEATERS

These are the most common gas heaters. A large flame rapidly heats a coil through which a small but fast-moving stream of water passes. Although they are more expensive because they consume the largest amount of fuel, coil heaters are suited for pools and spas of any size, as they heat a large body of water quickly.

ELECTRIC HEAT PUMPS

A heat pump for a pool is a lot like a heat pump for a house. In effect, it transfers heat from the outside air to the water. Warm outside air heats the refrigerant within the heat pump. Then the refrigerant is further heated and compressed by the compressor, resulting in a very hot gas. When the gas passes through a heat exchanger, its heat is transferred to the pool water.

The beauty of a heat pump is that although it runs on electricity, it actually yields many times more heat than could be produced by an electric heater alone. The downside is that heat pumps work best in hot climates and are of little use in warming a pool in a cold climate during spring and fall.

Solar Thermal Heating

Because of the big expense of heating pool water, solar energy is an increasingly appealing option. In part, you can use the heat from the sun by choosing a pool location with a southern or southwestern exposure and no shade from trees (this can be a bit too much in warm or hot climates, though). A solar thermal system, however, involves the use of a solar collector, typically on the roof. Pool water circulates directly through the collector, absorbs heat from the sun, and returns to the pool. A solar system can work on its own or together with a conventional heater, reducing the heater's energy use. When installing solar collectors or combination systems, choose a contractor with a significant track record working with solar heat.

As a general rule, the surface area of solar thermal collectors should add up to at least 75 percent of the surface of your pool.

Solar panels

Heated water out

Cool water in

Conventional heater (optional)

Spas & Hot Tubs

From a plumbing standpoint, spas and hot tubs may seem like miniature swimming pools, but there are some differences. Spas and hot tubs are generally heated to a much higher temperature than a swimming pool, and the force of the water flowing into them is much greater.

Safety Tip

Spas and hot tubs pose a drowning risk to unattended young children and some pets. Install and operate a spa or hot tub only in a fenced yard, and don't leave children or pets unattended near them. Check local codes for other requirements.

About Heaters

Spa water is heated much higher than pool water—in some cases, up to 104 degrees Fahrenheit. Gas heaters are by far the fastest, warming the water in minutes. Among electric heaters, those that run on 110 volts heat water very slowly, while those that run on 220 volts are comparatively quicker. However, electric heaters are far more expensive to operate than gas heaters in most parts of the country.

Here are two examples of spas that have been built into their surroundings. Mortared stone and a wood top give the portable spa at top left a very permanent appearance. The spa at left is set into a deck so that it can be entered easily.

Related Topics

Outdoor plumbing basics, 158–159
Pool filters & heaters, 184–185
Swimming pool basics, 182–183

Spa Designs

When installed next to a swimming pool, an in-ground spa uses the same equipment as the pool itself. The pool's basic equipment needs to be slightly larger to handle the additional load. Freestanding spas require their own pump, filter, and heater. That equipment can be smaller than for a swimming pool, since the workload is smaller.

Like a pool, a spa can be either above-ground, as with a portable spa, or in-ground. A hot tub is a specialized type of spa with characteristic materials and appearance.

PORTABLE SPA

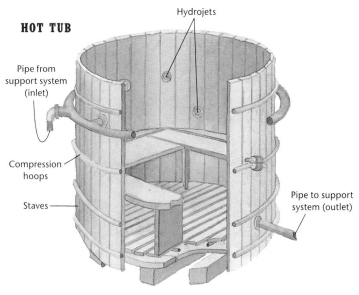

IN-GROUND SPA

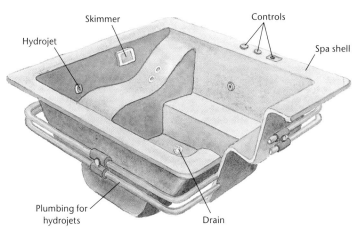

HOT TUB

Covers

A cover is an essential component of a spa, not just an option. First, covers provide safety by restricting access. Second, they keep out dirt and debris, which reduces the load on the pump and filter—especially important if the spa is outdoors. Third, covers save energy. Keeping the spa covered when it's not in use greatly reduces heat loss and therefore substantially lowers your energy bills.

Hydrojets

A signature difference between spas and swimming pools is that spas have hydrojets, providing high-pressure massage action. A hydrojet mixes a pressurized stream of water with air, then forces it into the spa to create a bubbling swirl. Each hydrojet pumps out between 12 and 15 gallons of water per minute, and most spas contain at least four jets.

Hydrojets do not have to be fixed in one orientation. Some move up and down to create a rippling massage. In many spas, you can choose the exact location of the hydrojets. If you can, sit in the spa before you purchase it, so the hydrojets can be placed according to your preference.

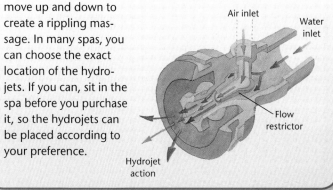

9 Help Section

In this chapter, we help you solve problems quickly, whether it's repairing a broken or frozen pipe, or unclogging a drain that's threatening to flood. Beyond dealing with emergencies, you'll also learn how to solve the nuisance of noisy pipes, anchor pipes to everything from joists to masonry, repair a wide variety of faucets, and troubleshoot disposers, toilets, and dishwashers.

Chapter Contents

Emergency Plumbing

Prompt action can limit the damage caused by many plumbing emergencies. The first step is to turn off the water, so locate your shutoffs ahead of time. Frozen pipes can cause havoc if they burst, but you can prevent bursting if you move quickly to thaw them.

Shutting Off Water

In most plumbing emergencies, you'll need to stop the flow of water quickly before it damages your floors, walls, or worldly possessions. You and your family need to know the location of the shutoff valves for fixtures and appliances, as well as the main shutoff for the house. Shutoff valves turn clockwise (toward the right) to close. Just remember: "righty tighty, lefty loosey."

If the emergency involves one fixture or appliance, locate its shutoff valve or valves (in the case of paired hot and cold supply lines) and cut off the water. The valve or valves are usually underneath a fixture such as a sink or a toilet, and behind an appliance such as a clothes washer.

If there is no shutoff valve for the appliance or fixture, or if the problem is elsewhere (as with a cracked pipe), use the main shutoff for the house. Locate this ahead of time as well. You'll find it either just inside or just outside your house, near where the main supply line enters. In cold climates, it is usually just inside the foundation wall in the basement or crawl space. If you need a wrench to turn it, keep a wrench near the valve with a special label on it.

If the main shutoff itself must be repaired, call your water utility company. They can send someone with a special tool to turn off the water at the street.

Water meter in sidewalk

Access to the water meter for this home is easy to spot in the sidewalk.

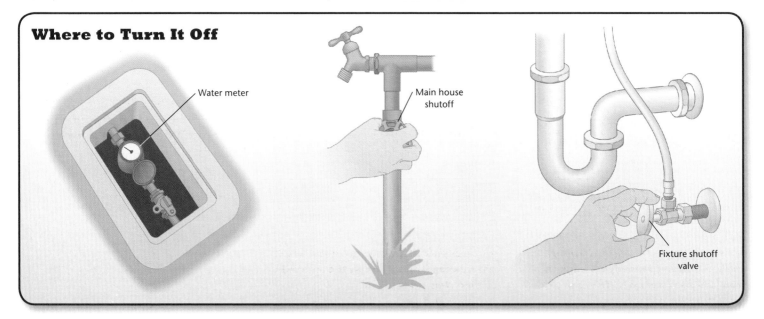

Where to Turn It Off

Water meter

Main house shutoff

Fixture shutoff valve

Tools You'll Need

Hair dryer
Heat lamp
Heating pad
Pan
Rags
Towels

Related Topics

Adding shutoff valves, 36–37
Home plumbing systems, 8–9
Money-saving upgrades, 196–197
The supply system, 10–11

Preventing Frozen Pipes

The best way to avoid frozen pipes is to winterize your plumbing. If a severe cold snap catches you off-guard, you can help to prevent the freezing and subsequent bursting of pipes with these precautions:

- Keep a constant trickle of water running from the faucets.
- Beam a heat lamp or aim a small heater at exposed pipes, but avoid overheating plastic pipes.
- Wrap uninsulated pipes with newspapers, heating wires, foam padding, or self-adhesive insulating tape.
- Keep doors ajar between heated and unheated rooms.
- Open the doors of an under-sink cabinet or vanity, but make sure hazardous materials like cleaners are not accessible to children or pets.

Thawing Frozen Pipes

The first sign of a frozen pipe is when you open a faucet and no water comes out. Turn off the water at the main house shutoff, then address the problem. First locate the frozen portion of the pipe. It's probably in the least insulated part of the house. Open the faucet or faucets nearest the frozen pipe so it can drain as you thaw it.

A CHOICE OF METHODS

Always work from the open faucet toward the iced-up area so that the melted water is released through the faucet. Don't rush. The more gradual the thaw, the better the chance of avoiding a burst pipe. Never use a torch or open flame to thaw a frozen pipe. Exercise extreme caution when using electrical appliances, such as a hair dryer or heat lamp, around water.

Thawing Plastic Pipe

Plastic pipe requires special consideration. Never heat plastic pipe above about 150 degrees Fahrenheit (roughly the temperature at which you can still grasp the pipe with your bare hand). Heat can damage plastic pipes, so do not try to thaw plastic pipe with boiling water, and be careful when using a heating pad or heat lamp.

HEATING PAD

Wrap a length of pipe with a heating pad. Check the pipe every 15 minutes or so to see whether it is warming up. For a plastic pipe, make sure not to overheat it. You can supplement a heating pad with a hair dryer.

HEAT LAMP

For pipes inside walls, floors, or ceilings, beam a heat lamp 8 inches or more from the surface of the pipe. Again, exercise extreme caution near water. Carefully work from the open faucet toward the frozen area so the water will be released as it melts, and avoid overheating a plastic pipe.

HOT WATER

For a metal pipe, the safest thawing method is to wrap the pipe in rags and pour boiling water on it. This is much too hot for a plastic pipe.

HAIR DRYER

A hair dryer will gently defrost the frozen pipe. Sweep it slowly across the affected section. You can use it on its own or with a heating pad. Be very careful near water.

Leaking or Cracked Pipes

Leaking or cracked pipes should be repaired immediately. You can locate them easily in an exposed space such as a basement. For pipes that are out of sight or buried, a high water bill may be the first sign of a leak.

Locating the Leak

To find a suspected leak, first make certain that the plumbing is not in use—that faucets are closed, that toilets aren't running, and so on. Then check your home's water meter. If the lowest-quantity dial is moving, you're losing water somewhere in the system.

If you don't have a water meter, you can buy or borrow a mechanic's stethoscope, which will amplify any sound of running water when held up to a pipe.

If you hear water running, follow the sound to its source. If you don't hear it, look for stains.

- If water has stained the ceiling or is dripping down, the leak is probably directly above. Occasionally, though, water may travel along a joist and then stain or drip at a point some distance from the leak.
- If water stains a wall, there's a leak in a vertical section of pipe. Since the stain is most likely below the leak, you'll probably need to remove an entire vertical section of the wall to find it.
- If you don't hear running water or see any drips or stains, the leak may be in the crawl space or the basement. Use a flashlight to check the pipes there.

A Fast, Temporary Solution

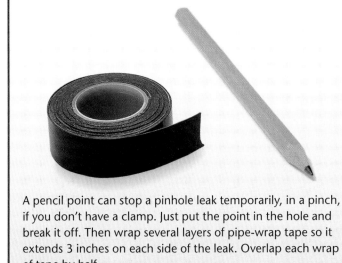

A pencil point can stop a pinhole leak temporarily, in a pinch, if you don't have a clamp. Just put the point in the hole and break it off. Then wrap several layers of pipe-wrap tape so it extends 3 inches on each side of the leak. Overlap each wrap of tape by half.

Temporary Fixes

Once you locate the leaking pipe, turn off the water at the main house shutoff valve. For a major leak, you'll probably have to replace the leaky section of pipe. If the leak is small, you may install a simple, temporary solution until you have time for the replacement job.

SLEEVE CLAMPS

Sleeve clamps should stop most leaks for some months, or even years; it's a good idea to keep some on hand. Sleeve clamps are usually sold with a built-in gasket. A clamp that fits the pipe diameter exactly works best.

HOSE CLAMPS

A hose clamp in size #12 or #16 will stop a pinhole leak on an average-size pipe. Use a piece of rubber, such as part of a bicycle inner tube or electrician's rubber tape, along with the clamp. In a pinch, you could use a household C-clamp, a small block of wood, and rubber or tape.

PUTTY

Epoxy putty will often stop leaks around joints where clamps won't, but it doesn't hold as long. The pipe must be clean and dry for the putty to adhere, so turn off the water supply to the leak to let the area dry.

Stuff to Buy

Epoxy putty
Fittings and short replacement
  pipes
Hose clamps
Pipe-wrap tape
Plastic pipe cement
Sleeve clamps
Solder supplies

**Time
Commitment**

1–2 hours

**Tools
You'll Need**

Mechanic's stethoscope
Screwdriver

**Related
Topics**

Assessing your water supply,
  16–17
Emergency plumbing, 190–191
Home plumbing systems, 8–9
Making the connections,
  118–119
Other copper connections,
  112–113
Soldering a copper joint,
  108–111
The supply system, 10–11
Working with plastic pipe,
  104–107

Replacing Pipe

The ultimate solution for any leak is to replace the pipe. The method you choose depends on whether the damaged pipe is copper, plastic, or galvanized steel. Brace the pipe run with your hand or with pipe hangers while you cut.

DWV Pipes

What if your drain-waste-vent system springs a leak? You'll find a selection of flexible repair fittings, like the elbow shown (right), at plumbing supply stores and home centers. These fittings, available in common DWV sizes, are designed to clamp onto existing cast-iron, plastic, and galvanized steel drainpipes just like no-hub couplings.

Flexible DWV
elbow

Copper Pipe

For rigid copper pipe with a small leak, you might be able to cut out the leaky spot, pull the pipes away from each other, slip on a repair coupling, and solder it in place. If the damage is more extensive, or if you can't get enough slack for the coupling, you'll need to cut out the damaged section and add a new piece of pipe and two slip (no-shoulder) couplings.

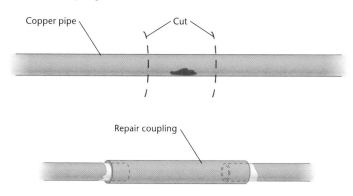

To replace a leaky copper pipe, first cut out a small section, then solder on a repair coupling.

Steel Pipe

For galvanized-steel pipes, you'll have to cut through the leaky pipe run, follow it back to the nearest fittings on both sides, and unscrew the pipe sections from each fitting. You'll need to replace the entire run with two new pipe lengths and a galvanized union.

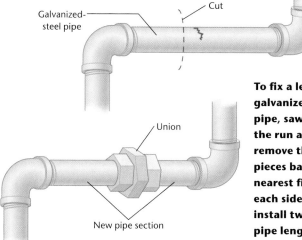

To fix a leaky galvanized-steel pipe, saw through the run and remove the cut pieces back to the nearest fitting on each side. Then install two new pipe lengths and join them with a union.

Plastic Pipe

For rigid plastic pipe with a small leak, try cutting out the leaky spot and slipping on a repair union. Otherwise, you'll need to cut out a section and patch in a new pipe.

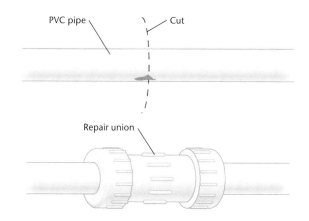

For a small leak in PVC plastic, saw through the center of the leaky spot and pull apart the sections of pipe. Then slip on a repair union and tighten its compression nuts.

Quieting Noisy Pipes

Degree of Difficulty
● Easy

Not all pipe noises are created equal, so listen carefully if your pipes make annoying sounds. The possibilities include loud water hammer when you turn off the water, banging when you open a tap, high-pitched squeaking, and faucet chatter.

Stopping Water Hammer

The most common pipe noise, water hammer, occurs when you quickly turn off the water at a faucet or an appliance. The water flowing through the pipes slams to a stop, causing a hammering noise.

To avoid this problem, many water systems have short, air-filled pipe sections rising above each faucet or appliance, known as air chambers or water-hammer arresters (below and right). These air-filled pipe sections serve as shock absorbers, allowing room for the moving water to rise within them instead of slamming to a stop.

Over time, old arresters can fill with water, losing their effectiveness. To revive them, take these steps:

- Check the toilet tank to make sure it is full, then close off the supply shutoff valve just below the tank.
- Close the main house shutoff.
- Open the highest and lowest faucets in the house to drain all water. Then close the two faucets and reopen the main house shutoff and the shutoff valve below the toilet tank.

Normal water flow will re-establish itself for each faucet when you turn it on.

How a Water-Hammer Arrester Works

Air chamber

When the faucet is open, water flows through the supply pipe and out the faucet, without moving up into the air chamber. When the faucet closes quickly, the moving water stops at the faucet and fills part of the air chamber, avoiding water hammer.

Comparing Water-Hammer Arresters

To minimize the loud bang and destructive shock known as water hammer, many codes require water-hammer arresters (also known as air chambers) near fixtures. These are installed at the top of a fixture's water supply risers, on the incoming side of shutoff valves and supply risers that serve the fixture or appliance.

You can buy a commercial arrester or make your own. Most installations place the arresters on T-fittings at the tops of supply risers inside the wall. Some plumbers prefer that the arresters be outside the wall for easy servicing. These can be concealed inside a kitchen sink cabinet or a bathroom vanity.

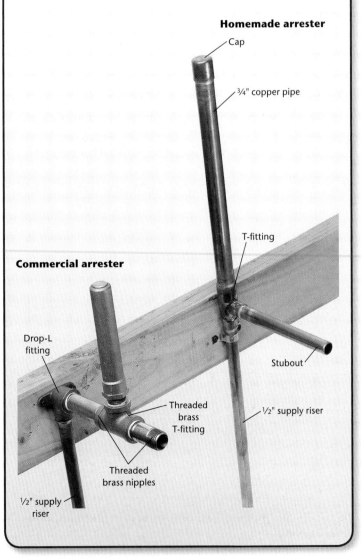

Homemade arrester

Cap

¾" copper pipe

T-fitting

Stubout

½" supply riser

Commercial arrester

Drop-L fitting

Threaded brass T-fitting

Threaded brass nipples

½" supply riser

Banging Pipes

If you hear a banging noise whenever you turn on the water, check the way the pipes are anchored. You may find that a vibration-causing section of pipe is inadequately supported.

If the noise continues, slit a piece of old hose or cut a patch of rubber and insert it into the hanger or strap as a cushion. For masonry walls, attach a block of wood to the wall with masonry fasteners, then anchor the pipe to it with a pipe hanger.

Be careful not to anchor a pipe, especially a plastic one, too securely. Leave room for expansion with temperature changes.

Squeaks & Chatter

Pipes that squeak are always hot-water pipes. As a pipe expands, it moves in its support and friction causes the squeak. To silence it, insert a piece of rubber between the pipe and its supports, as you would to eliminate banging.

Faucet chatter is the noise you hear when you partially open a compression faucet. To correct the problem, tighten or replace the seat washer on the bottom of the faucet stem.

PIPE & MASONRY

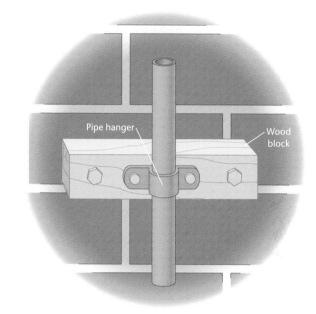

Pipe hanger • Wood block

Fasten a wood block to a masonry wall and strap on the pipe.

HANGERS

New pipe hanger

Old pipe hanger

Nail additional pipe supports to joists to stop horizontal pipes from banging.

CUSHIONING

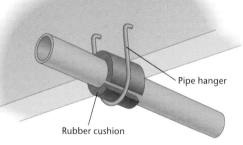

Pipe hanger • Rubber cushion

Wrap a rubber blanket or hose around a noisy pipe to cushion it in its strap.

Money-saving Upgrades

To avoid future problems and to save energy, winterize your plumbing system now. Also make sure the water pressure is neither too low nor too high. High pressure can damage fixtures over time, while low pressure is needlessly annoying.

If you live in a cold climate, you know the importance of insulating pipes, but even folks who live where winters are warm should protect their plumbing systems against the occasional deep freeze.

Preparing for Winter

Winterizing your pipes is an essential precaution in a cold-winter zone, and it saves energy by keeping hot-water pipes hot. Frozen pipes can also be a problem in warm-winter areas on exceptionally cold days. Pipes in such regions may be more vulnerable than you might think, because they are often in unheated and uninsulated spaces.

Planning for Travel

If you live in a cold climate, shut off your house water supply when you leave home in winter. Then open the valves and drain the system. What causes frozen pipes to burst is the buildup of water pressure. If no water is coming into the house, there's nothing in the pipes to freeze. So take that important extra step while you're turning down the water heater and the house thermostat.

Insulating Vulnerable Pipes

Winterizing begins with a survey of your supply lines. Start at the main line and then track pipe runs from there. If you have supply lines in unheated or uninsulated areas like the attic, garage, or crawl space, make those your first candidates for insulated pipe sleeves. These sleeves are made of foam, rubber, or fiberglass and easily fit over the pipes. The ends should butt together tightly and should be sealed with aluminum tape.

Winterizing Outdoor Plumbing

In a climate where occasional frost is possible, wrap aboveground pipes with insulating foam tubing or tape.

Always disconnect garden hoses or other items from your outdoor faucets before the first freeze. (To protect the hoses, drain them fully.) Shut off water to the faucets inside the house if there are indoor shutoffs, then open and drain the faucets. Some outdoor faucets have a feature to prevent backflow into the home system. Make sure such devices are not holding standing water inside the faucet valve, which could freeze and burst.

Also drain your sprinkler system before the first freeze to keep the pipes from bursting. First close the system's shutoff valve. Opening the drain valves at the low points in the system will extract most of the water in the pipes. The best way to remove any remaining water from a sprinkler system is to blow compressed air through it—usually a job for a professional. Disconnect and fully drain aboveground drip irrigation systems as well.

If you live in a mild-winter region with only occasional freezes, you might be able to simply wrap aboveground pipes or valves in winter. Check at your garden or home center to see what's customary in your area.

$ Stuff to Buy
Aluminum tape
Insulated pipe sleeves
Pressure-reducing valve

**Tools
You'll Need**
Water-pressure gauge
Wrenches to attach pressure-
reducing valve

**Related
Topics**
Assessing your water supply,
16–17
Emergency plumbing, 190–191
The supply system, 10–11
Valves & transitions, 34–35

Adjusting Water Pressure

Most appliances, valves, and fixtures that use water are engineered to take 50 to 60 pounds of pressure per square inch (psi). Mains deliver water at pressures as high as 150 psi and as low as 10 psi. You can determine your water pressure by attaching a water-pressure gauge to an outside hose bibb.

LOW PRESSURE

The telltale sign of low pressure is a very thin trickle of water from faucets throughout the house. Chronic low pressure is found typically in homes on hills near reservoir level. Periodic low pressure may occur during peak service hours.

The only way to increase water pressure to a home is to install a booster system. However, flushing rusted pipes or putting in larger sections of pipe will at least give you a greater volume of water. If your pipes are too small, consider replacing the section of pipe that leads from the outdoor utility shutoff valve to the main house shutoff. For example, if it's a ¾-inch pipe, replace it with a 1-inch pipe. If you have a water meter, you can also ask your utility company to install a larger meter.

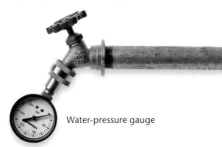

Water-pressure gauge

HIGH PRESSURE

The symptoms of high pressure are loud clangs when the dishwasher shuts off or wild sprays when faucets are first turned on. High pressure usually occurs in houses on low-lying slopes of steep hills or in subdivisions where high pressure is maintained for fire protection.

FLUSHING THE PIPES

Flushing the pipes will help you regain lost volume if the water flow in your house has become sluggish. Remove the faucet aerators, clean them, and set them aside. Then close the valve that controls the pipes you intend to clean. It may be the main house shutoff or a shutoff valve on the water heater.

Next, fully open the faucet that is farthest from the valve and open a second faucet nearer the valve. Plug the faucet near the valve with a rag (but don't shut off the faucet). Reopen the valve and let water run full force through the farther faucet for as long as sediment continues to appear—probably only a few minutes.

Finally, close both faucets, remove the rag, and replace the aerators.

Pressure-Reducing Valve

Above-normal pressure can be corrected inexpensively with a pressure-reducing valve. As the name suggests, the valve can reduce pipe pressure from 80 psi or more to 50 to 60 psi. If you'd like to retain high water pressure for outdoor use, install the valve downstream from your outdoor plumbing.

To add a pressure-reducing valve, first shut off the water supply. Assemble the valve with the fittings necessary to connect its threads to the existing pipe. Remove a length of pipe on the house side of the main house shutoff that's long enough to accommodate the valve and the assembled fittings. Install the pressure-reducing valve using the appropriate methods for your pipe material, and check for leaks after completing the job.

To reduce the water pressure, turn the adjusting screw at the top of the valve clockwise until the pressure is low enough to end bothersome pipe noises. Make sure the valve still supplies adequate water flow to upper floors or faraway fixtures.

Pressure-reducing
valve

Unclogging a Sink

If only one sink is blocked and no other drains are affected, you're probably dealing with a clog in the sink's trap or drainpipe. If multiple drains are blocked, you may need to clear the main drain instead.

A Range of Tactics

A kitchen sink usually clogs because of a buildup of grease and food particles. A dose of scalding water is often effective against grease buildups; keep running the water long enough to flush the pipes. Alternatively, a small object—a coin or small utensil—may be caught in the drain. To check, remove and thoroughly clean the strainer or, in the case of a bathroom sink, the pop-up stopper.

If these simple measures fail, try using a sink plunger to clear the pipe. If the plunger doesn't work, you'll need to use a drain-and-trap auger, also called a snake. This is a flexible metal coil that you feed through the pipes until it reaches the clog. The end of the coil snags the clog and dislodges it or pulls it out.

Good Auger Technique

Feed the drain-and-trap auger, or snake, into the drain, trap, or pipe until it stops. If you've simply encountered a turn in the pipe, which is likely, work past it carefully. Once you reach the clog, tighten the thumbscrew and rotate the handle clockwise to break the blockage. Never rotate counterclockwise, as that can damage the cable.

Once the head of the auger hooks the blockage, pull the auger back a short distance to free some material from the clog, then push the rest on through. After breaking up the clog, pull the auger out slowly. Have a pail ready to catch whatever is brought out. Flush the drain with hot water. Dry the auger and coat it with a lubricant before putting it away.

Drain Assembly

Use an adjustable wrench to remove the trap, and let the contents spill into a pail. Clean the trap. If you are lucky, the clog will be there. You won't need to take the entire drain assembly apart to clear a clog, but if you decide to replace old or corroded pieces while you are under the sink, here's how to put everything back together.

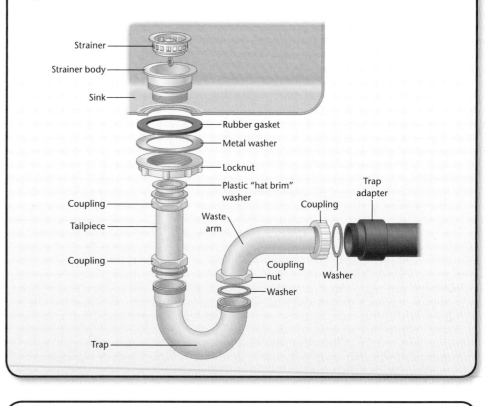

Preventing Drain Clogs

The best way to deal with clogs is to prevent them. Be alert to warning signs, such as sluggish drains. It's easier to clear a drain that's slowing down than one that's stopped completely. Some maintenance tips:
- Never pour grease down the kitchen drain. Most clogs are a buildup of grease and particles.
- Throw out coffee grounds. Don't wash them down the sink.
- Run the water for several seconds after using the garbage disposer.
- Clean strainers and pop-ups regularly.
- Chemical drain cleaners should never be used on drains that are stopped completely, but they can be used occasionally for clog prevention in an open drain. They may also help clear a partial block, where water is still draining somewhat. Choose an alkali cleaner (usually containing lye) to cut grease, and an acidic one to dissolve soap and hair.

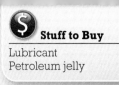

Stuff to Buy

Lubricant
Petroleum jelly

Time Commitment

Depends on the clog

Tools You'll Need

Plunger
Optional:
  Auger
  Bottle brush
  Rags
  Slip-joint pliers
  Spud wrench

Related Topics

Basin drain hookups, 52–53
Basin & tub pop-ups, 54–55
The DWV system, 12–13

Plunging

Make sure the suction cup on your plunger is big enough to cover the drain opening completely. Fill the sink a few inches deep, so the plunger cup will be under water. Use wet rags to block off all other nearby outlets, such as the second drain in a double sink or the overflow vent in a bathroom sink.

Coat the rim of the plunger cup with petroleum jelly to ensure a tight seal, and insert the plunger into the water at an angle so that little air gets trapped under it. Then, holding the plunger upright, apply 15 to 20 forceful downstrokes. The last motion should be a vigorous upstroke, snapping the plunger off the drain and, ideally, drawing the clog with it. Repeat the process two or three times before trying an auger.

Augering

To use an auger, first insert it down through the sink drain. If that doesn't clear the clog, put the auger in through the trap cleanout, if there is one.

If that doesn't work, remove the trap entirely, using a spud wrench or slip-joint pliers. Catch the water with a bucket and a drop cloth underneath. Try cleaning the trap with a flexible brush, such as a bottle brush, and soapy water.

If all of these methods fail, the clog is farther down the line and you'll need to insert the auger directly into the drainpipe. If the kitchen sink has a garbage disposer and the disposer drainpipe clogs, disassemble the trap and thread an auger into the drainpipe. If both basins of a double sink with a garbage disposer are clogged, snake the auger through the one without a disposer.

If running an auger through the sink drainpipe doesn't work, you're probably dealing with a clog in the main drain line.

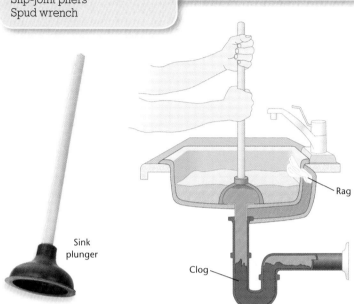

Sink plunger

Rag

Clog

Seat the plunger over the drain opening under a few inches of water and operate it forcefully 15 to 20 times, pulling it away at the end. Try a few more times if the drain doesn't unclog right away.

Safety Tips

- Wear gloves when unclogging a drain, and wash your hands with soap after completing the project.
- Chemical drain cleaners should never be used on a completely blocked drain. Don't plunge a blocked drain if a cleaner has been used. Cleaners can be useful for maintenance on an open drain, but they are hazardous and may cause injury to eyes and skin. Read and follow the instructions on the label.
- Don't mix an acid and an alkali cleaner, and don't look down the drain after pouring in a chemical.

To snake through the sink, first remove the pop-up mechanism or the sink strainer. Insert the auger into the drain opening and twist it down through the trap until you reach the clog.

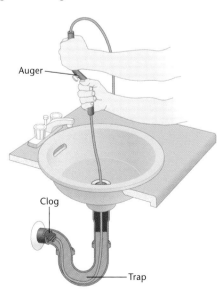

Auger

Clog

Trap

With the trap removed, feed the auger through the drainpipe as far as possible until it hits the clog.

Drain-and-trap auger

Clog

Elbow

Drainpipe

Unclogging Tub & Shower Drains

When a tub or shower drain won't clear, check whether other fixtures are affected. If they are, work on the main drain. If it is just the tub or shower, clear the clog as described on these pages, then install a strainer or hair trap to avoid the problem in the future.

First Things to Try

If your tub or shower won't drain at all, first try plunging the drain, using the same plunger and methods as you would for a sink. Don't use a drain cleaner. Fill the tub or shower pan a few inches (enough to cover the plunger cup), center the plunger over the drain, and pull up sharply 15 or 20 times. Try a second round of plunging if the first attempt fails.

If plunging doesn't work, remove the strainer or pop-up mechanism and clean it. If that wasn't the problem, use a drain-and-trap auger, or snake. A balloon bag and a garden hose, often used for main drains, might also work. If you use that method, however, never leave the hose in the drain, as a sudden drop in water pressure could siphon raw sewage back into the fresh-water supply.

Safety Tips

- Wear gloves when unclogging a drain, and wash your hands with soap after completing the project.
- Chemical drain cleaners should never be used on a completely blocked drain, and you should not plunge a blocked drain if a cleaner has been used. Cleaners can be useful for maintenance on an open drain, but they are hazardous and may cause injury to eyes and skin. Read and follow the instructions on the label.
- Don't mix an acid and an alkali cleaner, and don't look down the drain after pouring in a chemical.

Hair Trap

Install a hair trap, also called a strainer, to help prevent clogs in tubs and showers. This type sits inside the drain, so installation is a no-brainer. Others replace the pop-up.

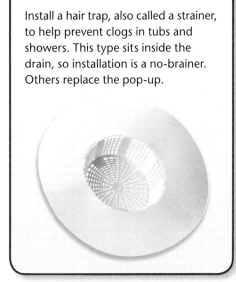

Unclogging a Tub Drain

REMOVE THE POP-UP

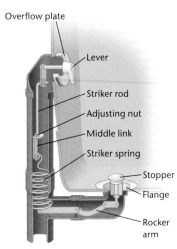

Overflow plate
Lever
Striker rod
Adjusting nut
Middle link
Striker spring
Stopper
Flange
Rocker arm

To take out the tub pop-up mechanism, remove the stopper and rocker arm by pulling the stopper straight up. Unscrew and remove the tub's overflow plate, then pull the entire assembly out through the overflow vent. Clear the parts of any hair or debris.

USING AN AUGER

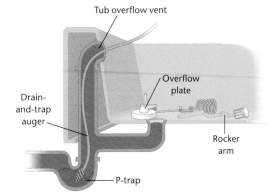

Tub overflow vent
Overflow plate
Drain-and-trap auger
Rocker arm
P-trap

To clear a tub P-trap, first remove the entire overflow and pop-up mechanism, if there is one. Then feed the auger down through the overflow pipe and into the trap.

If this does not clear the drain, remove the trap or its cleanout plug from below (if it's accessible) or through an access panel. Have a pail ready to catch water. Then insert the auger toward the main drain.

UNCLOGGING FROM A DRUM TRAP

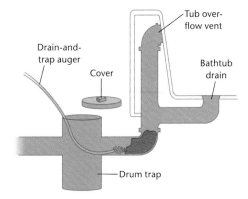

Tub over-flow vent
Drain-and-trap auger
Cover
Bathtub drain
Drum trap

Tubs in some older houses may have a drum trap. To clear a clog, bail all water from the tub and unscrew the drum trap's cover with an adjustable wrench. Watch for any water welling up around the threads. Remove the trap's cover and rubber gasket and clean out any debris. If the trap is still clogged, work the auger through the lower pipe toward the tub and, if necessary, in the opposite direction.

Tools You'll Need

Adjustable wrench
Auger
Garden hose
Plunger
Screwdriver

Related Topics

Basin & tub pop-ups, 54–55
The DWV system, 12–13
Roughing-in, 148–153
Unclogging a sink, 198–199

Unclogging a Shower Drain

Unclogging a shower drain is a lot like unclogging a bathtub drain but with fewer complications, as there is no overflow vent. As with any clogged drain, never use a chemical drain cleaner.

USING AN AUGER

You will probably need to unscrew and remove the strainer on the shower drain, as most augers are too wide to be threaded through it. To use the auger on a clog, probe the auger down the drain and through the trap until it hits the clog. Then turn the auger handle clockwise as you push on the clog.

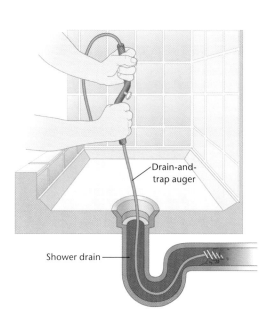

Drain-and-trap auger

Shower drain

USING A HOSE

You can also use a garden hose to clear a slow drain (but not a blocked drain). Attach the hose to a faucet with a threaded adapter, or run it to an outside hose bibb. Push the hose deep into the drain trap and pack wet rags tightly into the opening around

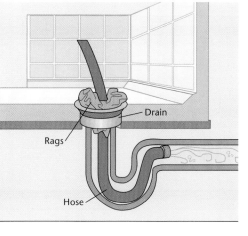

Drain

Rags

Hose

it. Hold the hose in the drain and turn the hose water alternately on full force and then abruptly off. Never leave the hose in a drain, as it could back-siphon wastewater into the water supply if the pressure suddenly dropped.

The source of a clog under this bathroom could be the shower or the tub, so plunge both before going to the trouble of removing either drain to make room for an auger.

Repairing Drains & Traps

Clogs in sinks, tubs, and showers sometimes result from mineral buildup in an old trap. Corrosion or stripped fittings can also cause traps to leak. In either case, the solution is to install a new trap and sometimes a new tailpiece.

Exposed plumbing need not be unattractive, as shown here. It also makes repairs to drains and traps a snap.

Buying Replacement Parts

Traps are often the first plumbing parts to cause leaks or clogs, so replacements are easy to find. Most home plumbing systems use P-traps, shaped like the letter P, which are the type generally shown in this book. If you discover an old-style S-trap, which exits the floor rather than the wall, you're not required to replace it with a P-trap unless you are remodeling or altering your plumbing system.

If possible, buy a new trap that's the same size as the old one. Brass and plastic traps last longest. New traps are sold as complete units, including washers and threaded couplings. You can also buy these fittings separately.

If the existing trap is attached to the tailpiece with a short extension and unthreaded slip couplings, you'll need to buy a new extension along with your new trap. A trap adapter is necessary to secure a waste arm to an unthreaded drain stubout.

A tailpiece that is cracked or corroded must be replaced. Replacements are available separately, not just as part of a trap assembly.

Fudging the Connections

As you replace older parts, you may be unable to find a standard replacement trap that readily lines up with your existing tailpiece, drain elbow, and wall stubout. Don't force unruly trap parts together and hope for the best, as they'll probably leak. Instead, try any of the other available options. A flexible trap can help bridge a mild misalignment between an existing tailpiece and a drain elbow. Tailpiece extensions are designed to fill vertical gaps between the tailpiece and the trap height. You can also buy 45-degree and 90-degree elbows to fine-tune a tricky angle between the trap and an off-center drain stubout.

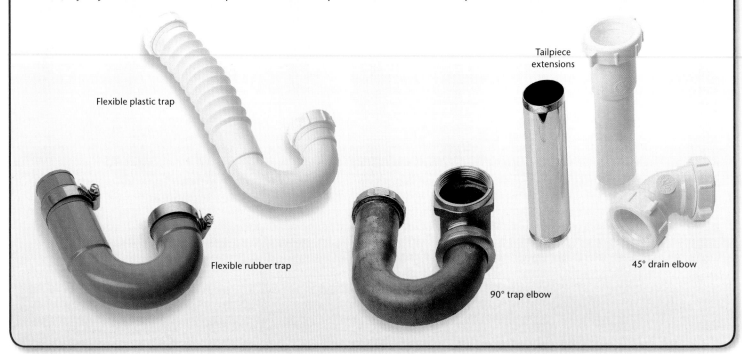

Flexible plastic trap

Flexible rubber trap

Tailpiece extensions

90° trap elbow

45° drain elbow

Stuff to Buy

Pipe-joint compound
Replacement tailpiece, if
   needed
Replacement trap

**Time
Commitment**

1–2 hours

**Tools
You'll Need**

Adjustable wrench
Slip-joint pliers
Spud wrench

**Related
Topics**

Adding a garbage disposer,
   80–81
Basin & drain hookups, 52–53
Basin & tub pop-ups, 54–55
Unclogging a sink, 198–199
Upgrading to a new sink, 76–79

Replacing a Trap

The first step in removing an old trap, after you've put a pail underneath it, is to remove the cleanout plug, if there is one, using an adjustable wrench. Use a spud wrench or taped slip-joint pliers to loosen the couplings that attach a swivel P-trap to the tailpiece and waste arm. Then take out the trap.

Slide the new couplings and washers into place, then install the new trap and tighten the couplings by hand. That should do it for plastic couplings. Finish tightening metal couplings with a spud wrench or slip-joint pliers. Be careful not to strip or overtighten the couplings. Run the water and check all connections for leaks while the fixture drains.

Replacing a Tailpiece

To remove the old tailpiece, unscrew the couplings that fasten it to the trap and the sink drain, then push the tailpiece down into the trap. Loosen the couplings at the drainpipe or waste arm and turn the entire trap at the drainpipe a quarter turn, just far enough to allow room to remove the tailpiece. You can now pull the old tailpiece out of the trap and replace it with a new one of the same length.

Coat all threads with pipe-joint compound to ensure a watertight seal, then tighten the couplings. Run some water and look for leaks.

1 Remove the old trap

- Place a pail to catch water
- Remove the cleanout plug, if there is one
- Loosen the couplings with a tape-wrapped wrench
- Remove the trap

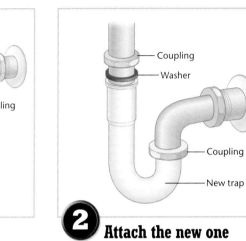

2 Attach the new one

- Slide a new coupling and washer over the tailpiece
- Slide another coupling over the waste arm
- If required, remove the waste arm to position the coupling
- Set the trap in place
- Tighten the couplings by hand
- For metal couplings, tighten further with a tool; don't overtighten

Replacing a Waste Arm

If the waste arm needs replacing along with the trap, loosen the coupling holding it to the drain stubout. For a plastic stubout, use a threaded adapter and coupling. For an unthreaded galvanized steel stubout, you can use a Mission coupling to bridge the gap.

PLASTIC STUBOUT

GALVANIZED STUBOUT

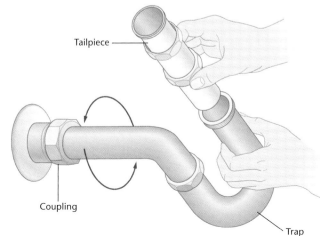

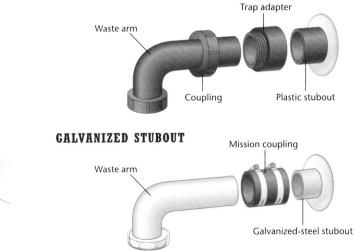

Unclogging a Toilet

The most common cause of a toilet clog is an obstruction in the trap. To dislodge it, first try using a toilet plunger. If that does not clear the clog, try a toilet auger, working with care to avoid scratching the bowl's finish.

STOP!
Wear gloves when unclogging a toilet, and wash your hands with soap after completing the project.

Avoiding an Overflow

As soon as you think a toilet bowl is overfilling, close the shutoff valve at the wall. You can also remove the tank lid and push the stopper or flapper into the flush valve, which will prevent more water from flowing out of the tank and into the bowl. Do these two steps in whichever order is fastest, but make sure the shutoff valve is closed when you are done. It's a good idea to check toilet shutoff valves periodically to make sure they will close easily when you need them to.

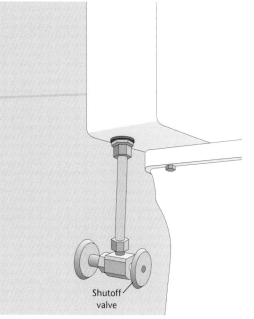

Shutoff valve

To help keep the tank from overflowing, close the shutoff valve by turning it clockwise.

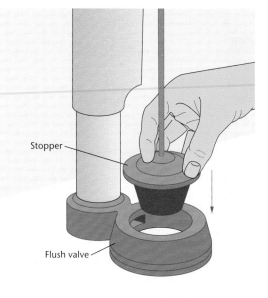

Stopper

Flush valve

If your toilet is about to overflow, remove the tank lid and push the flapper or stopper into the flush valve, then close the shutoff valve. Close the shutoff valve first if it's easier to reach and turn.

Tools You'll Need

Toilet auger, if needed
Toilet plunger

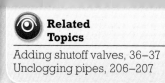

Related Topics

Adding shutoff valves, 36–37
Unclogging pipes, 206–207

Plunging

The best way to clear a toilet is with a plunger. A toilet plunger has a fold-out flange that fits snugly into the trap. To loosen a clog, pump the plunger up and down at least a dozen times and then pull it away sharply on the last stroke. The alternating pressure and suction should pull the obstruction back through the trap and into the bowl, allowing water to drain. Try this a few times if it doesn't work at first.

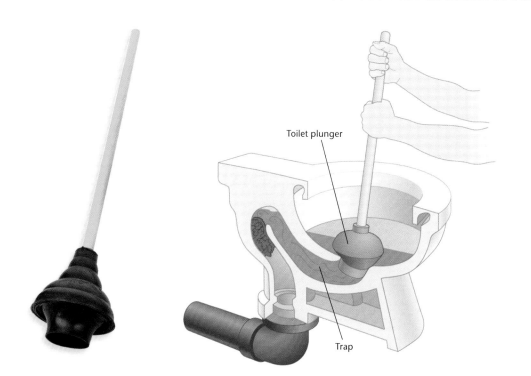

Toilet plunger

Trap

Using a Toilet Auger

If plunging merely pushes the obstruction a little deeper into the drain, use a toilet auger. Also called a closet auger, this tool reaches down well into the toilet trap. It has a curved tip that starts the auger with a minimum of mess, plus a protective housing to prevent the bowl from getting scratched. But you still need to take care to avoid marring the finish. Feed the auger into the trap, turning the handle clockwise as you go. Once you snag the clog, continue turning the handle as you pull out the debris.

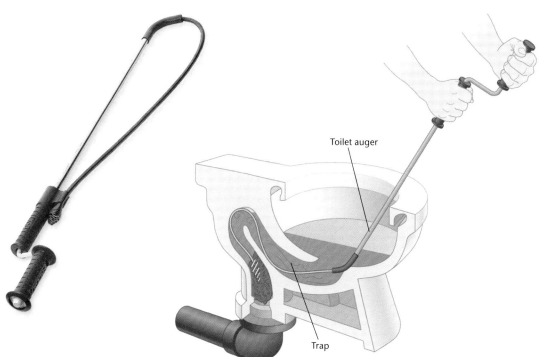

Toilet auger

Trap

Unclogging Pipes

If more than one drain won't clear, something is stuck farther along—in a branch drain, in the soil stack, or in the main drain—causing all of the fixtures upstream of the clog to stop up.

Troubleshooting a Clog

To troubleshoot a clog in your home's drain-waste-vent (DWV) pipes, first confirm that more than one fixture drain is affected. Otherwise, you're probably dealing with a local clog that can be cleared at the fixture.

Try using a drain-and-trap auger to reach the clog from a branch cleanout. In most new buildings, branch cleanouts are installed wherever a branch of the drainage system makes a sharp turn.

If that doesn't work, trace the pipes from the plugged fixtures to the main soil stack (the vertical pipe to which all the branches connect) and clear the soil stack. You can do so from the roof vent if you are comfortable working on a roof, if the roof is safe, and if you take all necessary precautions. Alternatively, you may be able to clear the soil stack from below, through the main cleanout.

A clog in the main drain can also be cleared through the main cleanout or the house trap.

Opening the Main Cleanout

The main cleanout, usually a Y- or T-shaped fitting, is near the bottom of the soil stack where it meets the main drain. Look for it in the basement or crawl space, or on an outside wall near a toilet.

Balloon bag

Put on rubber gloves and have pails, mops, and rags handy. Slowly remove the plug with a pipe wrench to release the backed-up water a little at a time and to prevent flooding.

Try to clear the clog first by using a hand-operated drain-and-trap auger. If that doesn't work, try a balloon bag (also called a blow bag) attached to a garden hose. The empty bag slips into a drainpipe, then fits snugly as it fills with water. Jets of water from the end of the bag then drive into the clog to break it apart. Don't leave the hose in the drain any longer than necessary, as a sudden drop in pressure could back-siphon sewage through the hose into the water supply.

Once the drain is clear, flush it with water. Coat the plug with pipe-joint compound and recap the cleanout. Clean and disinfect all tools and materials, and wash your hands.

Working from a Main Cleanout

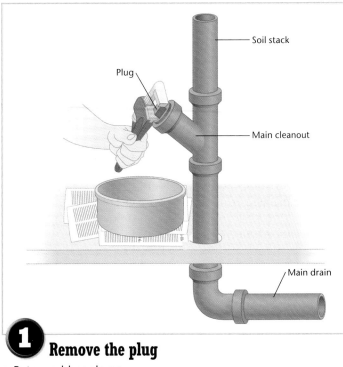

Soil stack
Plug
Main cleanout
Main drain

1 Remove the plug

• Put on rubber gloves
• Set up a pail on newspapers to catch wastewater
• Slowly remove the plug with a pipe wrench
• Release any water a little at a time

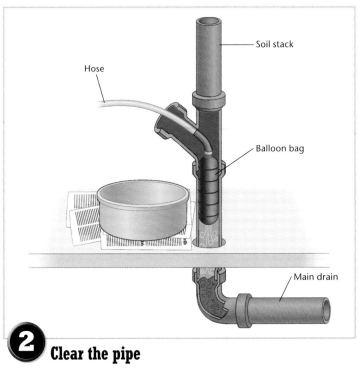

Soil stack
Hose
Balloon bag
Main drain

2 Clear the pipe

• Try using an auger, as you would for a clogged fixture
• If that doesn't work, try a balloon bag and a hose
• Make sure the balloon bag matches the drain diameter
• Once the drain is clear, flush it with water

Stuff to Buy

Balloon bag, also called
a blow bag

**Time
Commitment**

Depends on the clog

**Tools
You'll Need**

Auger
Garden hose
Pipe wrench
Wire brush

**Related
Topics**

Probing the House Trap

If your house has a trap, it's in the basement, crawl space, or yard near where the main drain leaves the house. Two cleanout plugs extend up to floor or ground level.

Before opening the house trap, put on rubber gloves and spread newspapers or rags around the cleanout. With a pipe wrench, slowly loosen the plug that's closer to the outside sewer line. Probe the trap and its connecting pipes with an auger.

Be prepared to withdraw the auger and cap the trap quickly when water starts to flow. When the flow subsides, open both ends of the trap and clean it out with an old wire brush.

Recap the pipes and flush them with water from an upstream cleanout.

Unclogging a Drain from the Roof

Don't work on a roof unless you feel comfortable with heights, and even then, be very careful. Assess the angle and condition of any roof before you stand or walk on it. Wear nonslip shoes, move carefully, avoid the edge, and wear a safety harness attached to a secure anchor.

Thread a hand-operated auger through the vent stack to the soil stack, working it from side to side. If the clog requires a power auger and the only access is from the roof, hire a professional.

Avoiding a Flood

Unlike a clogged sink drain, for example, where the pent-up water is confined to the sink basin in plain view, a clogged soil stack may be filled with backed-up wastewater, which can cause a small flood when you open a main cleanout or house trap, or after you release a clog. Work with care, as described here, by setting out newspapers and a bucket and releasing water into the bucket a little at a time.

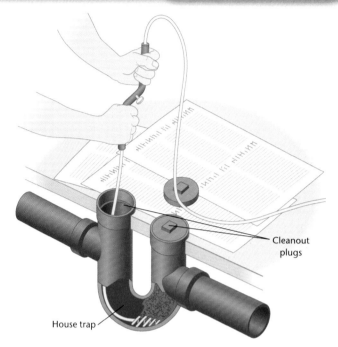

Cleanout plugs

House trap

WORKING FROM A HOUSE TRAP

Slowly loosen and remove the cleanout plug nearest the outside sewer line. Probe the trap and its connecting pipes with an auger. Work slowly, and be prepared to cap the trap quickly when water flows.

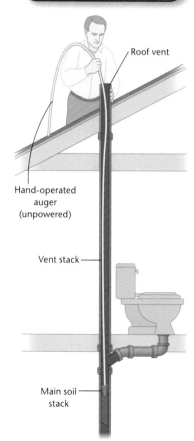

Roof vent

Hand-operated
auger
(unpowered)

Vent stack

Main soil
stack

About Power Augers

If these methods don't do the job, you might choose to rent a power auger, which is longer and more powerful than a hand-operated model.

Know your drain's diameter when you rent the auger, and ask for explicit safety instructions. Always plug the auger into a GFCI-protected receptacle, enlist a friend to help you run the auger, and be careful.

If you don't want to use a power auger, it's time to call a plumber or professional drain-cleaning company, which may decide to try cleaning the soil stack with a power auger through the vent stack from the roof. Because of the danger involved in working on a slick roof with an unwieldy power tool, you should not attempt this job yourself.

Fixing Compression Faucets

A compression faucet has separate hot- and cold-water handles that come to a spongy stop. When you turn a handle to close the faucet, it compresses a rubber seat washer. On the stem, compressed packing material prevents leaks.

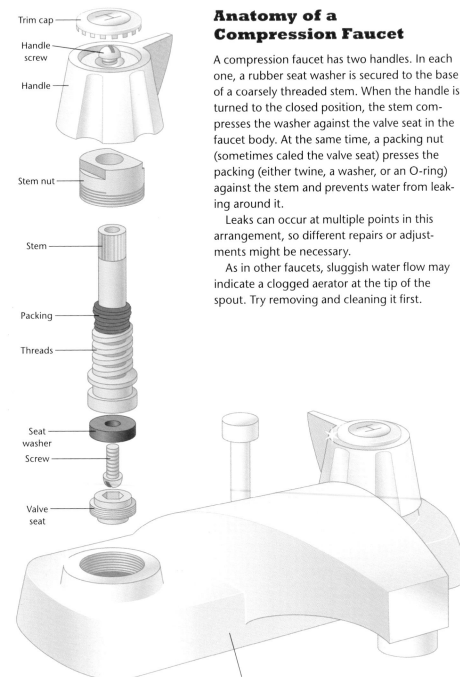

- Trim cap
- Handle screw
- Handle
- Stem nut
- Stem
- Packing
- Threads
- Seat washer
- Screw
- Valve seat
- Faucet body

Anatomy of a Compression Faucet

A compression faucet has two handles. In each one, a rubber seat washer is secured to the base of a coarsely threaded stem. When the handle is turned to the closed position, the stem compresses the washer against the valve seat in the faucet body. At the same time, a packing nut (sometimes caled the valve seat) presses the packing (either twine, a washer, or an O-ring) against the stem and prevents water from leaking around it.

Leaks can occur at multiple points in this arrangement, so different repairs or adjustments might be necessary.

As in other faucets, sluggish water flow may indicate a clogged aerator at the tip of the spout. Try removing and cleaning it first.

Leaks at a Handle

Leaks in compression faucets may occur around one of the handles or the spout. To fix a leak around a handle, first turn off the water at the sink's shutoff valves and open the faucet to drain the pipes. (If the sink does not have shutoffs, use the main house shutoff.)

Remove the handle and tighten the packing nut, then restore the water to see whether the leak has stopped. If that fails to solve the problem, remove the nut and replace the packing.

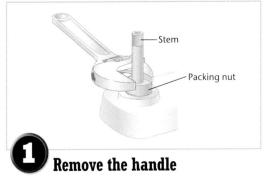

- Stem
- Packing nut

❶ Remove the handle

- Remove the trim cap
- Undo the handle screw
- Lift off the handle
- Tighten the packing nut and test to see whether the leak stops
- If it does not, turn off the water and remove the nut

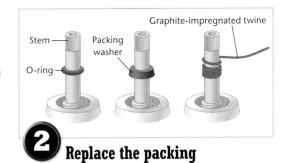

- Stem
- O-ring
- Packing washer
- Graphite-impregnated twine

❷ Replace the packing

- Remove an old O-ring or packing washer; scrape off old twine
- Replace an O-ring or packing washer with a new one
- For twine, wrap new packing twine clockwise around the stem
- Restore and tighten the packing nut
- Replace the handle and trim cap

Stuff to Buy

Pipe-joint compound
Replacement parts, as needed
Silicone grease

 **Tools You'll Need**

Screwdriver
Valve-seat dresser
Valve-seat wrench
Wrench

 **Related Topics**

Adding shutoff valves, 36–37
Installing bathroom faucets, 42–43
Installing a faucet, 70–71
Minor clogs & leaks, 218–219

Leaks at the Spout

If the faucet leaks from the spout, either a washer is defective or a valve seat is badly worn or corroded. First, find out whether the hot or cold side needs work by closing one of the shutoff valves at a time. Before proceeding, turn off water to the sink and drain the pipes by opening the faucet.

Take off the handle on the defective side and remove the stem. Check the washer first. If it's worn, replace it.

If the washer looks fine, a damaged valve seat could be causing the leak by preventing the seat washer from fitting properly. On most compression faucets, the valve

seat is replaceable, making for a relatively easy repair.

If the seat is built into the faucet, though, it may be possible to smooth it with a valve-seat dresser, which grinds down burrs. The valve seat is very soft, so smooth it just a little at a time with the dresser. If you do it too much, you might ruin the faucet.

Before you reassemble the faucet, lubricate the stem threads with silicone grease. If the threads are worn or stripped, consider replacing the stem.

Working on Valve Seats

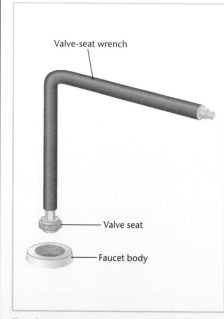

Replace a removable seat
- Insert a valve-seat wrench into the valve seat
- Turn it counterclockwise until the seat lifts out
- Coat the threads of an identical new one with pipe-joint compound
- Install the new seat

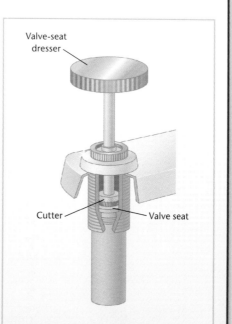

Dressing a nonremovable seat
- Insert the seat dresser
- Turn it clockwise once or twice until the seat is smooth—there's no need to overdo it
- Remove metal filings with a damp cloth

Inspecting the stem
- Remove the trim cap and handle
- Loosen the packing nut and stem with a wrench
- Unscrew the stem and lift it straight out
- Check the washer, stem threads, valve seat, and packing
- Replace bad components, including a stem with damaged or worn threads

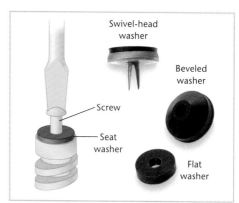

Replacing a seat washer
- Remove the screw and the cracked or worn washer
- Replace the old washer with an identical new one
- Replace the screw
- If the worn threads won't hold a screw, use a swivel-head washer

Fixing Disc Faucets

Disc faucets come in single-handle and double-handle versions. The core of a washerless disc faucet is a ceramic assembly that's sometimes called a cartridge. Openings in its disc line up with inlet holes, allowing water to flow through.

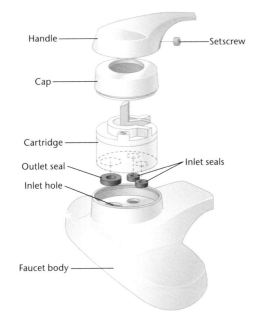

Handle — Setscrew
Cap
Cartridge
Outlet seal — Inlet seals
Inlet hole
Faucet body

Working on a Single-Handle Model

If there's a leak at the base of the faucet, one of the seals may be worn. Take the faucet apart as shown below. You'll find the set of seals under the cartridge. Replace all the seals with identical new ones.

Before You Begin

As in other faucets, sluggish water flow may indicate a clogged aerator at the tip of the spout. Try removing and cleaning it first. Before doing any other work on the faucet, turn off the water at the fixture shutoff valves or at the main house shutoff.

About Single-Handle Models

Two discs inside a sealed cartridge within a single-handle disc faucet control the mix and flow of hot and cold water. Raising the faucet handle lifts the upper disc, controlling the flow. Rotating the handle turns the lower disc, controlling the mix. The disc assembly seldom wears out, but if it does, you'll need to replace the entire cartridge. Most often, though, a worn inlet or outlet seal is the problem.

If the water flow is slow and you've already cleaned the aerator, there may be sediment built up in the inlet and outlet holes.

When you reassemble the dismantled faucet, be sure to realign the lugs in the disc assembly with slots in the base of the faucet.

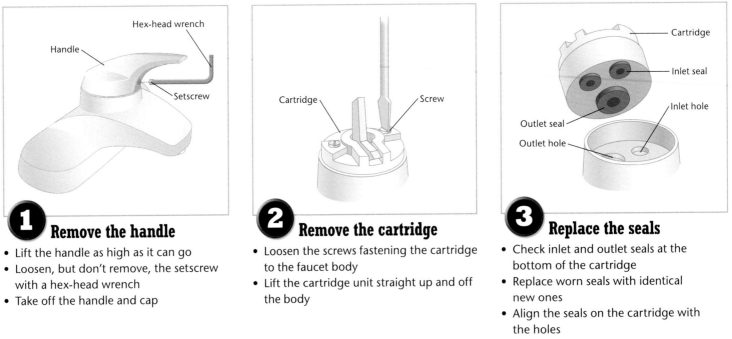

1 Remove the handle

Hex-head wrench
Handle
Setscrew

- Lift the handle as high as it can go
- Loosen, but don't remove, the setscrew with a hex-head wrench
- Take off the handle and cap

2 Remove the cartridge

Cartridge — Screw

- Loosen the screws fastening the cartridge to the faucet body
- Lift the cartridge unit straight up and off the body

3 Replace the seals

Cartridge
Inlet seal
Inlet hole
Outlet seal
Outlet hole

- Check inlet and outlet seals at the bottom of the cartridge
- Replace worn seals with identical new ones
- Align the seals on the cartridge with the holes
- Replace the cartridge
- Replace the cap and handle

Stuff to Buy

Replacement parts, as needed
Silicone grease

Tools You'll Need

Blunt knife
Hex-head wrench
Long-nose pliers
Screwdriver
Slip-joint pliers

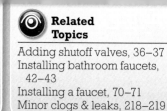

Related Topics

Adding shutoff valves, 36–37
Installing bathroom faucets, 42–43
Installing a faucet, 70–71
Minor clogs & leaks, 218–219

About Double-Handle Models

Double-handle models operate the same way as single-handle disc faucets, except they have a pair of cartridges, or stem-unit assemblies, plus a single rubber or plastic seal and a small spring on each side. Although cartridges in single-handle models rarely wear out, in double-handle models they may need to be replaced from time to time. More often, though, an inlet seal is the culprit.

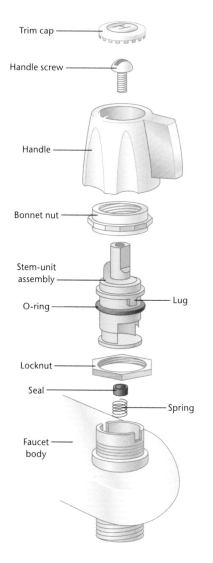

Working on a Double-Handle Model

If the faucet drips from the spout, the inlet seal and spring probably need replacing. If the faucet leaks from the handle, the O-ring or stem-unit assembly needs replacing.

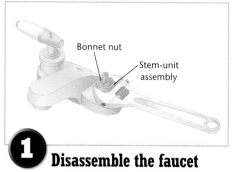

1 Disassemble the faucet

- If there's a trim cap, pop it off with a blunt knife or a screwdriver
- Undo the handle screw
- Pull off the handle
- Use a wrench to remove the bonnet nut

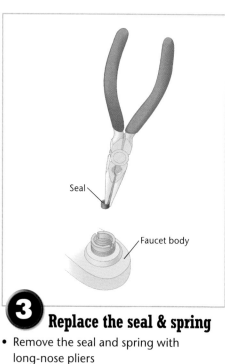

3 Replace the seal & spring

- Remove the seal and spring with long-nose pliers
- Replace them with parts for the same faucet model
- Put back the stem-unit assembly
- Line up the lugs with the slots in the faucet base
- Reassemble the faucet and handle

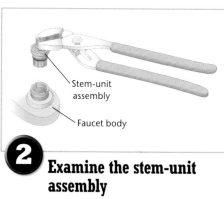

2 Examine the stem-unit assembly

- Pull out the stem-unit assembly with pliers
- Replace a worn O-ring with an identical new one
- Lubricate the new ring with silicone grease, then roll it on
- If the O-rings are good, replace the stem-unit assembly

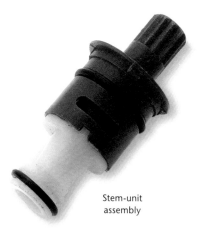

Stem-unit assembly

Fixing Ball Faucets

Degree of Difficulty
● Easy

Inside every ball faucet is a slotted metal ball atop two spring-loaded rubber seals. Water flows when openings in the rotating ball align with hot and cold inlets in the faucet body.

BALL FAUCET

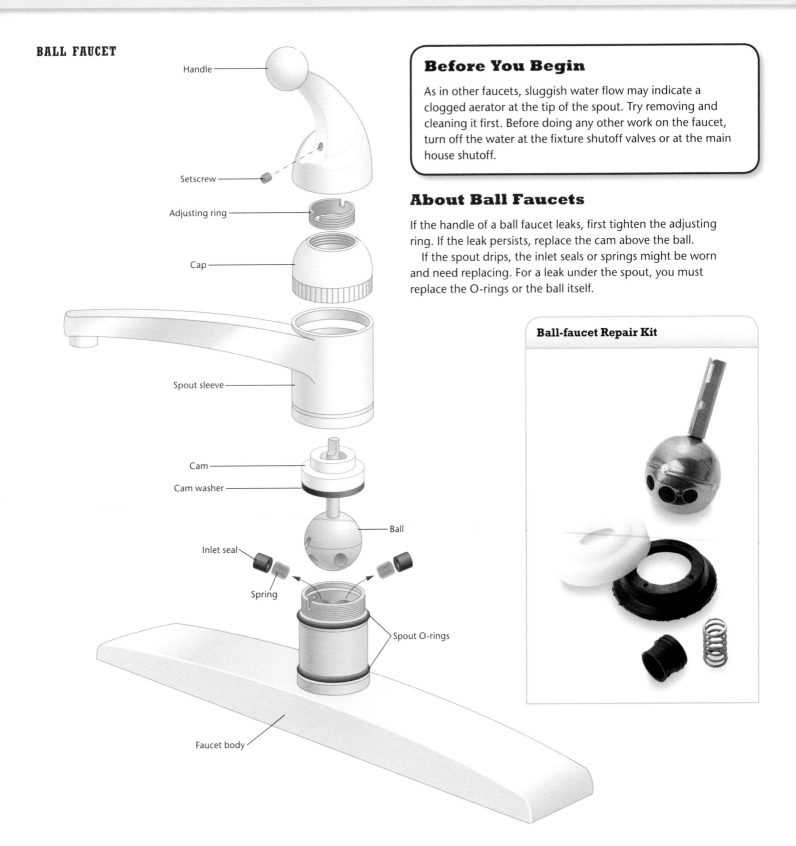

Handle

Setscrew

Adjusting ring

Cap

Spout sleeve

Cam

Cam washer

Ball

Inlet seal

Spring

Spout O-rings

Faucet body

Before You Begin

As in other faucets, sluggish water flow may indicate a clogged aerator at the tip of the spout. Try removing and cleaning it first. Before doing any other work on the faucet, turn off the water at the fixture shutoff valves or at the main house shutoff.

About Ball Faucets

If the handle of a ball faucet leaks, first tighten the adjusting ring. If the leak persists, replace the cam above the ball.

If the spout drips, the inlet seals or springs might be worn and need replacing. For a leak under the spout, you must replace the O-rings or the ball itself.

Ball-faucet Repair Kit

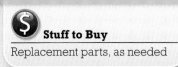

Tightening the Adjusting Ring

1 Remove the handle

- With a hex-head wrench, loosen the setscrew under the handle (leave the setscrew in the handle so it doesn't get lost in the drain)
- Lift off the handle

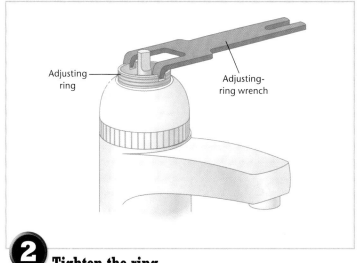

2 Tighten the ring

- Turn the ring clockwise to tighten it
- Use an adjusting-ring wrench as shown
- Alternatively, try a kitchen knife inserted into the notch

Replacing Faucet Parts

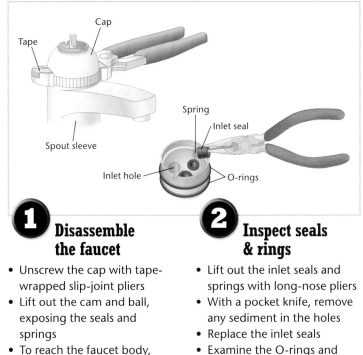

1 Disassemble the faucet

- Unscrew the cap with tape-wrapped slip-joint pliers
- Lift out the cam and ball, exposing the seals and springs
- To reach the faucet body, remove the spout sleeve

2 Inspect seals & rings

- Lift out the inlet seals and springs with long-nose pliers
- With a pocket knife, remove any sediment in the holes
- Replace the inlet seals
- Examine the O-rings and replace them if they're worn

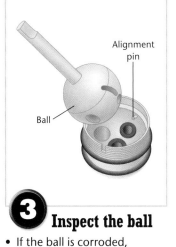

3 Inspect the ball

- If the ball is corroded, replace it
- Align the slot in the new ball with the alignment pin in the faucet body

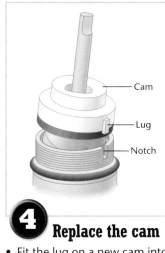

4 Replace the cam

- Fit the lug on a new cam into the notch on the faucet body
- Put the spout sleeve and cap back in place
- Tighten the adjusting ring and replace the handle

Fixing Cartridge Faucets

Also called washerless faucets, cartridge faucets have a series of holes in the stem-and-cartridge assembly that align to control the mix and flow of water. Usually, leaks occur because of worn O-rings or a faulty cartridge.

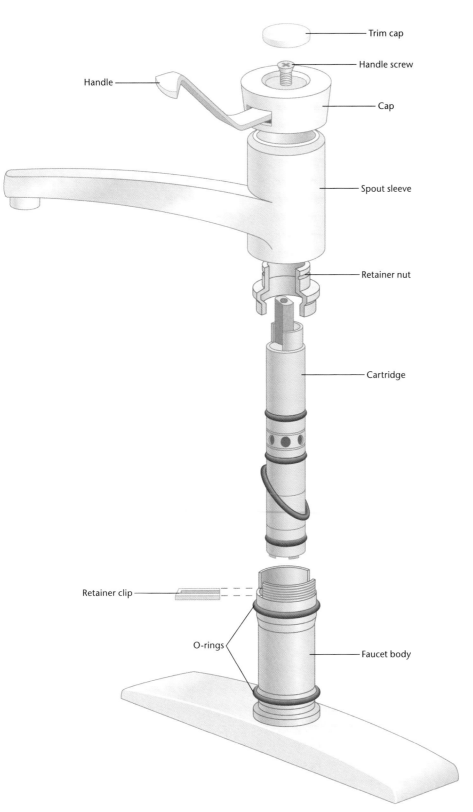

- Trim cap
- Handle screw
- Handle
- Cap
- Spout sleeve
- Retainer nut
- Cartridge
- Retainer clip
- O-rings
- Faucet body

Troubleshooting the Faucet

If the water flow is weak, try removing and cleaning the aerator. Before doing any other work, turn off the water at the sink shutoff valves or at the main house shutoff.

For a leaking faucet, look at the O-rings on the faucet body. If they're worn, replace them. If they're in good shape, remove the cartridge (for some cartridge brands, use a special tool designed for the purpose). If the cartridge is worn, replace it with an identical new one.

Cartridges vary, so read the manufacturer's instructions before installing one. The most common type has a flat side on the stem that must face the front. Otherwise, the hot and cold water supplies will be reversed. Be sure to fit the retainer clip snugly into its slot.

If a faucet is hard to turn, lubricating the cartridge O-rings with silicone grease should fix the problem.

Cartridge-faucet Replacement Parts

Stuff to Buy

Replacement parts, as needed
Silicone grease

Tools You'll Need

Cartridge remover (available
  for certain brands)
Pliers
Screwdriver

Related Topics

Adding shutoff valves, 36–37
Installing bathroom faucets,
  42–43
Installing a faucet, 70–71
Minor clogs & leaks, 218–219

Taking the Faucet Apart

Handle screw

Cap

1 Remove the handle

- Remove the handle screw with
  a screwdriver
- Lift off the cap and handle

Retainer clip

Retainer
nut

2 Remove the retainer clip

- Move the spout sleeve back and forth
- Gently pull the spout sleeve off the
  faucet body
- Pull out the retainer clip with a screwdriver or pliers

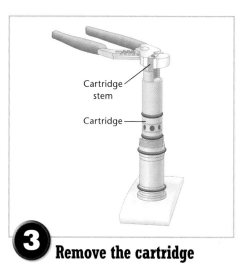

Cartridge
stem

Cartridge

3 Remove the cartridge

- Check the manufacturer's instructions
  for the specific cartridge
- For certain brands, use a special
  cartridge puller; otherwise, use pliers
- Grip the cartridge stem and pull
  it straight out; it might require a
  strong pull

Changing an O-Ring

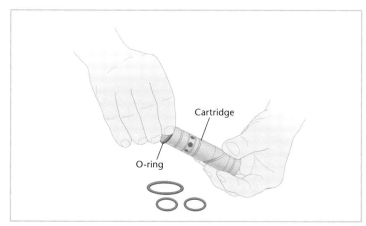

Cartridge

O-ring

- Examine the O-rings on the cartridge
- Replace them if they show signs of wear
- Apply silicone grease to the new O-rings before installing them

Replacing the Cartridge

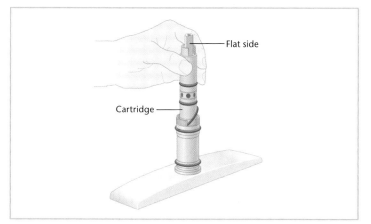

Flat side

Cartridge

- If the O-rings are in good shape, replace the cartridge
- Buy an identical replacement
- Read the instructions for removing the old one, as described
  above in Step 3
- Push the new cartridge down into the faucet body
- If there's a flat side, be sure it faces forward
- Fit the retainer clip snugly into its slot in the faucet body

Fixing Tub & Shower Faucets

Tub and shower faucets can be either compression or cartridge style (washerless) and are similar to sink faucets of those types. Water is directed from the faucet to the tub spout or showerhead by a diverter valve.

The spout in this bathtub has a diverter knob that forces water through the showerhead.

Before You Begin

Some tubs and showers have separate shut-offs that you can reach via an access panel. Open the access panel, close the valves, and then open the faucet to drain it before proceeding. If there's no local shutoff option, turn off the water at the main house shutoff and then drain the pipes by opening a faucet that is lower than the level of the tub faucet. You may also want to review some of the preceding pages on compression and cartridge sink faucets, which are similar to tub and shower faucets of the same types.

Useful Tool

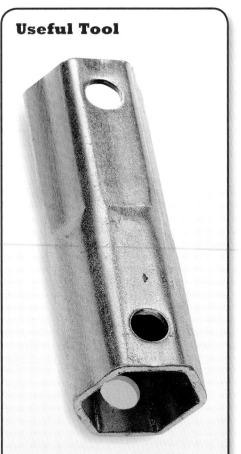

A shower socket, also called a tub wrench, will make short work of removing a tub faucet. The wrong tool could slip and damage the tub or the shower's tiles.

Stuff to Buy
Replacement parts, as needed

Tools You'll Need
Large wrench
Screwdriver
Shower socket, also called a tub wrench or bonnet wrench

Related Topics
Fixing cartridge faucets, 214–215
Fixing compression faucets, 208–209
Minor clogs & leaks, 218–219
Roughing-in, 148–153
Unclogging tub & shower drains, 200–201

TUB COMPRESSION FAUCET

TUB CARTRIDGE FAUCET

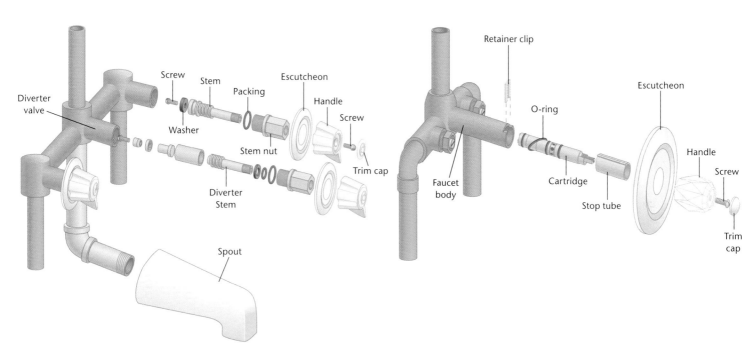

Spouts & Handles

Some tub and shower faucets have built-in diverter valves, while others have a knob on the tub spout. The latter type is easy to replace. Simply grip the old spout with a tape-wrapped wrench and turn it counterclockwise to remove, then hand-tighten the new spout into place.

To work on a recessed tub faucet, first unscrew the handle and remove the escutcheon. To access the packing nut (also called a stem nut) in a compression faucet, grip the nut with a deep shower socket (also known as a tub wrench or bonnet wrench).

Replacing a tub faucet

- Pry off the cap
- Unscrew the handle
- Remove the escutcheon
- Use a tub wrench to turn the packing nut
- Replace the faucet with a similar one
- Follow the manufacturer's instructions for the new faucet

Minor Clogs & Leaks

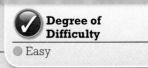

Degree of Difficulty
● Easy

When water is flowing slowly through faucet aerators, sink sprayers, or showerheads, the culprit is often built-up minerals or dirt. Also notice and correct small leaks at sprayers, showerheads, and sink strainers.

Cleaning Faucet Aerators

The aerator at the tip of most faucets mixes air and water for a smoother flow. But minerals or dirt particles in the water can clog the screen and disc over time. If dirt is the problem, unscrew the aerator from the end of the spout and clean the parts. To loosen stubborn connections, soak them with penetrating oil.

You might be able to clean an aerator as is, or you may need to disassemble it for a more thorough going over. Clean the screen with a brush and soapy water. Use a pin or toothpick to open any clogged holes in the disc. Flush all parts with water, then reassemble them if necessary.

If mineral deposits are present, try soaking the aerator in a mixture of vinegar and water. If the deposits won't go away, or if the aerator parts are damaged, it's best to replace the aerator.

Washer

Perforated disc

Screen

Body

Cleaning Sink Sprayers

Retaining screw   Perforated disc   Nozzle

Screw cover   Body   Washers

Spray head

Washer

Plastic ring

Retainer clip

Coupling

Hose

A sink sprayer is attached to a faucet by a coupling nut under the sink. Sprayers have nozzle aerators that sometimes clog, and you can clean one in the same way as a faucet aerator.

Leaks can occur at the spray head, in the hose, or at the diverter valve inside the base of the faucet, which reroutes water from the spout to the sprayer. Remember to turn off the water and drain the faucet before correcting leaks.

Common Problems & Solutions

FIXING A LEAKY SPRAY HEAD
If the hose leaks at the spray head, try tightening the fitting at the base of the head. If that doesn't work, unscrew the head from the fitting and check the washer under the spray head. Replace it if it's worn.

REPLACING A LEAKY HOSE
If the hose leaks where it attaches under the sink, undo the fitting from the end of the hose by removing the retainer clip. Then undo the coupling nut under the sink with slip-joint pliers or a basin wrench. If the hose connects directly under the faucet with no coupling nut, unthread the hose. Inspect the entire hose for kinks or cracks. Replace a worn hose with a new one. Nylon-reinforced vinyl is the most durable.

CLEANING THE DIVERTER VALVE
If the sink sprayer won't work or has reduced flow even with a clean aerator, the diverter valve might be clogged with deposits or scale. To get to the diverter, you'll need to take off the faucet spout. Some spouts simply unscrew, while on others you might have to take apart the handle. Once you have access to the inside of the faucet body, loosen the screw atop the diverter valve just enough to lift the valve from the seat. Take apart the valve and clean the outlets and surfaces with an old toothbrush and water. Soaking the parts in vinegar or commercial lime dissolver will help get rid of scale.

Stuff to Buy

Lime dissolver
Penetrating oil
Plumber's putty
Replacement parts, as needed
Vinegar

**Tools
You'll Need**

Basin wrench
Hammer
Pin or toothpick
Screwdriver
Slip-joint pliers
Spud wrench

**Related
Topics**

Adding a faucet & sprayer,
    72–73
Showerheads, 56–57
Upgrading to a new sink, 76–79

Cleaning Showerheads

A showerhead simply screws on and off the shower arm stubout. Whenever you remove or install one, hold the stubout steady so it doesn't turn pipes inside the wall and create a major new problem.

If a showerhead is leaking or spraying wildly, unscrew it and tighten all connections with slip-joint pliers (wrap the jaws with tape to avoid damaging the finish on the head and stubout). If that doesn't solve the problem, replace the washer between the showerhead and the swivel ball.

If water flow is sluggish, there's likely a clog in the screen or faceplate. Remove the center screw and clean the faceplate and screen with a toothbrush and vinegar.

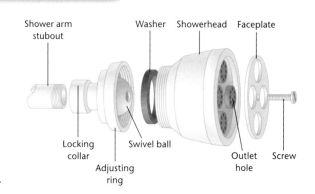

About Sink Strainers

There are two types of sink strainers. One is held in place by a locknut, the other by a retainer and three thumbscrews. An improper seal between the strainer body and the sink is the most common cause of leaks.

If the strainer body isn't loose, you'll likely need to replace the metal or fiber washer or rubber gasket between the locknut or retainer and the sink bottom. This requires disassembling the strainer from under the sink.

DISASSEMBLING A STRAINER

Unscrew the coupling with a spud wrench or slip-joint pliers to free the tailpiece. To loosen a locknut, use a hammer to tap an old screwdriver against the lugs, or use a spud wrench. To remove a retainer-type strainer, simply undo the three thumbscrews on the retainer. Remove the locknut or retainer, the washer, and the gasket and lift the strainer from the sink.

REINSTALLING THE STRAINER

Thoroughly clean the area around the opening and check the gasket and washer for wear. Purchase exact replacements if needed. Apply a 1-inch-thick bead of plumber's putty around the underlip of the strainer body and insert it into the sink opening. Press down firmly for a tight seal.

For a strainer with a locknut, work from beneath the sink to place the rubber gasket and metal washer onto the strainer body. Hand-tighten the locknut. Have a helper hold the strainer from above to prevent it from turning while you snug up the locknut with a spud wrench. If you're working alone, open the handles of a pair of pliers inside the strainer to hold it while you tighten the nut.

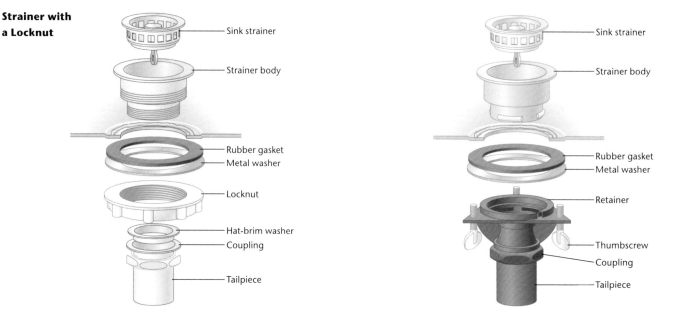

Strainer with a Locknut

Strainer with a Retainer

Fixing a Running Toilet

Degree of Difficulty
● Easy

The workings of a toilet might seem complex, but most aspects are quite simple. A constantly trickling toilet usually requires little more than adjustments to the float mechanism or the flush-valve assembly.

Three Common Adjustments

In an old-style toilet mechanism, you'll see a float ball at the end of a float arm. Bending the float arm downward or away from the back of the toilet tank may stop the water from running. Adjust it a bit at a time and don't overbend it. If a float ball is filled with water, it should be replaced.

In a toilet tank with a modern fill valve, there is usually a float cup on the valve assembly. Slide the float cup up or down to adjust the water level. Some toilets have a pressure-sensing device at the flush valve instead.

Tank water levels should be within about ¾ inch of the top of the overflow valve. Many tanks have the level marked on an inside surface.

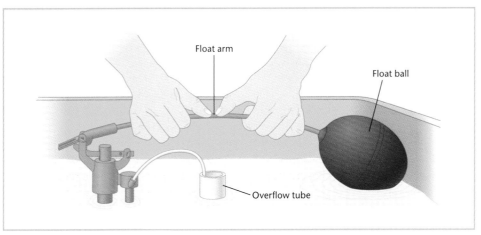

Float arm adjustment

- Bend a float arm up to raise the water level in a tank, or down to lower it
- Use both hands, working carefully to avoid damage
- Replace a cracked or water-filled float ball by unscrewing the old one
- Alternatively, put in a modern fill valve

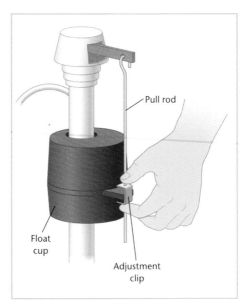

Float-cup adjustment

- Squeeze the adjustment clip on the pull rod
- Move the cup up or down to adjust the level

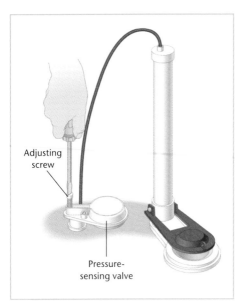

Pressure-sensing valve

- Turn the adjusting screw on a pressure-sensing valve to change the water level
- Turn it clockwise to raise the level, counterclockwise to drop it
- One turn should change the level by about 1 inch

Detecting Smaller Problems

A toilet that runs constantly can waste more than 1,000 gallons of water a day, though at least you can hear it. A toilet that seeps water into the bowl more slowly is harder to detect and can waste as much as 40 gallons a day.

To check your toilet, add about 12 drops of colored dye to the water in the tank (blue food coloring will work, or ask your water company for dye tablets). Then wait a few minutes to see whether the dye flows into the bowl. If it does, water is escaping either through the top of the overflow tube or past the tank flapper through the valve seat. Try the repairs on these pages to resolve the problem.

If you see blue water outside the tank, typically on the mounting bolts below it, you have a different kind of leak. Repair a leaking toilet as shown later in this book.

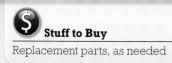
Stuff to Buy

Replacement parts, as needed

Tools You'll Need

Adjustable wrench
Fine steel wool
Screwdriver

Related Topics

Conserving water, 14–15
Replacing the fill valve, 222–223
Setting a toilet, 226–227
Stopping toilet leaks, 224–225
Toilets, 64–65

Replacing a Flapper Tank Stopper

A common cause of a continuously running toilet is a defective seal between the flapper (or, in older toilets, a stopper) and the flush-valve seat. To check for this, remove the lid and flush the toilet. Watch the flapper or stopper, which should fall straight down onto the valve seat. If it does not, make sure the chain (for a flapper) or the guide rod (for a stopper) is centered over the flush valve.

To make further repairs, turn off the water to the toilet, flush the toilet, and bail out or sponge out the remaining water. When the repairs are complete, turn the valve back on to refill the tank.

If the valve seat is rough and pitted, scour it smooth. If a stopper or flapper is worn, overly soft, or rigid and brittle, replace it. (Replace a stopper with a flapper setup.) Also replace a cracked overflow tube.

If those repairs don't solve the problem, you might need to replace the entire flush-valve assembly.

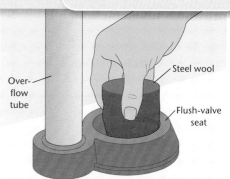

Touching up the valve seat

- Inspect the valve seat for corrosion or mineral buildup
- Gently scour it with fine steel wool

❶ Replace the flapper

- Remove the old flapper by detaching its collar from the overflow tube
- Install a new flapper

❷ Install & adjust the chain

- Attach the chain to the flapper
- Adjust the length of the chain, allowing about ½ inch of slack when the flapper is in place
- Hook the other end of the chain to the handle-operated trip lever

Fixing a Loose Handle

Another common problem related to a toilet's flush mechanism is a loose handle or trip lever, which can cause an inadequate or erratic flush cycle. Some handles have setscrews that might need tightening, so check that first. Otherwise, tighten the locknut that attaches the assembly to the tank, taking care to avoid cracking the tank through overtightening. This locknut tightens counterclockwise, unlike most nuts. If tightening the locknut doesn't fix the problem, replace the handle and the trip lever.

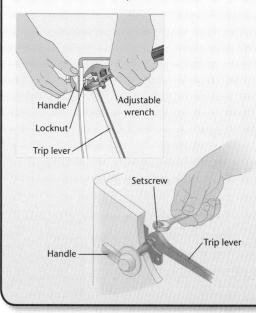

Handle
Adjustable wrench
Locknut
Trip lever

Setscrew
Trip lever
Handle

Replacing a Flush-valve Assembly

- Remove the tank's mounting bolts and gaskets
- Lift the tank off the toilet
- Remove the spud washer, then unscrew the locknut under the tank
- Remove the conical washer and the flush-valve assembly
- Assemble the replacement parts
- Reattach the tank as before

Conical washer
Mounting bolt
Locknut
Spud washer

Replacing the Fill Valve

Modern fill valves are fairly easy to install, either to replace an old-style ballcock and float arm or to replace a fill valve that has failed. Be sure your new fill valve is designed to prevent backflow (siphoning) from the tank into the water supply.

TOILET WITH BALLCOCK

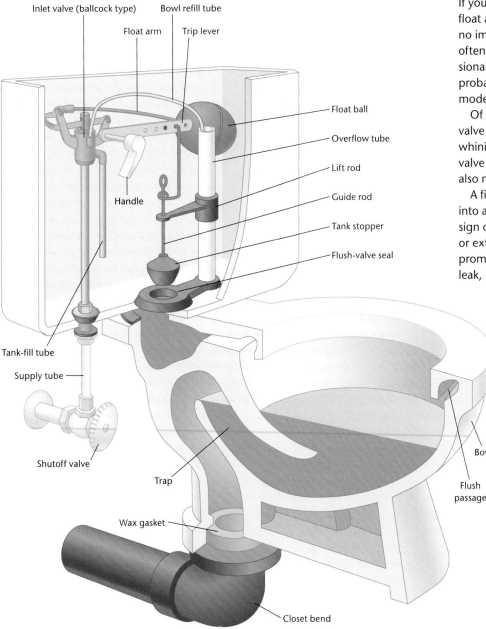

Inlet valve (ballcock type)
Bowl refill tube
Float arm
Trip lever
Float ball
Overflow tube
Lift rod
Guide rod
Tank stopper
Flush-valve seal
Handle
Tank-fill tube
Supply tube
Shutoff valve
Trap
Bowl
Flush passage
Wax gasket
Closet bend

Some toilets might still have the setup shown here, with a ballcock inlet valve and float arm. Most toilets today feature two updates: a modern fill valve (right) and a chain-operated flapper, rather than a stopper on a guide rod. Water flows from a shutoff valve at the wall through a supply tube and is controlled at the tank by the ballcock or fill valve, either of which fills the tank to a preset level. Water exits the tank into the bowl through the flush valve, which is sealed by the stopper or flapper when not in use. Waste exits the bowl through an internal trap that prevents noxious gases from entering the house.

When to Replace

If you have a toilet with a traditional ballcock and float arm (with a float ball) that work fine, there's no immediate reason to change them. You can often keep the mechanism going with an occasional new float ball. But if the mechanism fails, it's probably time to convert to a simpler, inexpensive modern fill valve.

Of course, you'll also need a replacement fill valve if the old one fails. If your toilet seems to be whining or whistling, that usually means a new fill valve is needed. A fill valve that runs continuously also needs to be replaced.

A fill valve that seems fine yet sometimes springs into action when no flush has occurred might be a sign of a problem elsewhere. It could be an internal or external leak that is lowering the water level, prompting the refill to occur. In that case, fix the leak, not the fill valve.

Modern Fill Valve

Modern fill valves are easier to install, simple, inexpensive, and relatively trouble-free. Be sure to buy one that protects against back-siphoning water from the tank into the water supply. Look for words like "antisiphon" or "meets plumbing codes." Follow the manufacturer's installation instructions. Note that most require you to hand-tighten the plastic nuts that hold them in place, rather than using a wrench.

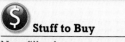
Stuff to Buy

New fill valve
Penetrating oil
Replacement washer, if needed
Supply tube

Time Commitment

1 hour

Tools You'll Need

Adjustable wrench
Locking-grip pliers

Related Topics

Fixing a running toilet, 220–221
Setting a toilet, 226–227
Stopping toilet leaks, 224–225
Toilets, 64–65

Replacing the Valve

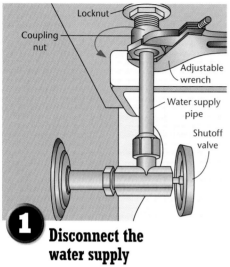

1 Disconnect the water supply

- Turn off the water and empty the tank
- Set a bucket and towels to catch water from the supply tube or pipe
- Use a wrench (carefully) on a metal coupling nut; penetrating oil helps loosen a corroded nut
- Loosen a plastic nut by hand
- Detach the supply tube or pipe from the tank, draining it into the bucket
- Replace a worn supply tube or pipe, preferably with a braided stainless-steel supply tube

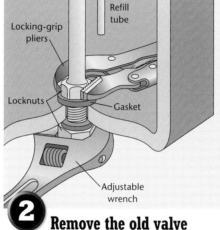

2 Remove the old valve

- For an old ballcock (shown here), use locking-grip pliers to secure the base of the assembly inside the tank
- Underneath the tank, carefully unfasten the locknut with an adjustable wrench
- For an old fill valve, loosen plastic nuts by hand, following the manufacturer's instructions
- Remove the ballcock or fill valve

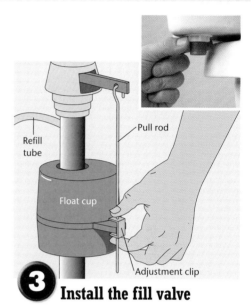

3 Install the fill valve

- Assemble and adjust the valve according to the manufacturer's directions
- Install it in the tank hole and tighten it with the interior and exterior locknuts (see inset)
- Place the refill tube as directed at the top of the overflow tube
- Below the tank, attach the supply tube or pipe, tightening the plastic nut by hand
- Turn on the water and check for leaks
- Adjust the water level with the float cup

Stopping Toilet Leaks

Degree of Difficulty
● Moderate

A leaking toilet wastes water, can cause mildew and rust stains, and can damage your bathroom's floor. In most cases, it is fairly easy to locate leaks and fix them, which is always going to be cheaper than waiting for things to get worse.

Is It Really Leaking?

Before you try to fix a leak, make sure the toilet isn't simply "sweating"—accumulating water beads as humid air contacts the porcelain. Water from a sweating toilet can run down to the bolts, creating the illusion of a leak. If you're not sure, use some blue food coloring in the tank water, then check with some toilet paper to see whether the color turns up on the bolts. If it does, there's a leak. Otherwise, the water is just condensation.

You can ignore a sweating toilet if the condensation occurs only rarely and mildly. Otherwise, the water could cause mildew or even some water damage. For heavier sweating, add a tank liner. Such liners insulate the exterior of the tank from the water inside, reducing the temperature difference that causes humid air to condense.

Where Toilets Leak

Toilet leaks can occur in several places, as shown at upper right. Water can escape from a worn supply tube, from the points where the tube connects to the shutoff or the tank; from around the base of the fill valve; from the mounting bolts connecting the tank to the bowl; from around the tank-to-bowl valve; and at the base of the bowl.

Within the toilet, water-wasting leaks can run from the tank into the bowl. Such leaks are dealt with on previous pages.

If a leak is coming from a crack in the tank or bowl, it is time for a new toilet.

LEAKS AT MOUNTING BOLTS

If the toilet tank is leaking at the mounting bolts, empty the tank and inspect the heads of the bolts and the gaskets inside. Replace worn gaskets and try gently tightening the bolts (overtightening could crack the toilet).

If there is a leak when the toilet is flushed, remove the tank and replace the spud washer on the bottom of the flush valve.

LEAKS AT THE BASE

Normally, leaks at the base of a toilet occur because the wax gasket needs replacing, either because it's deteriorated over time or because the bolts attaching the toilet to the floor have loosened, letting the toilet move enough to break the seal. If the leak has been there a while, the floor could be damaged, requiring structural repair. The best way to avoid such complications is to repair any leak right away.

Replacing a gasket is very much like setting a new toilet, as shown on pages 226 and 227. It's a heavy-lifting job you may prefer to leave to a plumber. The only difference when you're replacing a gasket is that you start by performing the installation steps in reverse—disconnecting the water supply,

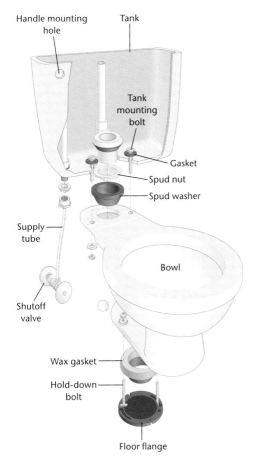

removing the tank, and detaching the bowl from the floor.

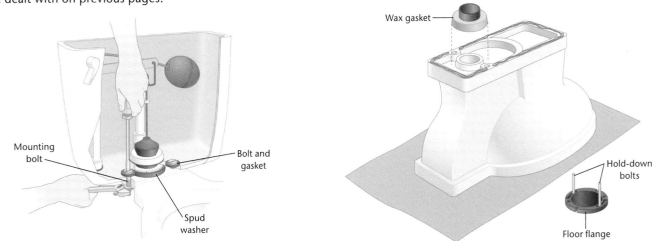

Stuff to Buy

Penetrating oil
Supply tube (braided stainless
   steel)

**Tools
You'll Need**

Adjustable wrenches
Screwdriver

**Related
Topics**

Fixing a running toilet, 220–221
Replacing the fill valve, 222–223
Setting a toilet, 226–227
Toilets, 64–65

Replacing the Supply Tube

Replace an old, leaking supply pipe or tube with a new flexible supply tube. Braided stainless steel is a good choice.

1 Close the shutoff valve
- Turn off the supply valve at the wall or floor
- Flush the toilet to empty most of the water from the tank

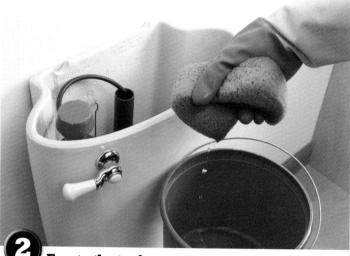

2 Empty the tank
- Bail out the rest of the tank water
- Swab up the leftover water with a sponge, rag, or towel

3 Detach the old supply tube
- Be sure to turn the coupling nut that attaches the supply tube (not the locknut above it)
- For an old metal nut, use an adjustable wrench, carefully
- Penetrating oil can help loosen a nut that's difficult to turn
- Remove an old plastic nut by hand
- Also detach the tube from the shutoff valve

4 Measure from the shutoff
- Take a quick measurement from the shutoff to the toilet tank
- Don't worry about being too precise; you're just confirming the length is typical for a toilet

5 Attach the new tube
- Buy the correct length of tube; this is usually a standard length for toilets
- Most braided stainless-steel tubes come with the nuts and washers already in place
- Attach the supply tube to the tank, tightening the plastic coupling nut by hand
- Attach the other end to the shutoff valve the same way
- Turn on the water and check for leaks

Setting a Toilet

Whether you're replacing the floor gasket on an old toilet or installing a new model, setting a toilet is a fairly straightforward task. Consider hiring a plumber if you don't want to maneuver the heavy bowl into place.

Degree of Difficulty
● Challenging

Before You Begin

Replacing a toilet or simply resetting your existing one to replace the gasket is generally an afternoon project. (Installing a toilet in a new location, of course, would be an entirely different, and far more ambitious, proposition, requiring a new supply line and drainpipe.)

For a new toilet, you might need to buy a few hold-down bolts, the wax gasket that seals around the drain, and a flexible supply tube. If you're replacing an existing toilet's wax gasket, this might be a good time to replace the supply tube as well. Wax gaskets are sold with and without plastic collars. Both work well.

Before beginning the installation, turn off the water at the shutoff valve or at the house's main shutoff. Flush the toilet to empty the bowl and tank, then sponge out any remaining water. Disconnect the supply tube from the tank. Detach the tank from the bowl and set it aside, leaving it upright (but securely supported) so that the mechanisms inside will be undisturbed.

Lining Up the Bolts

Before setting the toilet in place on the floor flange, push drinking straws onto the bolts. This will make it easier to line up the bolts with the holes at the toilet's base.

How to Do It

1 Remove the old bowl

- Pry the caps off the hold-down bolts attaching the bowl to the floor
- Remove the nuts with an adjustable wrench
- For corroded bolts, use penetrating oil or a hacksaw; avoid marring the bowl
- Rock the bowl gently to break the gasket seal
- Lift and remove the bowl, tilting it forward slightly to avoid spilling more water

YOU CAN BUILD

Stuff to Buy
Caulk
Penetrating oil
Plastic shims
Plumber's putty
Replacement parts, as needed
Wax gasket

Time Commitment
A few hours

Tools You'll Need
Adjustable wrench
Hacksaw
Level
Putty knife

Related Topics
Roughing-in, 148–153
Stopping toilet leaks, 224–225
Toilets, 64–65

2 Prepare the flange

- Stuff a rag into the drainpipe to keep out sewer gas
- Using an old putty knife, scrape the wax gasket's remains from the flange
- Replace any damaged hold-down bolts or a damaged flange
- Inspect the floor for rot and arrange for repairs if needed

3 Prepare the bowl

- Turn the new bowl upside down on a cushioned surface
- For a gasket with a plastic collar, confirm that the collar fits into the flange
- Place the new wax gasket over the horn on the bottom of the bowl
- Face the tapered side of the gasket away from the bowl
- For a gasket with a collar, face the collar away from the bowl
- Apply a thin bead of caulk around the toilet base

4 Place the bowl

- Remove the rag from the drainpipe
- Make sure the hold-down bolts are in place on the flange, pointing upright
- Gently lower the bowl into place on the flange, using the bolts as guides
- Press down firmly while gently twisting and rocking, but avoid any repositioning
- Using a level, check that the bowl is straight
- Use plastic shims if necessary for minor adjustments

5 Bolt the bowl into place

- Hand-tighten the washers and nuts onto the bolts
- Alternatively tighten the nuts with a wrench until the toilet is seated firmly
- Snug up the nuts, but don't overtighten them, as this can crack the bowl
- Fill the caps with plumber's putty and place them over the bolt ends

6 Add the tank

- For a new toilet, prepare the parts in the tank as needed
- Place a rubber tank cushion between the tank and the bowl
- Position the tank on the bowl
- Insert the mounting bolts, replacing the gaskets if they are worn
- Tighten the nuts and washers onto the mounting bolts
- Double-check that the mechanisms in the tank are in order

7 Hook up the supply tube

- Remember to hand-tighten the supply tube so you don't crack the tank
- Open the shutoff valve
- Check for leaks

First Aid for Disposers

The two types of garbage disposers are batch-feed, which is activated with the turn of a stopper, and continuous-feed, which is controlled by a wall switch. Problems with either type usually involve jams or clogs. Leaks are less common.

Maintaining Your Disposer

Taking care of your disposer mainly means using it appropriately—by not overloading it and by allowing water to run for several seconds to clear the drain after you operate the unit. See the manufacturer's instructions for additional tips.

You'll also need to clear jams when they occur, and perhaps clean the blades occasionally with a load of ice cubes. Water dripping from a disposer usually indicates one or more gaskets are worn and need replacing.

Many professionals will service disposers in your home. If you need to take a unit to a shop, first disconnect it from the power source. Then separate the disposer from the drain elbow and loosen the mounting screws to release it from the sink flange.

Safety Tips

- Before you start work, unplug the disposer or shut off power to it at the electrical service panel, not just at the local on-off switch.
- Never put your hand in the disposer. Use pliers or kitchen tongs to remove an object.
- Never pour a chemical drain cleaner into a disposer, as it could damage the unit.

DISPOSER DETAILS

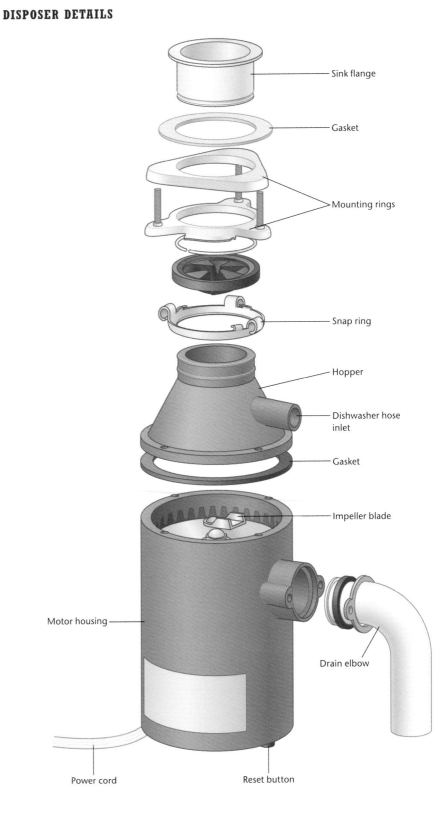

Sink flange

Gasket

Mounting rings

Snap ring

Hopper

Dishwasher hose inlet

Gasket

Impeller blade

Motor housing

Drain elbow

Power cord

Reset button

Tools You'll Need
Hex-head wrench
Kitchen tongs
Needle-nose pliers

Related Topics
Adding a garbage disposer, 80–81
Unclogging a sink, 198–199

Four Easy Solutions to Disposer Problems

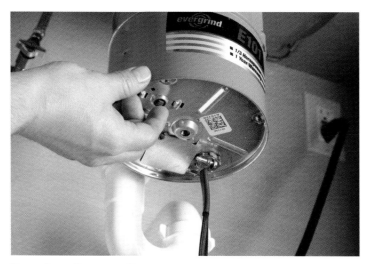

Pressing the reset button
- If your disposer jams, immediately turn it off
- Wait five minutes
- Firmly press and then release the reset button on the bottom of the motor housing
- Disposers with no button are designed to reset automatically
- Run water and try the disposer for a few seconds to see whether the jam is cleared

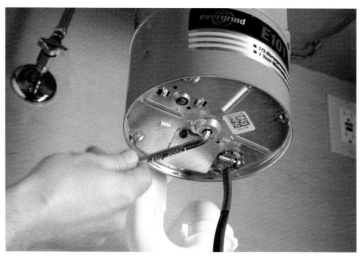

Crank the flywheel
- First try the reset button, if there is one
- Look for a small crank to turn the flywheel; if there is one, turn it
- Alternatively, look for an opening for a hex-head wrench
- Use the wrench to turn the flywheel
- Some disposers have a reversing switch you can try as well

Working from above
- If a metal bottle cap or similar item might be causing the problem, look down from above
- As always, confirm that the disposer's power is off
- Use tongs, needle-nose pliers, or a similar tool to grab and remove the item

Treating with ice cubes
- To clean the disposer blades, try using ice cubes
- Dump the cubes into the sink, push them down the drain, and run the disposer

Diagnosing Your Dishwasher

Plumbing-related problems in dishwashers involve leaks or clogs. If the dishes simply aren't getting clean, suspect low water temperature (140 degrees is ideal), hard water, or not enough detergent.

Checking the Air Gap

Many dishwashers today have an upward loop in the drain hose underneath the counter, just before it connects to a disposer or the sink drain. Some dishwashers, however, have a visible air gap with a cap beside the sink faucet. If yours does, you might need to clean it occasionally to dislodge bones, seeds, or bits of food. To clean an air gap, lift off the cap, unscrew its cover, and insert a long piece of wire, pushing it straight down. This may also help if the dishwasher is slow to drain or if suds ooze from the cap.

Safety Tips

- Before making dishwasher repairs, shut off power to the dishwasher at the electrical service panel.
- Turn off the dishwasher's water supply under the sink before working on the inlet valve or disconnecting the water hose.

A handsome dishwasher clad in stainless steel taps into the supply and drain lines of the kitchen's main sink.

Dishwasher Components

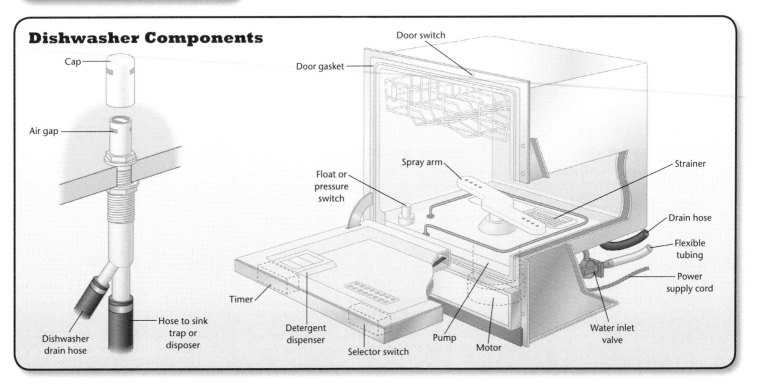

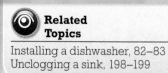

Stuff to Buy
Door gasket

Tools You'll Need
Adjustable wrench
Screwdriver

Related Topics
Installing a dishwasher, 82–83
Unclogging a sink, 198–199

Fixing Common Problems

If the dishwasher won't drain, the cause is probably a plugged strainer, a clogged drain, or a dirty air gap. Dishwasher leaks can usually be traced to either a faulty hose connection or a door gasket that isn't sealing. If your dishwasher won't fill, check to see whether the water-inlet valve is closed or whether the inlet-valve screen is simply clogged.

Clearing the strainer

- Open the dishwasher
- Empty the lower rack and remove it
- Lift out the sprayer arm
- Use a damp rag to pick up loose debris

- Examine the strainer and sprayer arm for blockages and remove them
- Return the arm and the lower rack

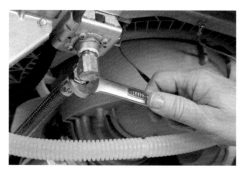

Correcting supply leaks

- Leaks under a dishwasher can be very small
- Ants are a common warning sign of a leak
- Remove the kick plate and the access panel (see lower photo at far right)
- Tighten plumbing connections with an adjustable wrench

Correcting door leaks

- For leaks from around the door, check to see whether the old gasket is worn, brittle, or cracked
- Purchase a replacement gasket
- Remove the old gasket; you may be able to pry it out, or you may have to unscrew it
- Soften the new gasket with hot water to make it flexible
- Carefully insert the new gasket around the door; don't twist it
- Close the door more firmly with a new gasket

To Solve Serious Problems

Detaching the dishwasher

- If you need to remove a dishwasher, unscrew it from the counter above
- Check for connections at each side and unscrew those as well
- You might also need to remove the kick plate and the access panel
- Protect the floor where you will move it

Gaining access below

- To reach plumbing connections under the dishwasher, unscrew the kick plate
- Then remove the access panel, which you'll need to lift off its supporting prongs

Glossary

ABS Acrylonitrile-butadiene-styrene; rigid plastic drainpipe.

adapter Connects one type of pipe to another.

antisiphon valve Device installed on a supply line to prevent siphoning of contaminated water back into potable water supply system.

back venting Vent looping up from a fixture and connecting to main soil stack or a secondary vent at a higher level.

branch Horizontal run of supply pipe that distributes hot and cold water to risers, which in turn feed individual fixtures and appliances.

branch drain Horizontal pipe that carries waste from a fixture or fixture group to the vertical soil stack.

cap Fitting with a solid end used for closing off a pipe.

center-to-center In mounting faucets: Distance between centers of holes on a sink deck. In pipefitting: Distance between centers of two consecutive pipes.

cleanout Opening providing access to a drain line or trap; closed with a threaded cleanout plug.

code Legal requirements for a plumbing installation.

Cleanout

compression fitting Easy-to-use fitting for copper or plastic tube. Pushed in and hand-tightened.

coupling Fitting used to connect two lengths of pipe in a straight run. Also a ring or nut that secures a trap to a tailpiece or drainpipe, or that holds a supply tube to a faucet or toilet inlet valve.

CPVC Chlorinated polyvinyl chloride; rigid plastic pipe for hot and cold water.

critical distance Maximum horizontal distance allowed between a fixture trap and a vent or soil stack.

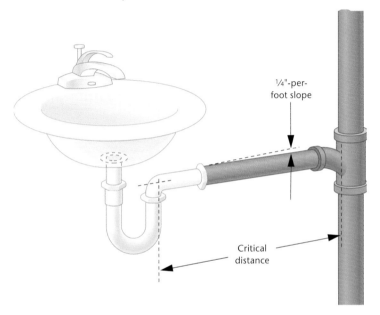

¼"-per-foot slope

Critical distance

cross connection Plumbing connection that could mix contaminated water with potable water supply.

DWV Drain-waste and vent; system that carries away waste water and solid waste, allows sewer gases to escape, and maintains atmospheric pressure in drainpipes.

elbow Fitting used for making turns in pipe runs (for example, a 90° elbow makes a right-angle turn). Also called an ell fitting.

emitter Water distribution device used in drip irrigation.

escutcheon Decorative trim piece that fits over a faucet body or pipe extending from a wall.

female Pipes, valves, or fittings with internal threads.

fitting Device used to join pipes.

fixture A non-powered water-using device such as a sink, bathtub, shower, or toilet.

fixture unit Equal to 7½ gallons or 1 cubic foot of waste water per minute. Used to rate fixture loads when sizing supply and DWV systems.

flange Flat fitting or integral edging with holes to permit bolting together (a toilet bowl is bolted to a floor flange) or fastening to another surface (a tub is fastened to wall through an integral flange).

flare fitting Threaded fitting used on copper and plastic pipe that requires enlarging one end of the pipe.

flexible supply tube Bendable piece of tubing that delivers water from a shutoff valve to a fixture or appliance.

flue Large pipe through which fumes escape from a gas water heater.

gasket Device (usually rubber) used to make a joint between two parts watertight. Term is sometimes used interchangeably with washer.

gray water Household waste water from showers, bathtubs, sinks, and washing machines; sometimes used to water landscaping.

hose bibb Valve with an external threaded outlet for accepting a hose fitting.

house trap U-shaped fitting in some older homes that has two adjacent cleanout plugs; visible at floor level if main drain runs under floor.

joist A horizontal wood-framing member placed on edge, as a floor or ceiling joist.

Locknut Nut used to secure a part, such as a toilet water inlet valve, in place.

main cleanout Fitting in shape of letter T near bottom of soil stack or where drain leaves house.

main supply pipe Cold water pipe that brings water into the house from the water meter; runs to the water heater, where it divides into hot and cold branches.

male Pipes, valves, or fittings with external threads.

nipple Short piece of pipe with male threads used to join two fittings.

no-hub Modern cast-iron pipe joined with neoprene gaskets and stainless-steel clamps.

O-ring Narrow rubber ring; used in some faucets as packing to prevent leaking around stem and in swivel-spout faucets to prevent leaking at base of spout.

233

packing Material that stops leaking around the stem of a faucet or valve.

PB Polybutylene; flexible plastic tubing for hot or cold water supply lines.

PE Polyethylene; flexible plastic tubing for cold water supply outdoors.

pipe-joint compound Sealing compound used on threaded fittings (applied to external threads).

pipe-thread tape Special tape used as a joint sealer in place of pipe joint compound.

plug Externally-threaded fitting for closing off a fitting that has internal threads.

PP Polypropylene; rigid plastic pipe used for traps.

Pressure-reducing valve Device installed in a water supply line to reduce water pressure.

PVC Polyvinyl chloride; off-white, rigid plastic pipe for cold water outdoors. Larger sizes are used in some areas for DWV systems.

reducer Fitting that connects pipe of one diameter with pipe of a smaller diameter.

riser Vertical run of supply pipe.

run Horizontal or vertical series of pipes.

saddle tee T-fitting that is fastened onto side of pipe, eliminating cutting and threading or soldering; usually requires drilling into pipe.

sanitary fitting A fitting with smooth bends and no inside shoulders to block flow of waste; used to join DWV pipe.

secondary venting Venting fixtures distant from main stack to roof through a second vent.

shoulder The ridge or stop inside a fitting's outlet that controls the depth to which a pipe can be inserted.

shutoff valve A valve that controls water flow through supply pipes. A fixture shutoff stops water to an adjacent fixture; the main house shutoff controls the entire system.

BALL VALVE

silicone grease A type of synthetic grease used to lubricate faucet parts; non-petroleum base won't break down rubber washers and other components.

siphoning Action occurring when atmospheric pressure forces water into a vacuum in a pipe.

slip coupling Used to join a new fitting into a run of copper or plastic tubing. Unthreaded, and without a center shoulder so it can slide along a tube. Also called a repair coupling.

soil stack Large DWV pipe that connects toilet and other drains to house drain and also extends up and out roof; upper portion serves as a vent.

solvent cement Compound used to join rigid plastic pipes and fittings.

spacer Short piece of unthreaded plastic or copper pipe cut to size; used when repairing or extending pipe. Some-times referred to as a nipple.

standpipe Special drainpipe for a washing machine.

street fitting A fitting that has one male and one female end. The male end slips directly into the shoulder of an adjacent fitting.

stubout End of a supply pipe or drainpipe that extends from a wall or floor.

stud A vertical wood framing member; also referred to as a wall stud. Attached to sole plate below and top plate above.

supply system Network of hot water and cold water pipes throughout the house. Runs from meter to water heater and on to individual fixtures and appliances.

sweat soldering A method of using heat to join copper tube and fittings.

STREET FITTING

T-fitting (or tee) T-shaped fitting with three openings.

transition fitting Adapter fitting that joins pipes of plastic and metal.

trap Device (most often a curved section of pipe) that holds a water seal to prevent sewer gases from escaping into a home through a fixture drain.

union Fitting that joins two lengths of pipe permitting assembly and disassembly without taking the entire section apart.

valve Device that controls the flow of water.

GATE VALVE

GLOBE VALVE

washer A flat thin ring of metal or rubber used to ensure a tight fit and prevent friction in joints and assemblies. Term is sometimes used interchangeably with gasket.

waste arm Elongated elbow fitting that connects a fixture's trap to the drainpipe.

water hammer Sound of pipes shuddering and banging. Water-hammer arresters (also called air chambers) are designed to stop water hammer.

wet venting Venting arrangement in which a fixture's drainpipe, tied directly to soil stack, vents fixture also.

Y-fitting (or wye) DWV fitting with three outlets in shape of letter Y.

Resources & Credits

Acknowledgments

We'd like to thank the professionals who helped us with this book:

Tom Bressan & John Stokes
The Urban Farmer Store
www.urbanfarmerstore.com

Christin Jolicoeur
Northern Virginia Soil and Water
    Conservation District
www.fairfaxcounty.gov/NVSWCD/

Doug Kirk
GreenPlumbersUSA
www.greenplumbersusa.com

Tim Miller
J. Kittelberger & Sons, Inc.
www.jkittelbergersons.ypgs.net/

Joe Teets
FCPS Adult and Community Education
www.fcps.edu/DIS/OACE/appren.htm

Resources

Cover-Pools
www.coverpools.com/

Dig Irrigation Products
www.digcorp.com/

Pentair Pool Products
www.pentairpool.com/index.htm

Rain Bird
www.rainbird.com/

Rigid
www.ridgid.com/

Rinnai Tankless Eater Heaters
www.rinnai.us/

Smith & Hawken
www.smithandhawken.com/

Spruce Creek Rainsaver
www.sprucecreekrainsaver.com/

Toto
www.totousa.com/

WaterPik
www.waterpik.com/

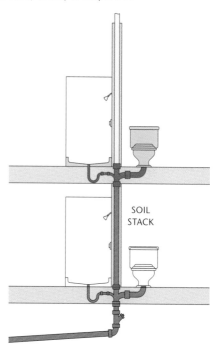

Index

You Can Build...
Do-it-yourself • Pro-level results
Step-by-step instructions

Sunset's all new *You Can Build* series was designed for today's Do-it-Yourselfer. Visually intuitive with hundreds of step-by-step photos and short, concise detailed instructions, you can easily tackle the most popular home improvement projects. You also get basic techniques, professional ideas, tips on avoiding costly mistakes, safety instruction, and troubleshooting advice.